SIMPLY NIGELLA

ALSO BY NIGELLA LAWSON

HOW TO EAT
The Pleasures and Principles of Good Food

HOW TO BE A DOMESTIC GODDESS
Baking and the Art of Comfort Cooking

NIGELLA BITES

NIGELLA SUMMER

FEAST
Food that Celebrates Life

NIGELLA EXPRESS
Good Food Fast

NIGELLA CHRISTMAS
Food, Family, Friends, Festivities

NIGELLA KITCHEN
Recipes from the Heart of the Home

NIGELLISSIMA
Instant Italian Inspiration

SIMPLY NIGELLA

NIGELLA LAWSON

Photographs by KEIKO OIKAWA

Chatto & Windus

LONDON

1 3 5 7 9 10 8 6 4 2

Chatto & Windus, an imprint of Vintage,
20 Vauxhall Bridge Road,
London SW1V 2SA

Chatto & Windus is part of the Penguin Random House group of companies whose
addresses can be found at global.penguinrandomhouse.com

Penguin
Random House
UK

First published by Chatto & Windus in 2015

www.vintage-books.co.uk

A CIP catalogue record for this book is available from the British Library

By arrangement with the BBC
BBC Logo © BBC 1996
BBC wordmark and logo are trade marks of
the British Broadcasting Corporation and are used under licence

ISBN 9780701189358

Design and Art Direction: Caz Hildebrand and Camille Blais
Cookery Assistant: Hettie Potter
Editorial Assistant: Zoe Wales
Home Economics Advisers: Caroline Stearns and Yasmin Othman
Props: Linda Berlin
Layout/Typesetting: Julie Martin
Index: Vicki Robinson

Penguin Random House is committed to a sustainable future for our business, our readers and our planet.
This book is made from Forest Stewardship Council® certified paper.

Printed and bound by Firmengruppe APPL, aprinta druck, Wemding, Germany

For Mimi and Bruno

CONTENTS

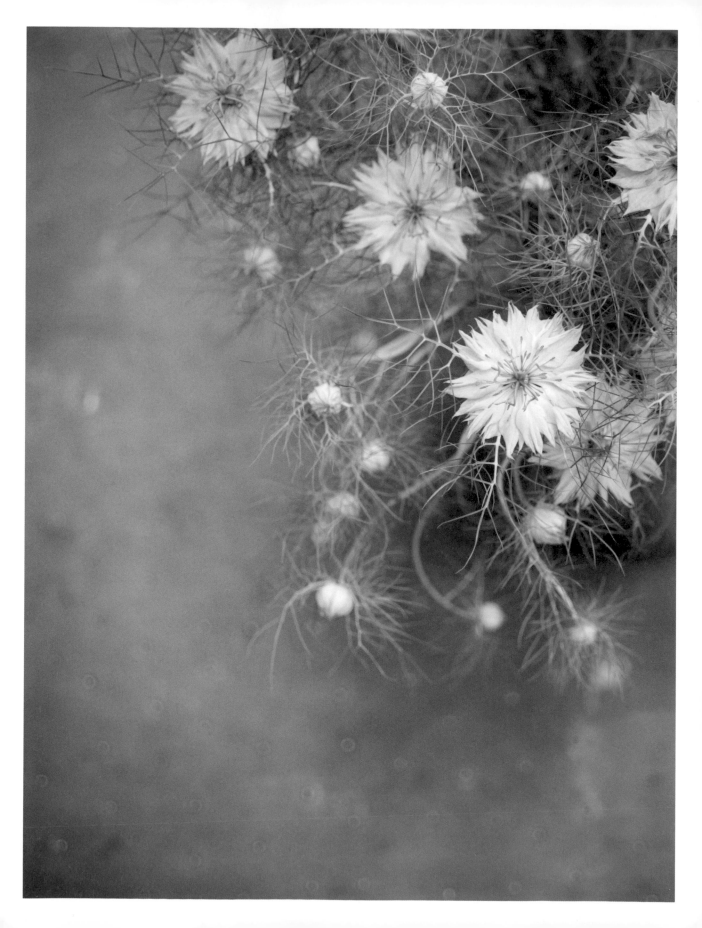

INTRODUCTION

It is a commonplace to talk of cooking as being therapeutic – and there are times when that is the case – but for me cooking stems from an engagement with life, which in itself combines hopefulness with playfulness. These gifts restored to me, this book began to emerge.

Of course, even when I felt I couldn't cook, or didn't have a kitchen of my own, I still needed to bring food to the table, and I am grateful for this. If cooking isn't hinged on necessity, it loses its context, and purpose. I cook to give pleasure, to myself and others, but first it is about sustaining life, and only then about forging a life.

We make worlds for ourselves all the time; for me, the locus has always been the kitchen. And while there have been times in my life when cooking has created a safe place, and a vital space where I could lose myself in creative concentration, all of which have been documented in my previous books, with this book it has been different. I first had to cook myself strong. Now, you will never hear me talking about "healthy" food. I loathe the term, but not as much as I am disgusted by the contemporary mantra of "clean eating". In *How To Eat*, written so long ago, I wrote: "What I hate is the new-age voodoo about eating, the notion that foods are either harmful or healing, that a good diet makes a good person and that that person is necessarily lean, limber, toned and fit... Such a view seems to me in danger of fusing Nazism (with its ideological cult of physical perfection) and Puritanism (with its horror of the flesh and belief in salvation through denial)."

The Clean-Eating brigade seems an embodiment of all my fears. Food is not dirty, the pleasures of the flesh are essential to life and, however we eat, we are not guaranteed immortality or immunity from loss. We cannot control life by controlling what we eat. But how we cook and, indeed, how we eat does give us – as much as anything can – mastery over ourselves.

The food in this book is what I've been cooking for myself and, although the impetus was certainly to seek out food that made me feel physically strong, I have always believed that food you cook for yourself is essentially good for you. This is not just because real ingredients are better for you than fake foods, but because the act of cooking for yourself is in itself a supremely positive act, an act of kindness. And while I have read much about mindful eating, I have not found much, if anything, on mindful cooking. When I cook, I am absorbed in the simple rituals of chopping, stirring, tasting, losing myself in the world of flavour, sensation and straightforward practicalities.

And as I progressed, this book became fused with the joyful realities of making a new home. It makes me smile to see the colours of my kitchen, and the house I have created around myself, reflected in the colours of this book. But, of course, it also necessarily tells the broader story of how I live: how I feed my friends and family, the aesthetic pleasure I derive from food, and my belief that what and how we cook can make our lives easier, make us feel better and more alive, and connect us to ourselves, to others, and the world.

A NOTE ON INGREDIENTS AND UTENSILS

The editor who commissioned my first book told me that he always thought of *How To Eat* as the "Pea, Marsala and Rhubarb Cookbook". And it's true that I am a person of enthusiasms, and go through bouts of extreme reliance on certain ingredients. This is manifested in *Simply Nigella* by the fulsome use of cold-pressed coconut oil, ginger, chilli and lime: I can't seem to cook without reaching for one of these in my kitchen right now. My books are nothing if not a diary of how I eat, and how I cook, so whatever my current passions are will always be reflected in their pages.

Sometimes the ingredients I require you to buy are not those stocked in every supermarket, but they are always easily available online, and I do ensure that any recherché ingredient gets proper use. I do not want to go shopping unnecessarily, and nor – I presume – do you. Much as I enjoy the ritual of cooking, I do feel it can be good to break out of one's normal routine and repertoire, even if it means adding to the clutter already in my kitchen cupboards. And I do want to stress that if I suggest a foray to, for example, an Asian supermarket – or its online equivalent – it is because the requisite ingredients there tend to be much cheaper, and of much higher quality, than the versions stocked in a local supermarket. A list of stockists for such ingredients can be found on **www.nigella.com/books/simply-nigella/stockists**. Rest assured, this refers to just a handful of recipes.

I have referred to short grain brown rice a number of times in these pages: this is different from regular brown rice, as it takes less time to cook, and absorbs liquid differently.

I have mentioned caramelized garlic in a number of recipes, and have always given instructions on how to make a batch using a very hot oven, but it makes sense to bake the garlic bulb when you already have something in the oven, and you can simply bake it for longer at a lower temperature at the same time. Thus, 45 minutes in a 220°C/gas mark 7 oven translates to 2 hours at 170°C/gas mark 3, or you can find some mid-point in between. At all times in the kitchen, you need to make your recipes work for you, not the other way around.

Ginger is required to be peeled and grated in many recipes in this book. The easiest way to peel ginger is to use the tip of a teaspoon, and a fine microplane grater is the best tool for grating ginger, as well as mincing garlic and zesting citrus fruit.

Coconut oil is specified as cold-pressed, and this is sometimes labelled as "raw" or "extra-virgin"; it is distinct from deodorized or refined types. Coconut oil is solid until the temperature reaches 24°C, at which point it liquifies.

Eggs are always large, and preferably free-range organic.

When baking, all ingredients – unless otherwise specified – should be at room temperature before you start.

Where appropriate, I have mentioned when a recipe is either dairy- or gluten-free, but only where one might expect it to contain dairy or gluten (such as the baking recipes). They are also indicated by coloured dots – green for dairy-free, pink for gluten-free – in the index.

I prefer sea salt flakes when I cook or eat, and the measurements given are not interchangeable with fine salt. If you are replacing them with fine salt, half the amount is required.

Where no freezing or make-ahead tip is given alongside a recipe, neither is recommended.

In some recipes, I find using American cup measures (now easily available over here) much simpler, and have consequently given cup measures, with their metric equivalents in brackets afterwards. It is important to remember that cup measures are a unit of volume, not weight, so it is not possible to give ready equivalents, except for liquid measurements.

Many recipes suggest using cast-iron frying pans (although alternatives are always given too). Treated well, and seasoned properly, they are the most effective non-stick frying pans, and can be used in the oven as well as on the hob. They also last a lifetime, while pans with a non-stick coating need to be replaced regularly. Mine are very basic and inexpensive, but they serve me well, and I find both the ancient ore they are forged from, and their steady heft, reassuring. Through them, I feel I am linked to a long line of cooks down the ages. The heavy-based casseroles I use in many recipes are enamelled cast iron and come with a tight-fitting lid; if you are using something less robust then the cooking times may need to be adjusted. A more luxurious and relatively new-fangled addition to the cast-ironware in my kitchen is a slow cooker. As with all cast iron, it retains the heat well and evenly, and avoids any problem of hot spots. Moreover, the pot part can be used in the oven and on the hob.

I often give measurements for pans used in a recipe: except for baking tins, which are specific, these are just to offer guidance.

I use a conventional electric oven; if you are using a fan or convection oven, consult the manual to adjust temperature.

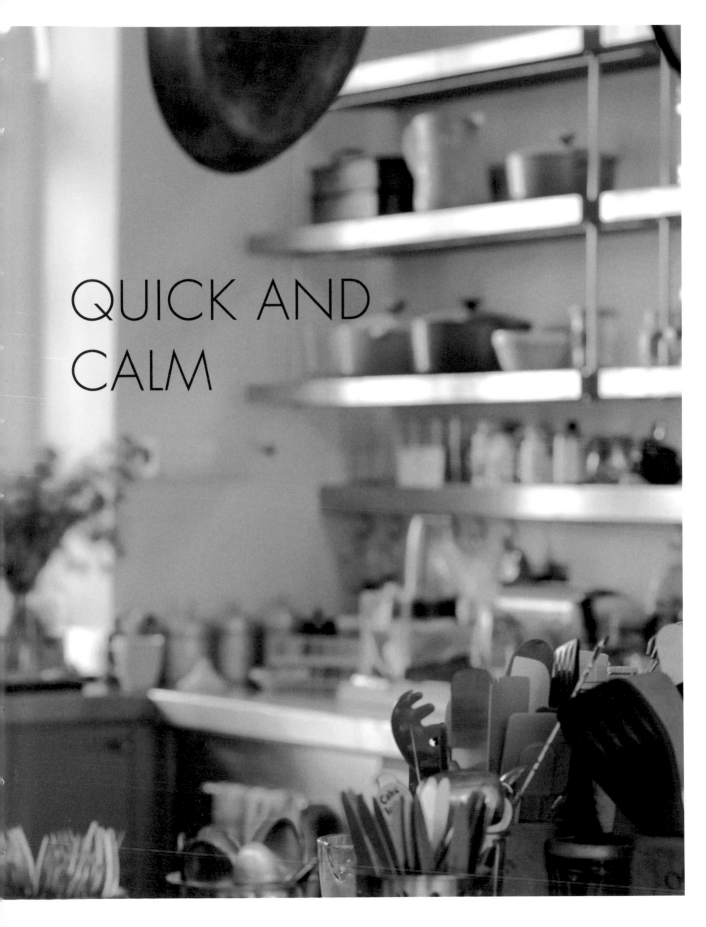

QUICK AND
CALM

A riff on a Caesar salad

There are those who hold the view that a classic recipe is just that: a dish that's earned its status because it, enduringly, works, and to fiddle with it is an act of desecration. It's not a dishonourable stance, but I think it essentially flawed. The classics, in food as in literature, are the very forms that can withstand and, indeed, spawn a plethora of interpretations.

I have subverted the Caesar Salad before. In *How To Eat*, I replaced the traditional croutons with some mini-cubes of potatoes, roasted till crunchy, and tossed – still hot – into the salad, and often still make it thus. My new, heat-blasted version here is a greater deviation and, for me, it's the perfect supper after a long working day, or a fine lunch on a leisurely Saturday. For those missing the crouton element, I suggest a large croûte, in the form of a piece of toast, brushed with extra-virgin olive oil, to munch alongside.

SERVES 2

1 romaine heart	zest and juice of ½ unwaxed lemon, plus ½ lemon to serve
2 x 15ml tablespoons regular olive oil	
1 clove garlic, peeled and finely grated or minced	2 x 15ml tablespoons sunflower oil
	2 eggs
4 anchovy fillets (the sort packed in oil), finely chopped	Parmesan to shave over

○ Preheat the oven to 220°C/gas mark 7.

○ Cut the romaine heart in half lengthways and lay both halves on a small baking or foil tray, cut-side up. Mix the olive oil, minced garlic and chopped anchovies in a bowl, and spoon over the lettuce. Put the tray in the oven to cook for 10 minutes, then add the finely grated lemon zest and the juice and pop back in the oven for another 5 minutes until wilted and slightly charred at the edges.

○ In a small cast-iron or heavy-based, non-stick frying pan that is just big enough to fry 2 eggs – I use a 20cm diameter one – pour in the sunflower oil. When hot, crack in 1 egg, followed by the other, and fry until the whites are cooked through but the yolks are still runny.

○ Put a romaine half on each serving plate and top with a fried egg. Using a vegetable peeler, shave strips of Parmesan over each plate, adding a ¼ lemon, too, in case more is needed to squeeze over.

Brocamole

I have borrowed the name – and inspiration for this recipe – from *mon cher confrère*, Ludo Lefebvre, and it is, as you've probably surmised, a broccolified guacamole (though his recipe contains no avocado). I don't feel too bad about pinching his title: it did, after all, come from his book *Ludo Bites*…

While the recipe is an obvious contender for a chip-and-dip arrangement when friends are over, I make it mostly for a quiet sofa-side supper, to be spread on sourdough toast or dipped into with crudités, or both. I make no apology for not eating all meals at the table. Some days just call for a slob-out on the sofa, but for me the food needs to be something that pulls me out of shattered collapse. This is such a recipe.

While it makes a lot, it does keep well (strangely, considering it has avocado in it) and also gives you a fantastic packed lunch for the next day, either with some raw vegetables to dip into it, or used as a sauce for cold soba – or indeed any other – noodles, in which case I add some toasted pumpkin seeds and toss them through the dressed noodles.

1 head broccoli (crown, not leggy tenderstem)

½ cup (125ml) vegetable oil

1 x 15ml tablespoon extra-virgin olive oil

1 ripe avocado

2 spring onions, trimmed and roughly chopped

small bunch coriander

1 fresh green chilli

juice of 2 limes

sea salt flakes to taste

° Trim the florets from the head of broccoli, and cook them in a big pan of salted boiling water for about 3 minutes (until what the Americans call crisp-tender).

° Drain and plunge straight into ice-cold water. Once the broccoli is cold, drain very well and tip into a food processor, adding the oils as you process to a thick purée.

° Halve the avocado, remove the stone and then spoon the flesh into the processor. Add the spring onions too, along with most of the coriander. If you don't want this too fiery, de-seed the chilli, then roughly chop it and add, along with half of the lime juice, and purée again.

° Taste to see if you want more lime juice – I generally find 1½ limes optimal, but it depends on their juiciness – and add salt to taste.

° Serve in a bowl, sprinkled with the remaining coriander, ready to be dipped into or spread onto toast.

MAKE AHEAD NOTE	STORE NOTE
Can be made up to 6 hours ahead. Cover with clingfilm or baking parchment and refrigerate until needed.	Leftovers can be stored, covered, in fridge for up to 2 days.

Feta and avocado salad with red onions, pomegranate and nigella seeds

My sister, Horatia, often puts hunks of feta on a plate, sprinkles with nigella seeds (family solidarity), douses in olive oil, and serves them alongside some flatbread with drinks. As you can, too. But I have parlayed this into a simple supper, as piquant as it is pretty. Since feta is the main ingredient here, it really does make a difference if you can get hold of chunky fresh feta from a deli or a Turkish store, but this still works with good-quality feta in packets. A bowl of baby spinach salad on the side is, along with puffy – rather than crisp – Turkish flatbread (or *pide*), my favourite accompaniment.

Steeping the onion in vinegar – an old trick of mine, which many of you may recognize – not only takes away the acrid rasp of raw onion, but also turns the red strips to a lambent crimson or, further, a positive puce if left to steep long enough. Two hours is optimum: longer is even better, and it does keep. If time is short, 20 minutes should be enough, in which case double the amount of vinegar, letting the onion drown rather than bathe in it.

Should nigella seeds (called *kalonji* in Indian cooking, where they are used a lot) elude you, and you have to leave them out, I promise I won't be offended. Black mustard seeds are a more-than-acceptable substitute here; or you can drop the spice element altogether. Liquid Gold Cretan extra-virgin olive oil is my anointing olive oil of choice, and it goes perfectly here, strong and true, despite the geo-political discordancy.

½ red onion, peeled

2 x 15ml tablespoons red wine vinegar

200–250g feta cheese

½ teaspoon nigella or black mustard seeds

1 ripe avocado

2 x 15ml tablespoons pomegranate seeds

1–2 x 15ml tablespoons extra-virgin olive oil (see Intro)

- Slice the red onion into fine half-moons and put this delicate tangle into a small, non-metallic bowl, pour the vinegar over this, and make sure all of the onion is submerged. Cover with clingfilm and leave to steep (see Intro).

- When the vinegar's done its trick and the onion strips are lit up like shards of a stained-glass window designed by Schiaparelli, get on with the rest of the salad.

- Get out 2 plates, and divide the feta between them, breaking it up into uneven chunks. Sprinkle it with the nigella or black mustard seeds.

- Peel and remove the stone from the avocado, then cut the flesh into long, thin, gondola-shaped slices, and arrange around the feta. Scatter with pomegranate seeds and trickle with a green gleam of extra-virgin olive oil. Serve with the onions, lifted from their steeping juice and draped over the plate.

MAKE AHEAD NOTE

The pickled onions can be made up to 1 week ahead. Put into a non-metallic container, cover and store in fridge until needed.

Halloumi with quick sweet chilli sauce

When I described halloumi once as "salt-flavoured Polystyrene", people thought I was being derogatory. Nothing could have been further from the truth. There is something so compelling about this squeaky cheese, and my fridge is stocked with it at all times. Most regularly I treat it as vegetarian bacon, dry-fried in a hot pan then dolloped with a peeled, soft-boiled egg (I'd rather peel an egg, even when it's hurty-hot, than poach one). But the idea for this recipe came to me one evening when I felt the need to counter the siren call of the halloumi's saltiness with some sweet-and-heat.

I use a copper pixie-pan for the quick sauce – which takes all of 4 minutes – but if you don't have one, just make more and keep it afterwards in a sealed jar, heating up what you need on further occasions.

3 fresh red chillies	TO SERVE:
2 x 15ml tablespoons runny honey	salad leaves of your choice
1 lime, halved	extra-virgin olive oil to taste
1 x 225g block halloumi cheese	

- Slice 2 of the chillies, leaving the seeds in, then de-seed the third and chop it into fine dice (this is for full-on fieriness; you may de-seed more cautiously if you wish) and add to a small pan – ideally, the sort sold as a butter-melting pan – along with the honey, and squeeze in 1 teaspoon of lime juice from one half of the lime. Put the pan on the smallest ring on the hob and bring to a bubble, then turn the heat down low, and let it foam away for 4 minutes. Stir frequently and do not leave the pan unattended, otherwise it will foam over the hob. Remove from the heat.

- Before you turn to the halloumi, arrange a few salad leaves on 2 plates, and pour as much or as little oil over them as you want. Cut the un-juiced half of the lime into wedges, and pop one on each plate if so wished.

- Slice the halloumi block into 8 pieces, and heat a cast-iron or heavy-based frying pan. When it's hot, add the slices and cook them – without any oil in the pan – for 30–60 seconds until they are tiger-striped underneath, then turn the slices over and cook until the underside is patchily bronzed, too.

- Remove the halloumi to the salad-lined plates and spoon the lipstick-red pieces of chilli in their honeyed glaze over the cheese. Eat immediately. Not hard to do.

STORE NOTE

Transfer cooled leftover chilli sauce to a jar, then seal and store in fridge for up to 2 weeks.

Roast radicchio with blue cheese

I have always held that what is true in the kitchen holds equally true out of the kitchen, but it occurs to me that there is one salient exception. In life, bitterness ("like drinking poison and expecting the other person to die" as I believe Carrie Fisher put it, though attribution is vexed) is to be avoided at all costs, but when it comes to eating, it is one of the greatest goods. As a mindset, I have never seen the allure of bitterness or been even momentarily tempted to succumb to it; in the kitchen, I am in its thrall. If you feel the same way, then you should definitely have the award-winning *Bitter* by Jennifer McLagan in your library. Those of you who are yet to be convinced, try this recipe first. Consider it an entry-level introduction, and one of the easiest, most elegant suppers I know. A few steamed new potatoes bolster it perfectly, their waxy sweetness providing a creamy foil to the muted pungency of the bitter leaves and blue cheese, though I love it as it is, or with the bitterness-boost provided by a tangle of watercress.

My favourite radicchio is not the round sort from Chioggia but the ultra-bitter, less tender-leaved, zeppelin-shaped Treviso Precoce. But it has a much shorter season (more costly, too), and the round radicchio, in all its plump Episcopal splendour, is not to be disparaged.

SERVES 2

1 large round radicchio or 2 Treviso Precoce if possible

1 x 15ml tablespoon regular olive oil

good grinding of pepper

1½ teaspoons balsamic vinegar

50g Gorgonzola Piccante or other blue cheese

2 x 15ml tablespoons pine nuts

1 x 15ml tablespoon chopped fresh chives

watercress, to serve (optional)

° Preheat the oven to 220°C/gas mark 7.

° If using the round radicchio, slice into quarters from bottom to tip (try to keep the quartered heads in whole pieces if you can). If you're using the long Treviso Precoce, then just halve them.

° Arrange them on a foil tray or a small, shallow baking tray lined with foil. Drizzle with the oil, grind some pepper over them, then sprinkle with the vinegar. Finally, crumble the cheese on top, or add blobs of it if the cheese is creamy, and then transfer to the hot oven to cook for 10 minutes.

∘ While the radicchio's in the oven, heat a small, heavy-based frying pan and toast the pine nuts by tossing them in the hot dry pan until they have coloured. Remove to a cold plate.

∘ Transfer the wilted, no-longer-crimson, but bronze-tipped radicchio with its molten pockets of cheese to a couple of plates, lined with watercress if so desired. Scatter with the toasted pine nuts and the chopped fresh chives.

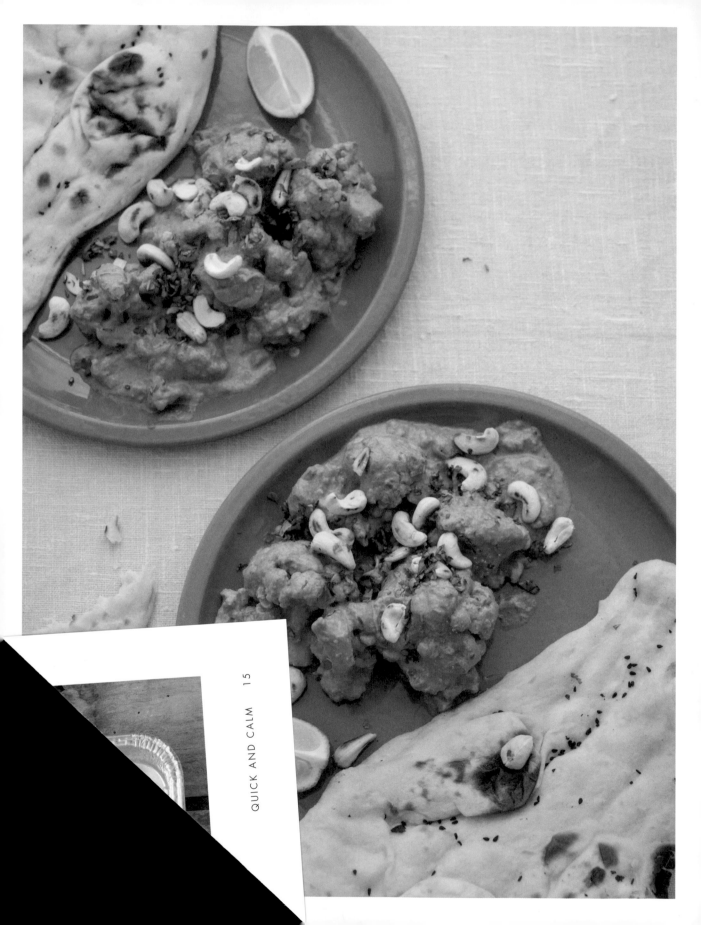

Cauliflower and cashew nut curry

You know I am never knowingly undercatered, and therefore are probably not surprised that I am suggesting turning a whole cauliflower into a curry for just 2 people. In my defence, I should say that I once made this for 4 people, and nearly hyperventilated as I saw the first 2 fill up their plates, and feared how meagre the portions would be for the 2 of us remaining. Besides, you cannot in all seriousness suggest that a quarter of a cauliflower is really enough for one person's supper: this is not a vegetable accompaniment; it is the main event. Yes, I know that it would be enough from a nutritional point of view, but blame my atavistic refugee mentality: I just can't do it. I feel part of the security I derive from cooking is knowing that there will be leftovers for later.

My suggestion would be to serve this just as it is, but with some pillowy naan warmed up in the oven for dippage as you eat. But if you want to, by all means rustle up some rice or – let me be a middle-class cliché – quinoa. This is, anyway, what you could term a Multi-Culti Curry: it shamelessly fuses Thai and Indian flavours (and you could indeed use an Indian curry paste in place of the Thai one here) but with honourable intent, and to most pleasing effect. I am a Londoner, after all, and a clashingly cosmopolitan kitchen comes naturally to me. I trust it causes no consternation beyond.

SERVES 2

1 medium-sized head cauliflower

2–3 teaspoons sea salt flakes, or to taste

2 bay leaves

1 x 15ml tablespoon cold-pressed coconut oil

2 spring onions, finely sliced

2 teaspoons finely chopped fresh ginger

seeds from 3 cardamom pods

1 teaspoon cumin seeds

1 x 15ml tablespoon finely chopped coriander stalks

¼ cup (4 x 15ml tablespoons) Thai red curry paste (see Intro)

1 x 400ml can coconut milk

75g cashew nuts

1 lime, halved

small handful chopped fresh coriander

naan, to serve (optional)

- Put a pan of water on to boil for the cauliflower. Cut said cauliflower into florets. Once the pan's boiling, add 2 teaspoons of sea salt flakes and the bay leaves, and cook the florets for 4–5 minutes or until they're cooked, but only just.

- While the cauliflower is bubbling away, heat the coconut oil in a wok – or pan into which all the ingredients will fit – that comes with a lid, and then add the spring onions, the chopped ginger, the cardamom and cumin seeds, and the finely chopped coriander stalks. Stir over a medium heat for 1 minute or so.

- Add the curry paste, stirring again before adding the coconut milk. Stir well, and bring to a bubble.

- Once the cauliflower florets have had their 5 minutes' boiling, check they are tender, drain and add to your wok or pan. Stir into the sauce and taste to see if you want to add the remaining salt; I always do. Then put on the lid, and simmer for another 10 minutes or so: you want the cauliflower to be tender, well-covered and soused by the sauce. This would be a good time to start warming the naan (if that's what you're having).

- Meanwhile, heat a small, heavy-based frying pan and toast the cashews until they have coloured. Stir half of them into the cauliflower pan, and tip the other half onto a cold saucer or plate for now.

- Taste the sauce again to see if you want to squeeze in some lime, and check the seasoning at the same time, then ladle the cauliflower and sauce onto 2 waiting plates. Scatter with the reserved cashews, sprinkle with the chopped coriander, and add a lime wedge to each plate.

STORE NOTE

Cool leftovers, then cover and refrigerate within 2 hours of making. Will keep in fridge for up to 3 days. Reheat gently in a saucepan, or in short blasts in a microwave, until piping hot.

Prawn and avocado lettuce wraps

I've taken what are essentially the shrimp and avocado tacos I've eaten whenever on the West Coast, and replaced the tortillas with lettuce leaves and subdued the traditional *pico de gallo* (the classic Mexican salsa of tomatoes, onion, jalapeños and coriander) by substituting the raw yellow onion with a modest amount of chopped spring onion. Still, it's plenty fiery enough; it's just that I don't like raw onion much. If you do, bung it in.

I love the softness of the lettuce wraps, but nothing's to stop you reverting to tortilla mode. Alas, the prawns I get here come frozen not fresh, but I simply take out what I need from the freezer in the morning and leave to thaw in the fridge during the day, which means I have the speediest supper when needed urgently, as I find it so often is, come the evening.

I like the scorch I get from using a cast-iron pan, but if you're using a heavy-based frying pan, put it over a slightly lower heat with the oil already in the pan.

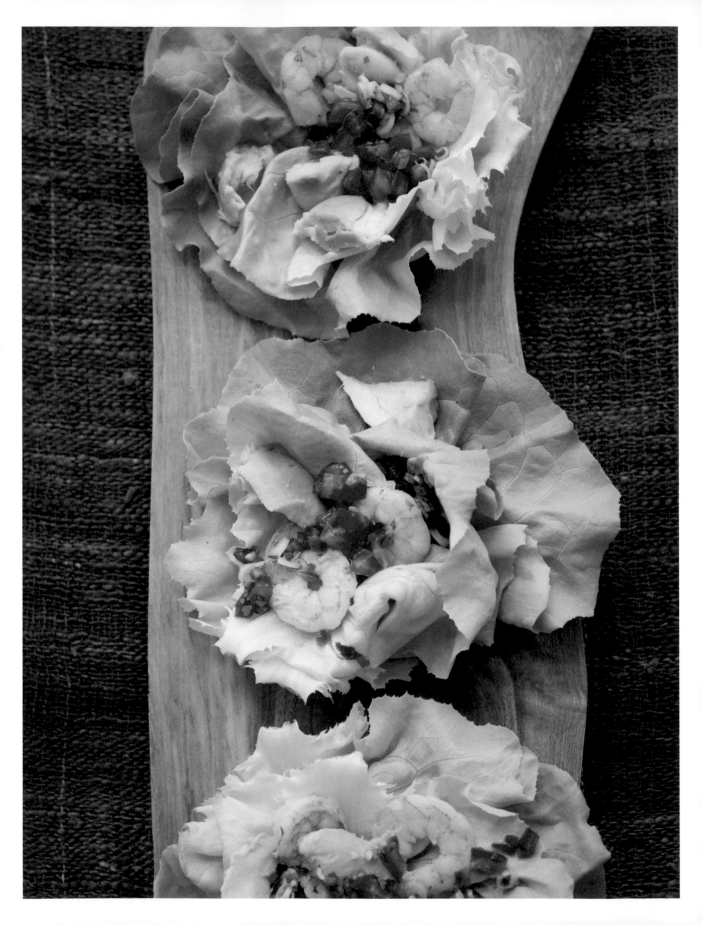

1 teaspoon cold-pressed coconut oil or regular olive oil	1 fresh jalapeño pepper
8 raw peeled king prawns, thawed if frozen	¼ cup (4 x 15ml tablespoons) chopped fresh coriander
zest and juice of 1 lime, preferably unwaxed	salt to taste
2 ripe tomatoes (75–100g total)	1 round lettuce
1 spring onion	1 ripe avocado

○ Heat a cast-iron pan (if you're using one) and add the oil (otherwise just warm the oil in a heavy-based frying pan). When it's sizzling, add the prawns and stir-fry until just cooked through. Using – for ease – a fine microplane, if you have one, grate the zest of the lime over the prawns and add a squeeze of lime juice, then stir and transfer to a plate for the moment.

○ De-seed and finely chop the tomatoes and drop into a small bowl. Thinly slice the white part of the spring onion, and add to the tomatoes. De-seed (or not if you want this properly hot, as I do) and finely chop the jalapeño and drop this into the bowl, too. Stir in the chopped coriander and squeeze 1½ teaspoons of lime juice over this, then mix gently and add salt to taste.

○ Get out a couple of plates. Tear 2 leaves – whole – from the lettuce and sit one on top of another to make a receptacle, then repeat 3 more times, so that each plate has 2 double-layer lettuce wraps on it. Slice each prawn in half lengthways – as if you were trying to open out each prawn like a book and then cutting down the spine – and divide between the lettuce wraps. Peel, stone and slice the avocado, and divide the pieces between the 4 prawn-filled lettuce cups. Spoon some of the salsa over the prawns and avocado slices, but do leave some in the bowl to spoon over as you, messily, eat.

Salmon, avocado, watercress and pumpkin seed salad

This is a regular lunch or supper at *casa mia*, as anyone who follows me on Twitter or Instagram will recognize. I sometimes poach the salmon and keep it in the fridge (see Make Ahead Note, overleaf), just so that I can make it even faster when the need hits. It's quick work anyway, so this is more of an aside than a piece of advice. Although you can always swiftly make a *salade tiède* by flaking the salmon onto the leaves while it's still warm.

I like to use wild Alaskan salmon, which accounts for the vivid hue here. It doesn't have an exceedingly strong taste – I always feel it's as if the salmon is frozen while still alive, the waters must be so cold – but nor does it have that spooky flabbiness of farmed salmon. And it isn't anywhere near as expensive as wild Scottish salmon, desirable and wholly delicious as that is.

If you have half an avocado that needs using up, you can put it to excellent use here, as you don't really need a whole one if this is to feed only two of you.

A final note: I love our British cold-pressed rapeseed oil, but should that not be available, please don't make the mistake of using regular vegetable oil in its place, but rather reach for good extra-virgin olive oil instead.

2 wild Alaskan salmon fillets (approx. 250g total)

2 spring onions, trimmed

1 teaspoon black peppercorns

2½ teaspoons lime juice

2 teaspoons sea salt flakes

FOR THE SALAD:

3 x 15ml tablespoons pumpkin seeds

100g watercress

1 teaspoon organic cloudy apple cider vinegar

1 small ripe avocado

1 x 15ml tablespoon cold-pressed rapeseed oil or extra-virgin olive oil

1 teaspoon sea salt flakes, or to taste

- Put the salmon fillets in a small frying pan (I use one with a 20cm diameter) and cover with cold water from the tap. Add the whole spring onions and peppercorns, squeeze in the lime juice and sprinkle in the salt, then bring to the boil, uncovered. When the pan is bubbling, turn the fillets over, then remove the pan from the heat and leave to stand for 7 minutes. Then take the fillets out of the liquid and leave to cool completely, which could take up to 1 hour. Once cool, the salmon will be cooked through, with its flesh desirably tender and coral inside.

- While the salmon's cooling, make a start on the salad. Toast the pumpkin seeds by tossing them in a dry, heavy-based frying pan on the hob. They will start jumping a little, and will darken and get a smokier taste. It doesn't take long to toast them, so don't leave the pan and, indeed, keep giving it a quick swirl. Then transfer to a cold plate.

- When you're ready to unite salmon with salad, put the watercress into a large shallow bowl (or split between 2 bowls), sprinkle with the vinegar, and toss. Now add the salmon, removing the skin and tearing the fish into bite-sized pieces or shreddy bits, as you wish.

- Halve the avocado and remove the stone, then spoon the flesh out onto the salmon and watercress, or cut it into slices if you prefer. Drizzle the oil over the salad, sprinkle with the salt and half of the toasted pumpkin seeds, and toss gently to mix. Scatter the remaining pumpkin seeds on top, and eat.

MAKE AHEAD NOTE

The salmon can be cooked up to 3 days ahead. Cool for up to 1 hour, then cover and refrigerate until needed.

Miso salmon

In *How To Eat*, I had a recipe for miso-steeped salmon that was very different from this, and in fact was my adaptation, more suited to our shores, of the Nobu black cod with miso that had just hit America and, so many years on, is still a fixed entry in the lexicon of would-be fashionable menus. This version is altogether simpler and quicker, and also lighter and sprightlier. Although I make this as an effortlessly exquisite supper for 2, you can see how easy it would be to up the numbers and make it when you have friends for supper. Were I cooking for more of a crowd, I'd advise you to make the Broccoli Two Ways (**p.230**) to go with it. As it is, I prefer to steam some pak choi, simply dressed with a few drops of toasted sesame oil. Some leggy tenderstem broccoli would work equally well.

1 x 15ml tablespoon sweet white miso

1 x 15ml tablespoon lime juice

1 x 15ml tablespoon soy sauce

1 x 15ml tablespoon fish sauce

1 clove garlic, peeled and finely grated or minced

2 salmon fillets or steaks (225–250g total)

1 fresh red chilli, de-seeded and finely sliced

○ Preheat the oven to 220°C/gas mark 7.

○ Place a freezer bag in a measuring jug, folding the edges over the top of the jug to make it easy to fill, then spoon in the white miso. Add the lime juice, soy sauce, fish sauce and grated or minced garlic to the bag, and then seal and massage the contents to create a smooth, paste-like marinade.

○ Open up the bag, slip in the salmon fillets, then seal it again and squidge it so that the fillets are covered with the marinade. Now lay the bag flat, leaving the salmon to steep for 15 minutes at room temperature.

○ Line a shallow baking tray with foil, then fish out your salmon from the bag, shaking off the marinade, and place, flattest-side down, on the foil.

○ Place the tin in the oven and cook the salmon for 7–10 minutes, depending on the thickness of your fish. You want it cooked through, but still juicy and coral within.

○ When they're cooked, transfer the fillets to a couple of warmed plates, then scatter with the chilli strips, dividing them between each fillet.

Indian-spiced cod

According to Rex, my excellent fishmonger, there is plenty of sustainable cod around Cornwall, and so I use it with an easy conscience here. Its price compared, say, to pollock or hake, certainly makes it a treat, but then so does its luscious, firm, silky-fleshed taste. But this recipe will accommodate any thick fillets of firm white fish and, indeed, would work (from a cooking point of view) with salmon, too. But if you are using cod, ask your fishmonger to cut from the loin, not the tail. And I urge you to go to a fishmonger if you can. It makes me feel much more assured about the fish I am using, in the first instance, and if we stop going to fishmongers, they will die out, which I do not want to see happen. Furthermore, it can be a mistake to presume that a supermarket will always be the cheaper choice.

I think of this as an Indian-inspired take on cod and mushy peas; my accompaniment of choice being the Quick Coconutty Dal on **p.234**, though feel free to serve with a simple salad if you prefer. And if you have your eye on the Pink-Pickled Eggs on **p.268**, then these would be splendid here too.

Similarly, if you want to use Greek yogurt rather than coconut-milk yogurt, which I adore, and extravagantly use whenever I can, please do (it's certainly less expensive), but in which case you will need only 1 teaspoon of lime juice along with the grated zest of the whole lime.

SERVES 2

3 x 15ml tablespoons coconut-milk yogurt, such as CoYo

zest and juice of 1 lime, preferably unwaxed

1 teaspoon garam masala

½ teaspoon hot chilli powder

½ teaspoon ground turmeric

1 teaspoon fine sea salt

4 teaspoons yellow mustard seeds

¼ teaspoon ground mace

2 skinless cod loin fillets (approx. 400g total)

TO SERVE:

lime wedges and either crushed pink peppercorns or dried chilli flakes from a jar

○ Preheat your oven to 200°C/gas mark 6. If you're making the dal on **p.234** to eat alongside, get started on that before the fish. Put the yogurt into a shallow dish, such as a small oblong Pyrex dish, then grate in – using a fine microplane for choice – the zest of the lime and squeeze in all the juice.

○ Whisk in the garam masala, chilli powder, turmeric, salt, mustard seeds and mace.

○ Coat each cod fillet in the spiced yogurt mixture, turning carefully to cover each one as evenly and thickly as you can.

○ Sit the fillets on a small, shallow baking tray and roast in the oven for 15 minutes. Check after this time that they are cooked through. The thickness of the fish will vary so it may need longer; you just need to check that the flesh is no longer glassy.

○ Transfer to 2 waiting plates, add some lime wedges and put some gently crushed pink peppercorns (or dried chilli flakes) nearby for tableside sprinkling, if so wished. Serve with a salad or the Quick Coconutty Dal.

Jackson Pollock

I'm sorry, but I just couldn't help myself. And while my little joke doesn't work should you use other firm white fish, the recipe does, so please use whatever fish you prefer. But there have been huge efforts to encourage us in Britain to eat our local pollock over recent years, though for some reason the name was seen to put people off. For a while, comic though this sounds, a supermarket rebranded pollock as "colin", though I can't believe that it helped matters much, and is slightly confusing given that *colin*, when not the man's name, is the French for hake (north of the Loire, that is; they call it *merlu* in the south). The chargrilled peppers in oil that I mention here (and elsewhere in this book) are the chopped, oil-steeped ones from Saclà.

SERVES 2

2 skinless pollock fillets (250–300g total)

250g spinach

¾ cup (about 15g) parsley leaves

1½ teaspoons sea salt flakes

zest and juice of ½ unwaxed lemon

3 x 15ml tablespoons sunflower oil

1 x 15ml tablespoon extra-virgin olive oil

2 teaspoons cold water (if needed)

1 x 290g jar chargrilled peppers in oil

1 clove garlic, peeled and finely grated or minced

○ Preheat the oven to 200°C/gas mark 6. Take the fish fillets out of the fridge. Tip the spinach leaves into a colander and rinse under the cold tap to clean, then shake the colander in the sink, pushing down on the spinach, to get rid of excess water.

○ Start by making the green sauce. You can use either a bowl and a stick blender, or the small bowl of a food processor. Blitz a cup and a half (about 45g) of the spinach with the parsley, ½ a teaspoon of sea salt flakes, the finely grated lemon zest and juice and the sunflower oil until you start to have an emulsified sauce. Add the extra-virgin olive oil, and blitz again, then taste for seasoning and add the cold water if the sauce needs thinning: it needs to have a certain amount of runniness for the artistic effect we have planned.

○ Tip the chargrilled peppers, and their oil, into a small oven tin – I use a shallow one measuring 23 x 30cm with a lip of 4cm. Add the grated garlic and sprinkle with ½ a teaspoon of sea salt flakes and stir to mix. Sit the pollock fillets on top and bake in the oven for 5–7 minutes, until the fish is cooked through.

○ While the fish is in the oven, heat up a wok or large saucepan (with a lid), and add the rest of the spinach along with the remaining salt, put on the lid and let the spinach wilt; this shouldn't take more than 2 minutes.

○ Check the fish is cooked and, when it is, take the tin out of the oven. Get out a large plate, and add the wilted spinach in dollops, using a slotted spoon, so that you're not making everything too watery. Now add the fish fillets, cutting each in half first, and – again using a slotted spoon – the peppers, arranging them around the fish and spinach, letting some chunks land on top, then dribble a little of the peppers' orange oil over the fish.

○ Spoon and streak the green sauce over as you wish; by all means, consult the picture here – or indeed an art book – for guidance.

Mackerel with ginger, soy and lime

I do delight in mackerel. Part of the pleasure, for me, is derived from the beauty of its blue-silver-gold-glinting skin with those almost otherworldly striations, but that doesn't mean I cook it for aesthetic reasons alone.

The sharp and feisty marinade here is the perfect foil to the mackerel's rich flesh, and if the marinating process means you don't get that crunchy, crisp skin, it's a trade-off I'm willing to make. Actually, if you grill this on a barbecue, at nuclear heat, for a mere-if-melting moment (after a yawningly long time a-heating) you may indeed get that Japanese-restaurant crispness, but a hot oven provides a tenderness so absorbingly complete, and without any frenzied interruption to the calmness of the occasion, that I can't suggest any better way to proceed than below.

I like to serve a little sushi ginger alongside, either out of a packet or, better still, made from the startlingly simple recipe on **p.266**. And a quick stir-fry of shredded Brussels sprouts works for me, too. Just heat a wok, add 2 teaspoons of sunflower oil and when it's sizzling, grate in (or mince and add) a clove of garlic and add 1 teaspoon of sesame seeds, stir, then quickly toss in about 150g Brussels sprouts, thinly sliced with a sharp knife, and stir-fry for 2–3 minutes. Finally, throw in a teaspoon of sea salt flakes mixed in a shot glass of water, and a spritz of lime, and stir-fry for 30 seconds to a minute, before seasoning to taste, and you're done. But nothing would be wrong in simply serving a crisp and astringently dressed salad alongside, instead.

zest of 1 lime, preferably unwaxed, and 2 teaspoons juice

2 x 15ml tablespoons soy sauce

1 x 15ml tablespoon grated fresh ginger

1 teaspoon maple syrup

drop toasted sesame oil

4 mackerel fillets

° Preheat the oven to 220°C/gas mark 7.

° Finely grate the zest of the lime (you'll need some of the juice later) and set this aside in a little bowl covered with clingfilm for the time being.

° Take out a freezer bag and put in all the marinade ingredients – 2 teaspoons of lime juice, the soy sauce, ginger, maple syrup and drop of sesame oil – then squish it around, before adding the mackerel fillets. Seal the bag, and give it another gentle squidge or two, then leave it flat for 10 minutes. Now would be the time to start slicing the Brussels sprouts, should you be wanting to eat them alongside (see Intro).

° Line a small, shallow baking tray – into which the fillets will fit neatly – with foil, and tip in the fillets, marinade and all, then turn the mackerel skin-side up before putting into the hot oven to roast for 10 minutes. Check, obviously, to see if the fish is cooked through before serving. If it needs only a tiny bit longer, just take the tray out of the oven and let it sit on a heatproof surface for a few more minutes.

° Get out a couple of plates and put 2 fillets on each, sprinkling most of the reserved lime zest over them. Add your vegetable accompaniment of choice, sprinkling the rest of the grated lime zest over that, and tuck in, adding sushi ginger as you go, should that make you happy. It makes me happy.

Spiced and fried haddock with broccoli purée

This recipe could hardly be easier, and requires no complication, nor any effort to keep it simple. Good fish, lightly dredged in spiced flour then flash-fried, is an old-fashioned pleasure, and one to be savoured. Here I use gluten-free flour in preference to regular plain flour to coat the fish. I had wanted the slight grittiness of rice flour, but had none in the house, and gluten-free flour (which I did have) contains rice flour and worked fabulously. Obviously, you can use plain flour if you wish. And while the verdiglorious accompaniment may look like old-time mushy peas, it is, in fact, broccoli, blitzed with a stick blender. I use frozen broccoli simply because I find that, cooked in this way, the taste is – counterintuitively – fresher and needs no more added to it than a little salt and pepper to taste, along with the mildest, yet emphatically creamy, hit of coconut. If you cringe at the idea of coconuttiness, however delicate, then use butter or a really good extra-virgin olive oil instead.

SERVES 2

FOR THE BROCCOLI PURÉE:

500g frozen broccoli florets

1–2 x 15ml tablespoons cold-pressed coconut oil
or butter or extra-virgin olive oil

salt and pepper to taste

FOR THE SPICED HADDOCK:

3 x 15ml tablespoons gluten-free or plain flour

1 teaspoon ground ginger

1 teaspoon paprika

1 teaspoon fine sea salt

2 haddock fillets, skin on (approx. 350g total)

1 x 15ml tablespoon sunflower oil

TO SERVE:

½ lemon, cut into wedges

○ Put a pan of water on for the broccoli, and when it comes to the boil, salt to taste and cook the frozen broccoli florets (unthawed) for 10 minutes from the time the water comes back to the boil, or until it's tender enough to be puréed. Drain and return to the pan, along with 1 tablespoonful of cold-pressed coconut oil, and set about it with your stick blender, adding salt and pepper and a further tablespoon of oil to taste. Put the lid on and leave while you fry the fish, which is the work of moments.

○ Get out a plate in which the fish fillets can lie flat, and in it mix the flour, spices and salt, then dredge the fish on both sides, so that the fillets are well coated. Place a cast-iron pan or a heavy-based, non-stick frying pan – into which the fillets will fit neatly – on the stovetop or hob. In the case of the cast-iron pan, heat it before adding the sunflower oil; if using a non-stick frying pan, add the oil first.

○ When the oil is hot, put both fillets in the pan, skin-side down, and cook for 3 minutes. Turn them over and cook for another 1½ minutes, or until the fish is just cooked through. These timings are based on fillets that are – as you can see – square-ish and quite thick. If yours are thinner, 2 minutes skin-side down, followed by 1 minute on the other side, should do it.

○ Once the fish is cooked, transfer to a plate lined with kitchen roll while you dollop the broccoli purée onto 2 dinner plates. Add the haddock fillets, crisp-skin-side-up, and eat with calm relish, and possibly a spritz of lemon.

Steamed sea bass with ginger and soy

While sea bass is undeniably a luxury, this recipe makes frugal use of it. I buy
1 wild sea bass fillet, and cut it in half so that it feeds 2. I should admit, though, that
the impetus here is not so much thrift, as concern about fitting the sea bass into the
steamer. And when I say steamer, I rig up a makeshift one by bringing water to boil
in my wok (which comes with a lid) and sitting a round cake-cooling rack on top of
it. The prepared fish goes on a heatproof plate, the plate goes on the rack, the lid
goes on, and it's as simple as that. Obviously, if you own a steamer, then it will be
even simpler. (And I suppose you could cook the fish, with its flavourings, wrapped in
a piece of lightly greased kitchen foil in a 200°C/gas mark 6 oven for 5 minutes, or
until just cooked through.) This fish is so delicate, and so lightly but beautifully sauced
– and its flavours, while gentle, are confident and resonant.

Alongside, I like a simple, undressed, salad made of ½ a cucumber (approx. 100g),
halved, de-seeded, then cut into juliennes or fine batons, along with 4–6 radishes
(depending on their size) cut into tiny red-tipped matchsticks, all tossed together. It
would also be perfect with some wilted spinach on the side.

SERVES 2

2cm piece (10g) fresh ginger, peeled	1 teaspoon toasted sesame oil
1 skinless sea bass fillet (approx. 200g)	coriander, to serve
1 x 15ml tablespoon soy sauce	

- Put a steamer on to boil. Make the cucumber and radish salad, and see Intro if
  you're going down that recommended route. Cut the peeled ginger into very thin
  slices across, then cut each slice into fine strips. Now cut the sea bass in two,
  across, so that you have a pair of shorter fillets.

- Get out a heatproof plate, with a lip, that will fit into the steamer (see Intro) and is
  also big enough for the 2 fillets. Sprinkle the plate with half of the ginger strips, sit
  the fish on top, and then add the rest of the ginger strips. Mix the soy sauce and
  sesame oil together and spoon over the fish. Sit the plate on the steamer rack, cover
  and steam for 5 minutes, or until the fillets are just cooked through.

- Divide the salad between 2 plates, then carefully transfer a fillet to each plate,
  pouring the scant but scented sauce over the fish, and making sure you get every bit
  of ginger, too. Sprinkle with a few coriander leaves and eat immediately, savouring
  each exquisite mouthful.

Devilled roes on toast

I love soft roes on toast. My mother often used to make them on a Saturday night – after the statutory chicken at lunch – and the contrast between the soft gaminess of the roes and the butteriness of the toast, and that essential, sharp squeeze of lemon, fills me not with a nostalgia for my childhood but for a taste that is now so rare, it feels as if it is about to slip into a historical archive or the exclusive province of the gentleman's club (or upmarket restaurants that aspire to that ungenerous estate).

For those too young to have grown up with them, I have to tell you that soft roes are the sperm of the herring. I see no place for squeamishness on the issue, but I know that many of you might not feel the same way. Your loss. And while so many fish are in declining numbers, the seas are awash with herring roes. Towards the end of the year, a third of a male herring's body weight is roe; this is because herrings mate by spraying their roes (the female has hard roes, with a granular rather than soft texture) into the sea. But enough of this now.

Herring roes are cheap and plentiful, and, out of season, you can buy frozen roes. Although they come in 1-kilo blocks, any good fishmonger will cut off the amount you need, and you don't need much. This is essentially an after-dinner savoury, which I like best eaten on its own. If you know what I'm talking about, you won't need further encouragement. If you don't, then please give it a go: this is such a lovely little supper for two.

1 x 15ml tablespoon cornflour

½ teaspoon cayenne pepper

½ teaspoon ground mace

200g soft herring roes

1 x 15ml tablespoon (15g) unsalted butter, plus more for the toast

drop regular olive oil

2 fat slices good bread (I like white sourdough)

juice of ½ lemon

smoked sea salt flakes or regular sea salt flakes, to sprinkle over

1 teaspoon finely chopped fresh chives (or other herb of your choice) to sprinkle over

° Mix the cornflour, cayenne and mace in a resealable freezer bag. Tear off a double sheet of kitchen roll, lay it flat and put the herring roes on top, then get another piece, place it on top and gently pat down to remove excess liquid. Now add the roes to the flour and spice mix in the freezer bag, seal and shake gently so that all the pieces are covered.

° In a small cast-iron pan (I use one of 20cm diameter) or heavy-based, non-stick frying pan, melt the tablespoonful of butter and drop of oil, and when bubbling, add the herring roes and cook for 2–3 minutes, turning them gently a few times, so that they're cooked through and bronzed in parts, but still keeping their shape.

° Meanwhile, put the bread in the toaster, and butter (generously for me) when ready.

° When the roes are cooked, spritz in the lemon juice, pushing the roes gently in the pan with a wooden spatula or whatever utensil you favour, then top the waiting pieces of buttered toast with the contents of the pan. Sprinkle with smoked sea salt flakes, should you be lucky enough to have some, or use regular sea salt flakes, and then scatter with the chopped chives. When I was a child, we ate this with a knife and fork, but now I like to cut the roe-topped toast in half and eat by hand.

Crunchy chicken cutlets

Chicken cutlets are what Americans call – give or take – what we'd describe as escalopes, but such is my alliteration addiction, I had to go for this nomenclature. I could have called them Cornflake-Crunchy Chicken Cutlets as the crisp coating is provided not by breadcrumbs, but by cornflakes. This is particularly handy if you want a gluten-free crunch, though do check the cornflake packet to be sure. In theory, cornflakes should by their very nature be gluten-free but, because of cross-contamination issues in factories, that isn't always the case. If this isn't an issue, then use any cornflakes you like.

You can buy chicken escalopes already beaten, but otherwise just buy a couple of chicken breasts and, one at a time, place them on a chopping board lined with clingfilm, cover the chicken with another layer of clingfilm and bash the living daylights out of them with a rolling pin. This is a gratifying way to de-stress at the end of a long day.

Once flattened, each breast provides a generously portioned escalope (you could use just one chicken breast and halve it across before bashing) but I like the expansiveness of a plateful of crunchy cutlet, and all I'd suggest you'd eat alongside is a handful of rocket, dotted with some halved cherry tomatoes, dressed simply. That's to say, I sprinkle a few sea salt flakes over the salad-lined plates, then squeeze some lemon juice on top, followed by a glug of excellent olive oil.

2 chicken escalopes or breast fillets (200–300g total), preferably organic

¼ cup (70g) Dijon mustard

1 clove garlic, peeled and finely grated or minced

½ teaspoon ground cinnamon

1 egg

3 cups (75g) cornflakes

1½ teaspoons pimentón picante or paprika

2 x 15ml tablespoons sunflower oil

cherry tomatoes and rocket or salad leaves of your choice, to serve

1 lemon, cut into wedges

- Take the chicken out of the fridge so that it isn't too cold by the time you get frying. If you are using filleted chicken breasts, rather than escalopes, then proceed as described in the Intro.

- Get out a shallow dish that, preferably, you can get both escalopes in, and spoon in the mustard and the garlic. Add the cinnamon and egg and whisk to combine. Put the escalopes in, turn them, and leave to sit in the mixture while you prepare the "crumbs".

- Put the cornflakes into a bowl and crush them by hand. This, sadly, is not as brutal as it sounds: merely break them up with your fingers to get coarsely crushed flakes, but not dust. Add the pimentón or paprika and use a fork to mix in.

- Dredge the egg-and-mustard-soaked escalopes, one by one, in the cornflake crumbs, so that they are well covered, and then transfer to a wire rack for 5–10 minutes so they can dry out.

- Heat the oil in a cast-iron pan or heavy-based frying pan in which the chicken pieces will fit neatly and, when hot, fry for 3 minutes on the first side, then turn them over carefully and give them another 3 minutes, by which time the chicken should be cooked through in the middle, though do check. Remove to waiting plates, already strewn with tomatoes and rocket or salad leaves of your choice.

MAKE AHEAD NOTE

Coat escalopes, then put on a baking sheet lined with baking parchment, and freeze. Once solid, transfer to a resealable bag and freeze for up to 3 months. Cook directly from frozen, adding 1–2 minutes to the cooking time, and ensure cutlets are cooked through before serving.

Spiced chicken escalopes with watercress, fennel and radish salad

When it comes to chicken, I am most decidedly a thigh rather than a breast woman, so trust me when I say that I am very happily using the white meat in preference to the dark here.

The vinegary, robustly spiced marinade may take an initial leap of faith. But jump: jump now. It tangily tenderizes meat that is so often dry when cooked, and the warmth of the spicing makes this a richly filling supper, while not detracting at all from its lightness. This is why I suggest using 1 breast portion to make 2 escalopes, which makes it a thrifty choice at the same time. And it is oh-so-speedy to cook.

The salad that nestles alongside is the perfect accompaniment: the watercress and radishes peppery, the fennel fragrant. And this salad is worth bringing out on other occasions, too. Ideally, the fennel and radishes should be sliced wafer-thin with a mandoline, but I'm far too clumsy to be safe with one and, besides, this is home, not restaurant food, and all the better for it.

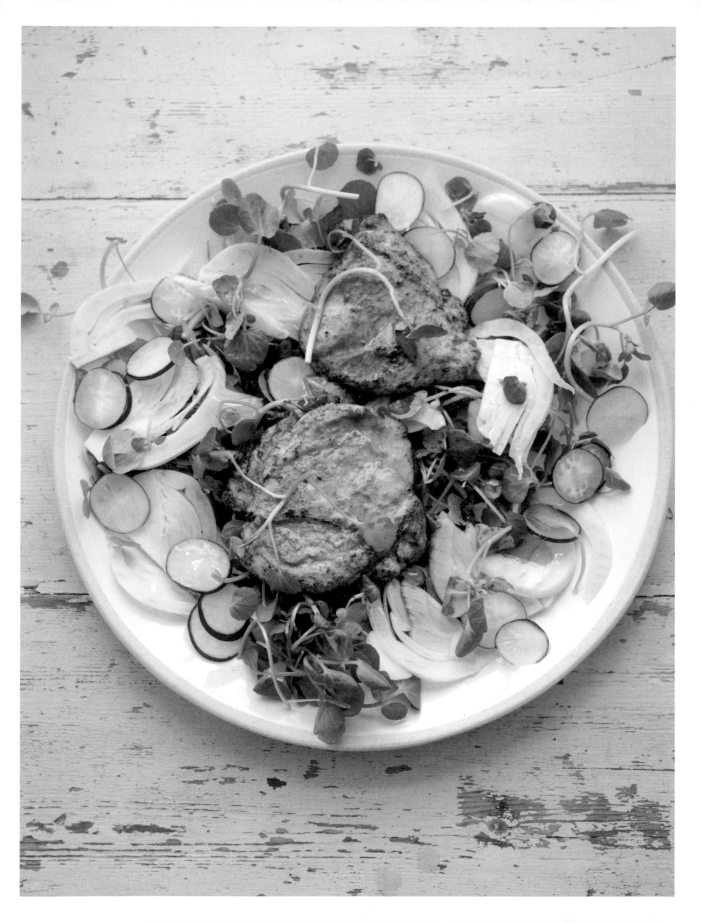

1 chicken breast, preferably organic

1 x 15ml tablespoon rice vinegar

2 teaspoons sunflower oil

½ teaspoon ground turmeric

1 teaspoon ground ginger

¼ teaspoon cayenne pepper

1 small bulb fennel

4–6 radishes

2 handfuls (approx. 50g) watercress

½ teaspoon sea salt flakes

1–1½ x 15ml tablespoons cold-pressed rapeseed oil or extra-virgin olive oil

2 teaspoons cold-pressed coconut oil or regular olive oil or sunflower oil

1 lime, to serve

- Line a chopping board with clingfilm, though do not cut off the piece from the roll quite yet. On another chopping board, cut the chicken breast in half across, and put half on top of the clingfilmed board, then cover with more of the clingfilm and tear off from the roll. With a rolling pin, bash the chicken until it's as thin as a veal escalope. Remove, then repeat this process with the as-yet-unbashed piece of chicken breast.

- Put the vinegar, sunflower oil, turmeric, ginger and cayenne into a resealable freezer bag, add the chicken escalopes, then seal and leave on a plate to marinate for 10 minutes.

- While the chicken marinates, halve the fennel, cut out the core, and cut each half into thin slices, then slice the radishes as thin as you can without stressing or cutting yourself. Put the watercress into a large bowl with the fennel and radishes, add the salt and the rapeseed or olive oil and toss lightly – I use my hands for this – to combine. I don't add vinegar here, but there will be lime to squeeze over if you feel the salad needs it once you're eating. Arrange the lightly dressed salad on a serving platter or divide between 2 dinner plates.

- Heat the 2 teaspoons of coconut (or other) oil in a cast-iron pan or a heavy-based, non-stick frying pan that will take both pieces of chicken, and when hot, add the escalopes and cook for 2 minutes on each side. You will need to cut into a thicker part to check they're cooked through, before removing to the platter. Halve the lime, and squeeze the juice from one half over the escalopes, then cut the remaining half into 2 wedges and put one on each person's plate.

Strapatsada

This is a Greek recipe given to me by Alex Andreou (of Squid and Orzo (**p.141**) and Old Rag Pie (**p.318**) fame). Actually, strictly speaking it's Italian, or of Italian derivation: *strapazzare* meaning, in the context of eggs, "to scramble". And really that's what this is: eggs scrambled with tomatoes. I have long since dropped my "no red with egg" rule – my Eggs in Purgatory from *Nigellissima* saw to that – but eating this makes me regret ever having voiced such an opinion in the first place.

True, I was initially hesitant about this, as the notion of tomatoes mixed into scrambled eggs didn't seem appealing. But the thing is, it doesn't quite taste like that. This is what cooking is all about: what the ingredients do together in the pan, not what they sound like on the page. A simple alchemy.

This is the sort of supper you need when you get home and the fridge is bare, or you're too tired to cook. And it's just the thing for those nights when you come home late, possibly a little worse for wear, or even not. Please don't wait for exhaustion or excessive alcohol consumption to make this.

Now, were you to be blessed with wonderful tomatoes, the sort you'd get in Greece, I would add another couple and dispense with the tomato purée element. And I give you the choice of basil or thyme, as the strapatsada is wonderful with either, but I'd tend to use the former in summer and the latter in winter. I am reliably informed that the cheese you would eat with it is Xynotyro, but since there's no way I have of getting my hands on that in my neighbourhood, I go for Wensleydale as the closest substitute available locally. What you want is a sharp and salty cheese that will crumble and melt a little, if that helps.

8 small (not cherry) tomatoes (300–350g total)

3 x 15ml tablespoons regular olive oil

1 x 15ml tablespoon tomato purée

pinch salt

pinch sugar

2 large eggs

25g Xynotyro cheese, or sharp, salty, crumbly cheese such as Wensleydale

small handful basil leaves or leaves stripped from few sprigs thyme

4 slices good bread, such as sourdough, or whatever you like

- ○ Cut the tomatoes in half – a Greek person would now cut out the cores; this English person is too lazy – and then cut them into rough chunks.

- ○ Warm the oil in a heavy-based frying pan (I use a cast-iron pan of 25cm diameter, heating the pan before adding the oil) and tumble in the chunks of tomato. Cook, stirring every now and again, for about 5 minutes, by which time the tomatoes will have started to break down into the oil and be oozing oranginess. If you want your bread toasted, now's the time.

- ○ Add the tomato purée, salt and sugar, and cook for another 5 minutes, by which time the tomato skins will be coming away from the flesh. Crack in the eggs and then stir, just as if you were scrambling them, until they are creamy, which is hardly any time at all (obviously, if you like your scrambled eggs set, cook the egg and tomato mixture here for longer).

- ○ Take the pan off the heat, crumble the salty cheese over the mixture and sprinkle with the basil or thyme leaves. Dollop some on your toast, or just eat straight from the pan using bread as your cutlery. For the record, I have one helping on toast, and another with just the bread. There's enough for 4 slices of bread here, but if you're eating solo and can't finish it all (really?), then know that this is also fabulous cold.

STORE NOTE

Leftovers can be refrigerated for up to 2 days.

BOWLFOOD

BOWLFOOD

If I could, I'd eat everything out of a bowl. For me "bowlfood" is a simple shorthand
for food that is simultaneously soothing, bolstering, undemanding and sustaining.
I'm not talking about comfort food in the traditional sense, with its implications
of nostalgia, the nursery and indiscriminate stodge. And I'm certainly not talking
about comfort eating, which I've always held to be the greatest misnomer. Rather,
discomfort eating is what that term always implies to me, with its random, rushed,
unassuageable hungers – eating, dislocated from appetite, as a means of self-
persecution, holds no comfort for me. But bowlfood is comfort eating in a more
innocent sense and, yes, perhaps infantile, too. Just as babies are weaned with
foods that provide an unchanging taste and texture, repeated from spoonful to
spoonful, so I derive succour from the food I eat out of a bowl, with fork or spoon,
each mouthful satisfyingly the same as the one before. And there are lazy days when
even chewing is too much, and then I turn gratefully to the solace of soup. But the
bowls of noodles I slurp, the shepherd's pie or meatballs I spoon gratefully into my
mouth, are neither bland and numbing – as comfort food tends to imply – nor about
offering some edible antidote to life's miseries or disappointments, but rather a glad
and calm celebration of the simple ritual of eating, and the quiet joys of both food
and existence alike. Om!

Ramen

This is one of my favourite solo suppers. I have made it for the family, but then, what with the multiplied chopping, prepping and dishing up, a certain frantic note can be introduced into the proceedings. For the same reason, although my photographer here, Keiko, admonished me gently, telling me that no Japanese person makes ramen at home, I find the chaos and noise at noodle joints is not what I want when I'm in the mood for ramen, and so I sacrifice authenticity for pleasure. But I felt that I was sacrificing a little too much authenticity for Keiko's comfort when I told her that I liked my ramen with soba noodles. This was a step too far, and so I tried to ingratiate myself with her by using the noodles she picked out of my Carb Cupboard (I have such a thing), but I do love soba noodles in my ramen, and am afraid will persist in this incorrect habit.

I found fresh dashi, a Japanese broth infused with seaweed and bonito fish, in a pouch, at my local supermarket, but otherwise there are plenty of instant dashi granules or cubes around and if I haven't got any, I just use Marigold Swiss vegetable bouillon powder. The flavour from the dried shitake mushroom is so beautiful, that any light broth is a good choice. Talking of which, if I have time, I use 4 dried whole shitake mushrooms and soak them for a couple of hours after the 15 minutes' bubbling – indeed, I sometimes get them soaking at breakfast so that the flavours deepen all day and I'm ramen'd up in no time at all in the evening. But I am not that organized often enough, in which case I use dried ready-sliced shitake, as below, and suggest you do, too. When I'm ramen-ready, I want no one or nothing to hold me up.

5g dried ready-sliced shitake mushrooms (see Intro)

3cm piece (15g) fresh ginger, peeled and cut into fine matchsticks

500ml cold dashi or vegetable stock

1 x 70g sheet instant ramen noodles or 50g soba noodles

1 egg

100g baby pak choi (about 3 little bundles)

2 radishes

2 teaspoons sweet white miso

½ teaspoon soy sauce, or to taste

drop toasted sesame oil

1 spring onion (green part only), thinly sliced

¼ teaspoon dried chilli flakes

- Put the dried shitake in a saucepan that has a tight-fitting lid. Add the ginger matchsticks and pour in the cold dashi, bring to the boil, then clamp on the lid, lower the heat, and let it simmer for 15 minutes.

- Meanwhile, put a saucepan of water on for the noodles; these take hardly any time. So, towards the end of the broth's 15 minutes' simmering time, cook the noodles according to packet instructions, then drain and refresh under a cold running tap and leave in the sieve or colander. Fill the saucepan with water again, bring to the boil, add the egg and simmer for 6½ minutes, by which time the yolk will be set around the edge, but still have a bit of ooze in the middle.

- While the broth's simmering, trim the ends of the pak choi, tear off the leaves and separate the stems into one pile and the leaves into another. Quarter the radishes, lengthways. When the broth's had its 15 minutes, bring it to a rolling boil, and add the pak choi stems and the quartered radishes. Let it come back to the boil, then add the pak choi leaves and turn off the heat. Now add the miso and soy sauce and a drop of sesame oil, and put the lid back on.

- When the egg is ready, pour out the boiling water, then run cold water from the tap into the pan until the egg has cooled enough to peel.

- Put the drained noodles into a bowl and pour the broth and vegetables over them. Cut the egg in half lengthways, then add both halves to the soup. (And yes, I know the bowl you see here only has one half.) Sprinkle the sliced spring onion and dried chilli flakes over the top, and eat yourself into Zen bliss.

Thai noodles with cinnamon and prawns

I have been alive a long time and, at least when it comes to eating, have spent that time wisely and well. So, it's not often that I eat something that tastes so different to anything I've come across before. But this is such a dish. A gorgeous and mesmerically talented chef called, so perfectly, Tum, cooked it when I was on holiday in Thailand last year, and I made him cook it again and again, and then finally asked him if I could video his making it, so I could try and recreate it at home.

I was apprehensive about doing so, not least because I was frightened of facing up to my inadequate camera work and the lesser ingredients found at home. And yet, even with frozen prawns, the substitution of regular celery for the Chinese celery (which is all leaf, no stalk to speak of, and stronger-tasting) and a less-experienced hand at the wok, the very first mouthful brought back the magical enchantment of its taste in Thailand.

You do need to buy leafy celery, and even though the stalks don't get a look-in, you chop the slender stems to which the leaves are attached and add them to the wok along with the other flavourings at the very beginning.

Apart from having to make geographically enforced changes, I have stuck to Tum's recipe, including the ready-ground pepper and chicken stock concentrate (actually, he used chicken powder). I just had to share this spectacularly unfamiliar but compelling recipe with you. I hope you will be as bowled over by it as I was.

1 x 15ml tablespoon sunflower oil

2 cloves garlic, peeled and roughly chopped

3cm piece (15g) fresh ginger, peeled and cut into fine matchsticks

1 star anise

½ long or 1 short stick cinnamon, broken into shards

2–3 leafy stems at the top of 1 stick celery (see Intro), stems cut into short lengths, leaves roughly chopped

1½ x 15ml tablespoons light soy sauce

1 x 15ml tablespoon dark soy sauce

1 x 15ml tablespoon oyster sauce

¼ teaspoon ground white pepper

100ml cold water

1 teaspoon chicken stock concentrate

1 x 15ml tablespoon ketjap manis, or 1 x 15ml tablespoon dark soy sauce mixed with 1 tablespoon soft dark brown sugar

10 raw peeled king prawns, thawed if frozen

80g mung bean (glass) noodles or rice vermicelli, soaked and drained as per packet instructions

fat pinch ground cinnamon

fat pinch ground cloves

○ On a high heat, heat the oil in a large wok. Add the garlic, ginger, star anise, cinnamon and the sliced leafy stems of celery, and cook, stirring, for 1 minute.

○ Stir in both soy sauces and leave to simmer for 30 seconds, then stir in the oyster sauce and ground pepper.

○ Add the water, followed by the chicken stock concentrate and the ketjap manis (or the mixture of dark soy sauce with soft brown sugar), stir until everything's well combined and bring to the boil.

○ Now add the king prawns, immersing them in the liquid. Simmer until the prawns are cooked through.

○ Finally, add the drained noodles and stir well – I find a couple of pasta forks, one in each hand, best for this – so that everything is combined, and most of the dark liquid is absorbed. Add the pinches of ground cinnamon and cloves, stir again, and if you're not serving straight from the wok, decant into a serving bowl, and sprinkle with the reserved chopped celery leaves.

STORE NOTE

Cool leftovers, then cover and refrigerate within 2 hours of making. Will keep for up to 2 days. Delicious cold.

Thai steamed clams

This is another recipe from my Thai holidays, although I had to recreate it from taste memory rather than from any actual record. I have, knowingly, made some changes, as the original uses a chilli paste and also had a scanter broth. But I keep good-quality, authentic Thai curry pastes in the house at all times, and I wanted the delicate sweetness of the coconut water, even though it's out of a carton. And I greedily wanted more of the richly flavoured but light broth: it is quite lovely just to bring the bowl of aromatic clam liquor to your lips once you've eaten the clams; besides, Chef Tum made this as part of a huge feast, but I eat it just as it is, for supper, enjoying the trance-inducing ritual of picking out the sweet flesh of the clams. You can, of course, make an accompanying bowl of jasmine rice (which takes about 10–15 minutes) and eat the broth-soused rice as a second course, after a delicate starter of steamed clams.

For me, the scent of Thai basil is crucial here. But I suppose if I hadn't eaten it in situ, with Thai basil, I would be perfectly happy with some chopped fresh coriander in its stead.

SERVES 2–4

1kg palourde clams

2 teaspoons Thai red curry paste

½ cup (125ml) coconut water

1 teaspoon lime juice

handful Thai basil leaves or coriander

○ Tip the clams into a large bowl, cover with cold water and leave to soak for 15 minutes. At the end of the 15 minutes, drain the clams, discarding any that remain open.

○ Get out a wok with a lid, and spoon in the Thai curry paste, then pour in the coconut water, add the lime juice and stir or whisk to mix. Now turn on the heat and, when the coral-tinted liquid comes to a bubble, tip in the clams and cover with the lid. They should take about 5 minutes to cook – by which time they should be gaping and open, revealing plump golden flesh within – but shake the pan sporadically to make sure the clams move about in the liquid so that they steam equally.

○ Transfer to a large bowl, discarding any clams that have stayed closed. Distribute most of the gorgeously scented Thai basil leaves throughout the bowl and either serve from this bowl or decant into individual bowls, scattering a few extra leaves on top, and making sure that each of you has an empty bowl for the shells, too.

Thai turkey meatballs

This is not a souvenir from my holiday, but an adaptation of a wonderful supper I ate at an American friend's house. It is Thai only so far as it uses green Thai curry paste and related ingredients, but I have no reason to believe there are even turkeys in Thailand, let alone turkey meatballs. In other words, it isn't Thai at all, but it tastes so good and is so easy to make, that I go with it willingly. I do, however, use authentic Thai curry paste and coconut milk, both of which are inestimably better and much cheaper from online Thai food shops than they are from the supermarket. And ever since I saw the amount of chicken powder they get through in Thailand, I unapologetically use chicken broth made from concentrate. Not that I have ever felt bad about using stock cubes or concentrate, actually. Maybe that's bravado. I do feel a bit sheepish about it, but I refuse to pretend to be more virtuous and less lazy than I am.

Talking of laziness, please don't be put off by a bit of meatball-rolling – the thought is worse than the deed. In fact, I find it immensely gratifying and soothing work, absorbing without being challenging. Think of it as a mindfulness exercise, if you like. I could write a whole book about mindfulness in the kitchen. But another time, maybe…

One final note: I like to eat this straight out of a bowl, but I do sometimes serve flat rice noodles alongside or, rather, nestling underneath, too.

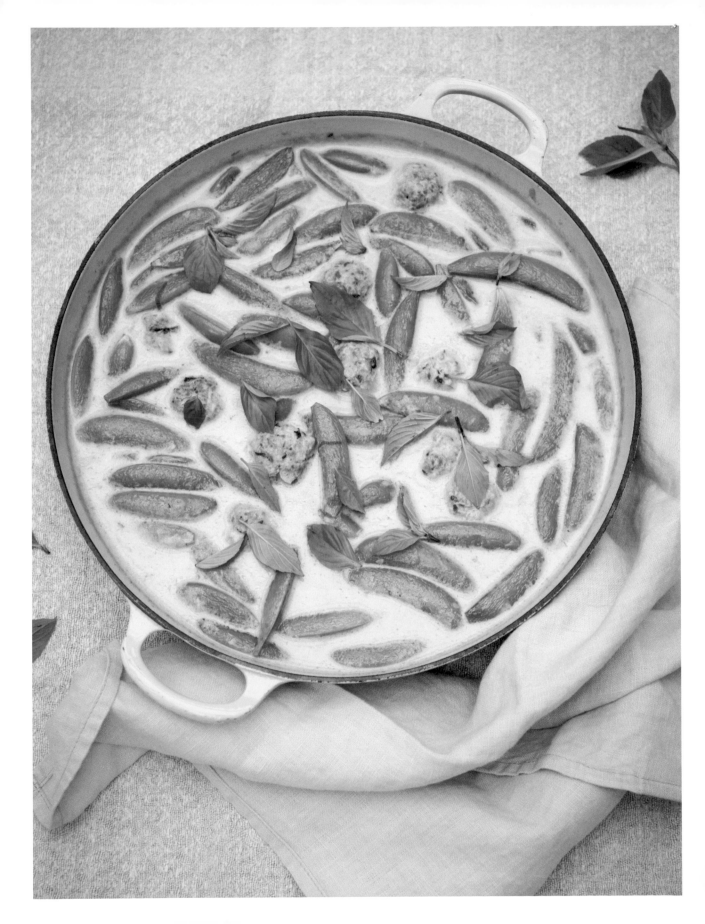

4 courgettes (approx. 750g)

500g turkey mince

3 spring onions

1 clove garlic, peeled and finely grated or minced

2cm piece (10g) fresh ginger, peeled and finely grated

small bunch fresh coriander, chopped

1 teaspoon dried chilli flakes

zest and juice of 1 lime, preferably unwaxed

1 teaspoon sea salt flakes, plus more to taste

2 teaspoons sunflower oil

3 x 15ml tablespoons Thai green curry paste, or to taste

1 x 400ml can coconut milk

500ml chicken stock

3 x 15ml tablespoons fish sauce

350g sugar snap peas

TO SERVE:

small handful Thai basil leaves

2–3 limes, cut into wedges

○ To make the meatballs, take one of the courgettes (approx. 200g) and trim the ends. Using a vegetable peeler, remove some of the skin in stripes, and then coarsely grate the courgette onto a piece of kitchen roll: I recommend you use a coarse box cheese grater here; if the grater's too fine, the courgette will just turn to mush. Press as much water as you can out of the grated courgette.

○ Put the grated courgette, and any excess liquid now squeezed out of it, into a big bowl, and add the turkey mince, breaking it up as you tip it in.

○ Trim the spring onions and halve lengthways, then finely chop them, putting the white part in with your mince and reserving the green part for later.

○ Add the garlic and ginger, then add 2 tablespoons of the chopped coriander, along with the chilli flakes, lime zest and salt.

○ Using a fork or your hands (the latter being my preference), mix the meatball mixture thoroughly but lightly. If you handle it too much, you will make heavy, dense meatballs, which you don't want. Once the mixture's gently combined, shape into small meatballs, using a heaped teaspoonful as a guide. You should get about 30 meatballs, provided you don't start making ever bigger ones as you go, which is easily done.

○ Heat the oil in a large casserole or pan (with a lid), and fry the chopped green part of the spring onion briefly, just turning it in the hot pan. Now add the Thai green curry paste, and then use the cream from the top of the coconut milk, whisking it into the paste over the heat.

○ Pour in the rest of the coconut milk, along with the chicken stock and fish sauce, and let it come to the boil.

- Peel the rest of the courgettes in stripes as before, then halve them lengthways, quarter them in the same way, and slice into (roughly) 1cm pieces. Add these to the bubbling pan, then gently drop in the meatballs, letting them fall in circles as you work around the pan from the outer edge inwards, and leaving them unprodded, as they will be very tender and easy to break up.

- Wait for the pan to come to a bubble again, then clamp on the lid, turn down the heat and leave to simmer for 20 minutes. Check that the courgettes are tender and the meatballs are cooked through, before stirring in the sugar snap peas and the juice of the zested lime. Check the seasoning, and adjust as you wish.

- Take off the heat and scatter with Thai basil (if you have some) or just sprinkle with a little more of the chopped coriander. And I like to chop some limes into wedges and bring to the table for people to spritz over as they eat.

MAKE AHEAD NOTE	FREEZE NOTE
The meatballs and sauce can be made 1 day ahead. Cool, cover and refrigerate within 2 hours of making. Reheat gently until piping hot, being careful not to break up the meatballs.	The cooked and cooled meatballs and sauce can be frozen, in an airtight container, for up to 3 months. Defrost overnight in fridge before reheating as Make Ahead Note.

Black rice noodles with ginger and chilli

I can't get enough of spicy noodles, and this is another example that breathes its seductive fire into my soul. I concede that the ingredients list is long, but I like to do a comprehensive shop at the Asian supermarket, and this means I have everything to hand when the mood strikes, which is often. I know I've gone a little fancy with the black rice noodles, but I saw these – along with green tea noodles and a panoply of other flavours – and just had to buy them. If you can get the black rice noodles, they do have a certain hardiness which means you can leave leftovers to get cold and then box them up for a mean packed lunch the next day. But soba noodles, or any other noodles of your choice, can be substituted without loss of face or flavour.

SERVES 1–2

2 x 15ml tablespoons chopped unsalted peanuts

1 fat clove garlic, peeled and finely chopped

6cm piece (30g) fresh ginger, peeled and finely chopped

1 teaspoon sunflower oil

2 teaspoons toasted sesame oil

2 x 15ml tablespoons soy sauce

2 x 15ml tablespoons Chinese (Shaoxing) rice wine

1½ x 15ml tablespoons hot sauce, such as Sriracha

2 x 15ml tablespoons cold water

200g black rice noodles (see Intro)

2 spring onions, trimmed

2 x 15ml tablespoons chopped fresh coriander, plus some whole leaves to put on top

° Toast the peanuts in a dry frying pan until golden, then tip onto a plate to cool.

° Put the garlic and ginger in a cold heavy-based pan with the sunflower and sesame oils, heat them gently then increase the heat a little and give the pan a minute's sizzling – not letting anything burn – and take off the heat.

° Now, carefully – as the hot oil could spit – add the soy sauce, Chinese rice wine, hot sauce and the 2 tablespoons of cold water. Put back on the heat and bring to a bubble, then immediately take off the heat and pour into a large bowl to cool.

° Cook or soak the noodles in boiling water, until they are tender, or according to packet instructions, then refresh under cold water, drain, and toss with the sauce.

° Cut each spring onion into 3 pieces and then shred lengthways into strips, adding to the noodles, along with the chopped coriander and most of the toasted peanuts.

° Divide the cold dressed noodles between 2 small bowls, and top each with a few coriander leaves and the rest of the nuts.

Chinese-inspired chicken noodle soup

Actually, there are dual inspirations for this soup, for it is really a version of My Mother's Praised Chicken from *Kitchen* infused with Chinese flavours. What you end up with is the sort of soup you want to eat in bowls held up inelegantly close to your mouth so that you are in easy slurping distance. I am embarrassed to say that I can't use chopsticks, unless they're the children's sort held together with a piece of card and a rubber band, but this soup really makes me want to learn.

I always recommend organic chicken (or organic meat generally) but I am mindful of the fact that not everyone can afford the luxury. Even so, if you use an intensively farmed chicken here (and lack of taste is only one concern), you just won't get a flavoursome enough soup, in which case add some stock cubes or concentrate to the water.

I've given an exuberant list of ingredients for sprinkling on at the end, as I love that final fling of flavour. And though I haven't added them here, should you be making a fresh foray to an Asian food shop to make this, and you see Chinese flowering chives about, they would be a real treat, and are so beautiful. Despite the Asian inspiration for the soup's flavour, I make a steep geographical about-turn and use golden nests (one per person) of De Cecco Taglierini all'uovo for the noodle element, though I do also love this with those very thin mung bean or rice vermicelli. In fact, I just can't think of a bad way of eating this: even noodle-less, and thus rather not living up to its title, this is bliss in a bowl.

3 leeks, cleaned and trimmed

3 carrots, peeled and trimmed

3 sticks celery, trimmed

7cm piece (35g) fresh ginger, peeled and finely grated

1 small or medium chicken, preferably organic

1 x 15ml tablespoon sunflower oil

125ml Chinese (Shaoxing) rice wine

tied stalks from bunch of coriander, plus leaves to serve (see below)

2.5 litres cold water

2 teaspoons sea salt flakes

1 teaspoon Szechuan pepper or dried chilli flakes

2 x 15ml tablespoons soy sauce, plus more to serve

2 fat cloves garlic, peeled and finely grated or minced

zest and juice of 1 lime, preferably unwaxed

300g baby pak choi, tatsoi, choi sum, or other greens of choice

100g radishes

1 nest (approx. 50g) dried fine egg noodles or vermicelli per person

salt for noodle water to taste

½ teaspoon toasted sesame oil, plus more to serve (see below)

TO SERVE:

toasted sesame oil

2 (or more to taste) fresh red chillies, de-seeded and finely diced (optional)

leaves from bunch of coriander (see above)

finely chopped chives (optional)

○ Slice each trimmed leek in half lengthways, and cut into 1cm slices. Set aside. Cut the carrots into 4cm lengths and quarter each log lengthways. Chop the celery into 1cm slices, reserving any leaves to add to the soup at the end. Grate the ginger onto a plate for the time being. I use a fine microplane grater and get 4–5 teaspoons of fiery pulp out of this. Don't wash up the grater yet, as you'll need it for the garlic and lime later.

○ Now, with your veg prepped, untruss your chicken, cut off (but do not discard) the ankle part of the leg (I find kitchen scissors more than adequate to the task) and put the chicken, breast-side down, on a chopping board, then press down until you hear the breastbone crack – perhaps I shouldn't like this as much as I do – and the chicken is slightly flattened. Wash your hands, and then warm the tablespoon of sunflower oil in a pan that comes with a lid and that's big enough to take all the ingredients comfortably; I use a saucepan of 28cm diameter, 12cm deep, which is a tight, but good, fit.

○ When the oil is hot, put the chicken in, breast-side down, and leave to brown for 3 minutes; the heat should not be too high for this or it'll start burning. Turn the chicken the other way up, then turn up the heat to high and chuck in the rice wine. While it's bubbling, throw in the chicken ankle pieces along with the tied coriander stalks, sliced carrots and celery.

- Pour in the water, then add the sea salt flakes, Szechuan pepper (or chilli flakes), soy sauce and finely grated ginger. Add the garlic, then grate in the zest of the lime, and squeeze in the juice of half of it. Let this come to the boil.

- Once it's bubbling, clamp on the lid, turn the heat to low and let it simmer, covered, for 1 hour. Once the hour is up, take the lid off, then turn up the heat and bring it back to the boil again, and, once it is, add the leeks you sliced earlier. Cover partially with the lid and cook for 10 minutes, then let the broth simmer uncovered and confidently for another 10 minutes. This is to let the broth strengthen a bit. Then turn off the heat altogether, though keep the pan on the hob, clamp the lid back on and leave for at least 20 minutes and up to 1 hour. While this is going on, I'd put a pan of water on to boil the noodles later, and salt it when it comes to the boil.

- When you want to eat, remove the chicken to a board: it may be falling to pieces, but so much the better. Remove the chicken skin (I discard it, as for me there's no joy in chicken skin unless it's crisp), then take the meat off the bone and shred it. And by the way, should you not use up all the chicken for the soup, know that it is magnificent – flavoursome and tender – in a salad or sandwich the next day.

- Chop the stems of the greens you're using, and put the leaves into a separate pile. Quarter the radishes top to tail. Bring the pan of soup back to the boil, add the stalks of the greens and the quartered radishes, and let it come back to the boil once more. At the same time, add the noodles to the pan of boiling salted water, and cook them (if you're using the fine noodles or vermicelli they shouldn't take more than 2–3 minutes).

- Add the leafy parts of the greens to the bubbling soup and drain the noodles. Put the noodles and shredded chicken into your serving bowls. Taste the soup for seasoning, and add more salt (or soy) and the juice of the remaining half of lime, if you think it needs it. When satisfied, ladle the fragrant broth, with its vegetables, on top of the chicken and noodles, add a drop of sesame oil to each bowl, then sprinkle with chopped chillies, coriander or chives, as you wish. Bring the bottles of soy sauce and sesame oil, and some more of the chopped chilli and herbs to the table for people to add as they eat. Warning: don't burn your mouth; this smells so good, I'm afraid it's easy to be dangerously impatient and eat while the soup's still scaldingly hot.

STORE NOTE	FREEZE NOTE
Transfer leftover cooked chicken to a container, cover, and chill within 1 hour. It will keep in fridge for up to 3 days.	The cooked and cooled chicken can be frozen, in airtight containers or resealable bags, for up to 2 months. Defrost overnight in fridge before using.

Drunken noodles

The general explanation given for why Thai drunken noodles are so called is that they have enough chilli in them to shake you out of even the worst hangover. The only difficulty here – prepared though I am to believe it – is that making a traditional *pad kee mao* is not an undertaking I'd recommend while worse for wear. So this is my simplified version. I've cut to the chase – no meat, fish or veg, just highly seasoned, searingly hot noodles.

Not that you need to be hung-over to eat them. Why give yourself all that pain, in order to get to the pleasure? Mind you, I say that as someone for whom a glass and a half of white wine is too much, though I could cope with a beer, so cold it hurts, while going for the blissful burn of these addictively hot noodles.

Anyway, I make them so often when in serenely sober Bowlfood Mood. Most of the ingredients come from the storecupboard, and the finished dish is in front of you in 10 minutes. I find these hot noodles hard to beat, and they do really blow your head off: if you want less of a fiery fright, then halve the chilli flakes. To start with, at least…

SERVES 2, OR A VERY DRINK-SOAKED OR GREEDY 1

150g dried flat rice noodles (the pad thai sort)

2 x 15ml tablespoons cold water

1 x 15ml tablespoon oyster sauce

1 teaspoon toasted sesame oil

2 teaspoons sunflower oil

3cm piece (15g) fresh ginger, peeled and finely grated

1 clove garlic, peeled and finely grated or minced

1 lime, preferably unwaxed

½ teaspoon dried chilli flakes

4 x 15ml tablespoons soy sauce

handful chopped fresh coriander

° Soak the rice noodles in hot water for 8 minutes, or according to packet instructions, then drain and refresh under a cold running tap.

° Put the 2 tablespoons of water into a cup and stir in the oyster sauce, then set aside for a mo.

° Put the oils in a wok, turn on the heat and add the ginger, garlic and grate in the zest of the lime – I use a coarse microplane grater here, only because it's faster than a fine one. Sprinkle in the chilli flakes. Stir well, then tip in the soaked, drained rice noodles and stir them – I find this easier with an implement in each hand – quickly in the hotly seasoned oil.

○ Add the watered-down oyster sauce, the juice of ½ the lime and the soy sauce, then transfer to a waiting bowl (or bowls) and toss with the chopped coriander. Keep the bottle of soy sauce and the remaining ½ lime close at hand, should you need either of them as you eat. I am such a pyrophile, I like to keep some extra chilli flakes to hand, too.

Rice bowl with ginger, radish and avocado

A rice bowl is a wondrous thing, but often – despite the simplicity of its title – a rather cluttered and complicated one. Here, I have pared it back, to make a gorgeously seasoned rice bowl, with nothing more than a few seeds, herbs and radishes stirred through it, and an avocado to top it. It's a simple take on an inspiringly expansive idea. So please use this as a starting point only. It's very much a non-recipe recipe, and every time I make it, I add something different, depending on what's to hand.

The only constant is the rice. I cannot get enough of short grain brown rice – so much more nubbly and delicious than regular wholegrain rice or white rice – but I find it doesn't cook quite like rice does normally. That's to say, usually the unswerving rule when cooking rice is 1 part rice to 2 parts water. I have found that with short grain brown rice it is 1 part rice to 1½ parts water (despite what it says on the packet). Anyway, whatever rice you're using, I find it much simpler to use cups rather than weights – though I've given those, too – as it is ratio of volumes that is crucial. Actually, I use cups for the seed-element here, too, as I find it very calming not getting the scales out. And even though I've given a weight for the ginger, in reality, I just shave off slices with the vegetable peeler until I feel I have enough.

Raw radishes are my usual go-to, but I had some cold leftover roast radishes, so that's what you see in the picture. If you want to have them hot, just roast halved radishes, cut-side down, with a little oil in a hot oven (about 220°C/gas mark 7) for 10 minutes.

¾ cup (150g) short grain brown rice

1 cup (250ml) cold water

5cm piece (25g) fresh ginger, peeled

4–6 radishes

1½ x 15ml tablespoons tamari or soy sauce

1 teaspoon organic cloudy apple cider vinegar

¼ cup (4 x 15ml tablespoons) mixed seeds, such as pumpkin, sunflower, sesame

3–4 x 15ml tablespoons chopped fresh coriander

1 small ripe avocado

- Put the rice and water in a heavy-based saucepan that comes with a tight-fitting lid, and bring to the boil. Once it's bubbling, clamp on the lid, turn the heat down very low and simmer for 25 minutes. Then turn off the heat, leaving the lid on, and let it stand for a further 5 minutes, by which time the rice will be cooked – but still nutty – and the water absorbed.

- While the rice is cooking, use a vegetable peeler to shave the ginger into very thin strips. Cut the radishes into quarters or eighths lengthways, depending on their size.

- When the rice is cooked, spoon into a mixing bowl. Add the tamari or soy sauce and the cider vinegar to the bowl and toss with a fork to combine, and then do the same with the ginger shavings, radishes and seeds. Stir all but a little of the chopped coriander into the rice, still using a fork.

- Divide between 2 smallish bowls and top with avocado, cut either into gondola-shaped slices or chunks, as wished. Sprinkle each with the remaining coriander, and eat serenely.

MAKE AHEAD NOTE

If you want to eat this cold, the rice can be cooked 1 day ahead. Spread cooked rice out on a large plate to cool quickly. Cover and refrigerate within 1 hour.

Sweet potato macaroni cheese

I'm just going to say it: this is the best macaroni cheese I've ever eaten – better than the macaroni cheese I ate as a child; better than the macaroni cheese I brought my own children up on when they were little (they don't agree); better than any fancy restaurant macaroni cheese with white truffle or lobster; better than any macaroni cheese I have loved in my life thus far, and there have been many.

I don't feel it's boastful to say as much, as the greatness lies not in any brilliance on my part, but in the simple tastes of the ingredients as they fuse in the heat. That's home cooking for you.

I do rather love the way these little macaroni cheeses, with their pixie-penne, look like they've been made with artificially coloured, cheap squeezy cheese or out of a box, when in fact their exotic glow comes courtesy of the earthy goodness of a sweet potato.

SERVES 4

500g sweet potatoes	¼ teaspoon paprika, plus ¼ teaspoon to sprinkle on top
300g pennette or other small short pasta	75g feta cheese
4 x 15ml tablespoons (60g) soft unsalted butter	125g mature Cheddar, grated, plus 25g to sprinkle on top
3 x 15ml tablespoons plain flour	
500ml full-fat milk	4 fresh sage leaves
1 teaspoon English mustard	salt and pepper to taste

° Preheat the oven to 200°C/gas mark 6. Put on a large-ish pan of water to boil, with the lid on to make it come to the boil faster.

° Peel the sweet potatoes and cut them roughly into 2–3cm pieces. When the water's boiling, add salt to taste, and then the sweet potato pieces, and cook them for about 10 minutes or until they are soft. Scoop them out of the water into a bowl – using a "spider" or slotted spoon – and lightly mash with a fork, without turning them into a purée. Don't get rid of this water, as you will need it to cook your pasta in later.

° In another saucepan, gently melt the butter and add the flour, whisking to form a roux, then take the pan off the heat, slowly whisk in the milk and, when it's all combined and smooth, put back on the heat. Exchange your whisk for a wooden spoon, and continue to stir until your gently bubbling sauce has lost any floury taste and has thickened. Add the mustard and the ¼ teaspoon of paprika. Season to taste, but do remember that you will be adding Cheddar and salty feta later, so underdo it for now.

○ Cook the pennette in the sweet-potato water, starting to check 2 minutes earlier than packet instructions dictate, as you want to make sure it doesn't lose its bite entirely. Drain (reserving some of the pasta cooking water first) and then add the pennette to the mashed sweet potato, and fold in to combine; the heat of the pasta will make the mash easier to mix in.

○ Add the feta cheese to the sweet potato and pasta mixture, crumbling it in so that it is easier to disperse evenly, then fold in the white sauce, adding the 125g grated Cheddar as you go. Add some of the pasta cooking water, should you feel it needs loosening up at all.

○ Check for seasoning again, then, when you're happy, spoon the brightly sauced macaroni cheese into 4 small ovenproof dishes of approx. 375–425ml capacity (or 1 large rectangular dish measuring approx. 30 x 20 x 5cm deep and 1.6 litre capacity). Sprinkle the remaining Cheddar over each one, dust with the remaining ¼ teaspoon of paprika, then shred the sage leaves and scatter the skinny green ribbons over the top, too.

○ Put the pots on a baking tray, pop into the oven and bake for 20 minutes (or, if you're making this in a larger dish, bake for 30–35 minutes), by which time they will be piping hot and bubbling, and begging you to eat them.

MAKE AHEAD NOTE

The macaroni cheese can be made 1 day ahead. When the pasta has cooked, reserve 100ml of the cooking water and add this to the white sauce (it may look a little thin but the pasta absorbs the sauce as it cools). Transfer to the ovenproof dishes (without the sage topping). Once cool, cover and refrigerate within 2 hours of making. Sprinkle with the Cheddar, paprika and sage just before baking and cook for an extra 5–10 minutes, checking that the macaroni cheese is piping hot in the centre before serving.

Pasta alla Bruno

Since this book contains a recipe for Chicken Cosima (**p.149**), inspired by my daughter, it seems only fair to include a recipe for my son as well. This is his favoured pasta – which can also be made with chorizo, should that be to hand – and I have been greeted on many mornings with the tell-tale signs of it in the kitchen from the late night before. A variant also includes fresh mozzarella, added at the end of the cooking time, while the pasta is sitting, calmly absorbing its sauce, but I think it better without. Not that, at home, it's my call. You must do as you wish.

SERVES 2, OR 1 TEENAGE BOY

200g casarecce pasta or pasta of your choice

1 teaspoon salt for pasta water, or to taste

1 teaspoon regular olive oil

6 rashers thin-cut smoked streaky bacon

1 clove garlic, peeled and finely grated or minced

200g ripe cherry tomatoes, quartered

1 teaspoon dried chilli flakes

Parmesan or mozzarella, to serve

- Put a pan of water on to boil for the pasta, and when it's bubbling, add a teaspoon of salt, or to taste, and put the casarecce on to cook. The make I use stipulates 11 minutes' cooking time, but I feel it needs rather less, so keep testing. Get on with the sauce when the pasta goes in, or even before, should you prefer, as it can stand, with the lid on, once it's cooked.

- Heat the oil in a wok or heavy-based frying pan that comes with a lid, then scissor in the bacon, and stir-fry until crisp. (If you want the bacon to stay crisp, remove now to a plate, uncovered, and toss back in just before eating.) Remove the pan from the heat, just while you add the garlic, then stir, and place back on the heat. Tumble in the quartered cherry tomatoes and the dried chilli flakes, stir well and put on the lid. Shake the wok from time to time while cooking, and lift the lid once or twice to give a stir, and a check.

- Once the pasta is cooked, but still with a bit of bite to it, use a "spider" or wire basket ladle to scoop out the pasta into the wok, stirring in a little of the pasta cooking water just to help the sauce amalgamate. Put the lid on and leave to stand on the ring it cooked on, though with the heat turned off, for 5 minutes.

- Stir the bacon back in, check for seasoning, then tip into a bowl, and eat heartily.

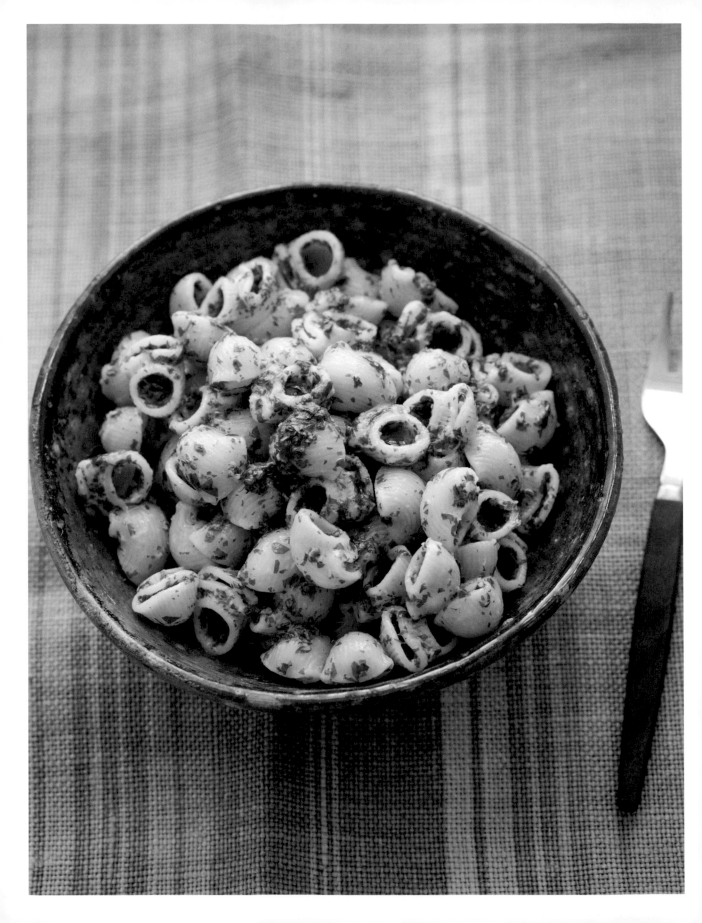

Pasta snails with garlic butter

I have rather a weakness for the culinary pun, and find this one particularly pleasing. This is snails in garlic butter, only the snails are pasta. Since, really, the reason people eat snails is for the garlic butter, it seems to me that this is no second best. And while it is obviously rich, the pasta snails make it rather less so than the original escargots. I'm afraid it's all too easy to eat, and copiously.

SERVES 2

150g pasta snails (lumache rigate)

salt for pasta water to taste

50g soft unsalted butter

2 fat or 4 smaller cloves garlic, peeled and finely grated or minced

pinch sea salt flakes, plus more to taste

1 cup (30g) finely chopped parsley

- Put on a pan of water for the pasta, salt it, and then cook the pasta according to packet instructions, though do start to taste 2 minutes before it says it'll be ready.

- In a saucepan that will take the pasta later, melt the butter over a lowish heat, then add the garlic and a pinch of sea salt flakes and fry for 1 minute, making sure the garlic doesn't colour. Add the parsley, and stir over the heat for another minute, until you have a velvety green sauce.

- When the pasta's cooked, but still has a bit of bite, reserve some of the pasta cooking water and then drain.

- Add the drained pasta to the pan of sauce, then add a tablespoonful of the pasta cooking water, and stir again — with the pan still over the heat — adding another tablespoonful or so, as much as is needed to make the sauce coat the pasta well. Season to taste and eat immediately.

Merguez meatballs

This is a recipe of fabulous ease and speed, but you'd never guess it to eat it. These meatballs taste as if they had been slowly and lovingly tended, and their deeply spiced sauce tastes as if it had been cooked over days. I make no apology for the shortcuts – the meatballs are made of squeezed-out merguez sausages, and the sauce's rich base is a jar of chargrilled peppers – because what you end up with is honest and flavourful and just so good.

500g merguez sausages

2 x 15ml tablespoons regular olive oil

1 x 400g can chopped tomatoes

1 x 290g jar chargrilled peppers in oil

2 teaspoons cumin seeds

1 teaspoon ground allspice

1 teaspoon ground cinnamon

2 teaspoons sea salt flakes

1 x 15ml tablespoon runny honey

- Squeeze the sausagemeat out of the casings and then form into small meatballs, using about 2 teaspoonfuls per ball. I get 34 out of this mixture, but I have to concentrate on not making the meatballs bigger as I go – they should each be about the size of a cherry tomato.

- Heat the oil in a wide, heavy-based saucepan or casserole (with a lid), and fry the meatballs for about 3 minutes or so, then spoon out as much excess oil as you can and discard.

- Add the chopped tomatoes, then drain the jar of peppers and snip or chop them into pieces, before adding to the pan as well.

- Sprinkle the spices over the contents of the pan, add the salt and – oiling the tablespoon first – the honey, then bring up to a bubble before partially covering the pan with its lid, and leaving to simmer for 10 minutes. Obviously, you can make rice or couscous to eat with this, or just get some good bread to dunk in.

MAKE AHEAD NOTE	FREEZE NOTE
The meatballs and sauce can be made 1 day ahead. Cool, cover and refrigerate within 2 hours of making. Reheat gently until piping hot, being careful not to break up the meatballs.	The cooked and cooled meatballs and sauce can be frozen, in an airtight container, for up to 3 months. Defrost overnight in fridge before reheating as Make Ahead Note.

Indian-spiced shepherd's pie

A reader kindly sent me her recipe for 'Indian Shepherd's Pie' (at my request, as I'd seen her mention it on Twitter), which certainly inspired this, although the recipe here is totally different. And cooking is like this: we each play out the themes differently in our own kitchens, but carrying with us, gratefully, the ideas and practices of others.

My children love this. Actually, I don't know anyone who's eaten it and doesn't. While it's spicy (though you can reduce the heat to taste) and vibrant, it is also cosy and comforting, and blends the familiar with the less traditional in a way that gives me quiet satisfaction.

The impetus to use a sweet potato mash for the topping was simply because it was so much easier than peeling and mashing regular potatoes, and they work so well against the hot, exuberantly spiced meat, especially when tempered with lime and ginger juice. And see overleaf for my ginger-juicing trick, which can be brought into play on any number of occasions – I often squeeze this juice into soups or stews at the end if I feel they need gingering up.

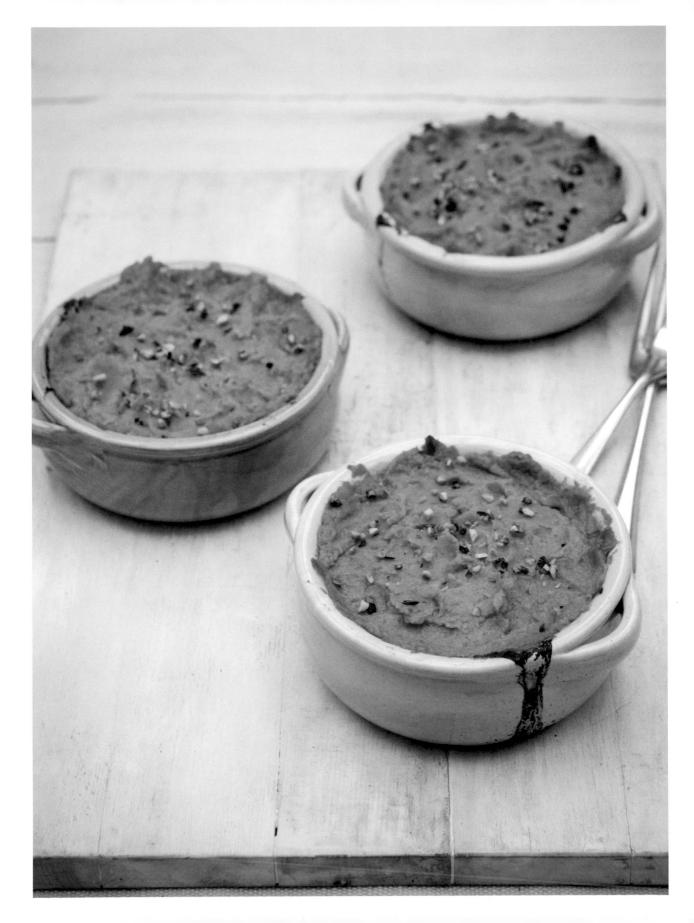

SERVES 4

FOR THE TOPPING:

1kg sweet potatoes

2 teaspoons sea salt flakes

2 x 15ml tablespoons white peppercorns

6 cardamom pods, cracked

peeled strips from 1 lime, preferably unwaxed, and juice of ½ lime

approx. 1 litre cold water

4cm piece (20g) fresh ginger, peeled, plus more for filling (see below)

FOR THE FILLING:

3 cloves garlic, peeled

4cm piece (20g) fresh ginger, peeled

1 onion, peeled

seeds from 6 cardamom pods

2 teaspoons cumin seeds

2 teaspoons coriander seeds

2 x 15ml tablespoons cold-pressed coconut oil

2 teaspoons garam masala

1 teaspoon dried chilli flakes

1 teaspoon ground turmeric

500g minced lamb, preferably organic

1 x 400g can chopped tomatoes

100g red lentils

1 teaspoon sea salt flakes

2 x 15ml tablespoons Worcestershire sauce

TO DECORATE:

4 teaspoons nibbed or finely chopped pistachios

- Preheat your oven to 220°C/gas mark 7. Start with the topping, cutting each of the sweet potatoes into approx. 4–5cm chunks.

- Put the unpeeled potato chunks into a large saucepan (with a lid) and add the salt, peppercorns, cracked cardamom pods and lime strips (you don't need the ginger just yet), then add just enough cold water (about 1 litre) to cover.

- Bring to the boil, then reduce the heat slightly, put the lid on and cook for about 30 minutes – or until the sweet potato is tender – while you get on with the filling.

- Slice the garlic and ginger roughly, quarter the onion, and put them all into the bowl of a food processor with the cardamom, cumin and coriander seeds, and whizz until finely chopped. Alternatively use a bowl and a stick blender, or just chop everything very finely by hand.

- Heat the coconut oil in a heavy-based pan (with a lid), and then tip this paste in.

- Cook for a few minutes or so to soften, stirring frequently, then stir in the garam masala, chilli flakes and turmeric, and tip in the lamb mince, turning it in the spiced onion mixture and breaking it up gently.

- Add the chopped tomatoes, then fill the empty can with cold water and, swilling it around, pour this in as well. Stir in the red lentils.

○ Season with the salt and Worcestershire sauce, then bring to a bubble, clamp on the lid, lower the heat and simmer for about 25 minutes, stirring once or twice to stop it catching on the bottom of the saucepan.

○ When the sweet potatoes are cooked, drain them, reserving the liquid, and leave until cool enough to peel away the skins. Put the flesh into a wide bowl.

○ Mash the sweet potatoes, using a potato masher, or any gadget of your choice (even a fork would do) and slowly beat in some of the potato cooking water – adding as much as you need to make the mash a less dense, more spreadable consistency – and squeeze in the juice of half the lime.

○ Grate the peeled ginger onto a plate – I use a coarse microplane grater – then spoon the grated ginger into the centre of a piece of kitchen roll. Moving quickly, pull up the edges of the paper and twizzle them, so you have a little wrapped swag-bag, then squeeze and wring out over the mash (an intense ginger juice will drip out). Beat this juice into the mash below. Check the seasoning, tasting to see if you want any more lime or ginger, too.

○ Once the lamb filling has had its time, ladle equally between 4 small ovenproof bowls or dishes of approx. 400ml capacity (or a larger rectangular dish, measuring approx. 30 x 20 x 5cm deep and 1.6 litre capacity), and then top with the mash, also dividing this equally between the bowls, spreading it to cover the rim of the dishes.

○ Sit the dishes on an oven tray and place in the oven for 10–15 minutes (or, if you're cooking this in one larger dish, it will need 30–35 minutes). The mash should be piping hot (though it won't get a crust) with the mince bubbling underneath.

○ On serving, sprinkle 1 teaspoon of nibbed pistachios over each bowl.

MAKE AHEAD NOTE	FREEZE NOTE
The pies can be assembled up to 2 days ahead. As soon as the pies are cool (and within 2 hours of making), cover each one and refrigerate until needed. Bake for an extra 10–15 minutes, making sure that the pies are piping hot in the centre before serving.	Wrap each pie tightly in a double layer of clingfilm and a layer of foil, and freeze for up to 3 months. Defrost overnight in fridge and bake as Make Ahead Note.

Warm spiced cauliflower and chickpea salad with pomegranate seeds

This is one of my favourite suppers, although there's nothing that says you can't serve this as a vegetable side as part of a more conventional meal. And you could also bolster it further by crumbling in some feta. But for me, it is perfect just as it is: the tomatoes almost ooze into a dressing in the oven, and the cauliflower softens, but not soggily. For choice, I'd always use home-cooked chickpeas (I cook batches in my slow cooker and freeze them in 250g portions for everyday use; see **p.211**), but otherwise I like the pre-cooked Spanish chickpeas in jars. Yes, they are more expensive than the canned variety, but the cheapest option is always to buy dried. Don't feel bad about using chickpeas out of a tin, though – I have been known to, myself. One can't always be so organized to have the freezer stashed with cooked chickpeas, and so I am always well stocked with canned chickpeas. They do work here, it's just that they won't be as soft; but then, you don't necessarily need them to be. The cauliflower and juicy tomatoes can stand some nubbliness.

The parsley is not a garnish – ugh, that word – but used, here, as a salad leaf. And this is also very, very good cold, so if you have some left over, it makes a fabulous packed lunch, or provides instant gratification on those days you have to eat fridge-side, with your coat still on, you're so hungry.

1 small head cauliflower

3 x 15ml tablespoons regular olive oil

½ teaspoon ground cinnamon

2 teaspoons cumin seeds

250g home-cooked chickpeas or drained weight from a jar or can (400g) of chickpeas

1–2 x 15ml tablespoons harissa, to taste (and depending on the heat of the harissa)

4 smallish ripe vine tomatoes (approx. 150g total)

1 teaspoon sea salt flakes, or to taste

3–4 x 15ml tablespoons pomegranate seeds

large bunch (approx. 100g) flat-leaf parsley

○ Preheat the oven to 220C /gas mark 7. Trim the cauliflower and divide into small florets. Pour the oil into a large bowl, add the cinnamon and cumin seeds, and stir or whisk to help the spices disperse. Tip in the prepared cauliflower and toss to coat. Pour the contents of the bowl into a small oven tray (I mostly use a disposable foil baking tray measuring 30 x 20cm) and place in the oven for 15 minutes. Don't wash out the bowl you've been using just yet.

○ Add the chickpeas to this bowl, and add the harissa, tasting it first to see if you want both tablespoonfuls, and, at the risk of being repetitive, toss to coat. Quarter the tomatoes and add them to the bowl, and shake or stir to mix. When the cauliflower has had its 15 minutes, remove the tray, quickly tip the chickpeas and tomatoes over the cauliflower, and toss to combine before returning to the oven for a further 15 minutes until the cauliflower is tender.

○ When it's ready, remove from the oven and sprinkle the salt over the vegetables, then (and this isn't the last time) toss to combine with half of the pomegranate seeds before dividing between 2 bowls. Divide the parsley leaves – without chopping them – between the 2 bowls and toss to mix. Scatter with the remaining pomegranate seeds.

STORE NOTE

Cool leftovers, then cover and refrigerate within 2 hours of making. Will keep in fridge for up to 2 days. Serve cold.

Stir-fried rice with double sprouts, chilli and pineapple

This is one of my quick-fire, bowlfood specials – instant comfort, instant joy. And here's what I'm not ashamed of doing: I use those pouches of ready-cooked brown basmati rice and supermarket packs of ready-cubed fresh pineapple. There, I've said it. And although I've stated (truthfully enough) that it will feed 2–4, I often make the full quantity for myself and, with a glad heart, stash any leftovers in the fridge to be eaten cold later. But if you want to make this as an accompaniment to a plate of cold ham or suchlike, then know that this amount will happily feed 6.

250g Brussels sprouts, trimmed	2 x 15ml tablespoons cold-pressed coconut oil
2 spring onions, trimmed	250g cooked and cooled brown rice
150g fresh pineapple cubes	250g beansprouts
3cm piece (15g) fresh ginger, peeled and finely grated	2 x 15ml tablespoons soy sauce
	2 x 15ml tablespoons lime juice
½ teaspoon dried chilli flakes	3 x 15ml tablespoons chopped fresh coriander

- With a sharp knife and a patient frame of mind, slice the Brussels sprouts thinly. Also thinly slice the spring onions, and mix the two together.

- Cut the pineapple cubes into 1cm dice and put in a bowl. Add the ginger and dried chilli flakes and stir to mix.

- Get out a wok (or similar) and over a vigorous heat, melt the coconut oil. Toss in the sliced Brussels sprouts and spring onions and stir-fry (I use a spatula-type implement in each hand) for about 3 minutes (the sprouts will start scorching in parts).

- Add the rice and toss to mix quickly, then add the beansprouts and the chillified, gingery pineapple (and any juice that has collected) and stir-fry for a minute or so, before adding the soy sauce, lime juice and 2 tablespoons of chopped coriander. Stir-fry for another minute, or until everything (most importantly the rice) is hot, and transfer to a warmed bowl or bowls, sprinkling the top with the remaining tablespoon of coriander.

STORE NOTE

Cool leftovers, then cover and refrigerate within 1 hour. Will keep in fridge for up to 1 day. Serve cold.

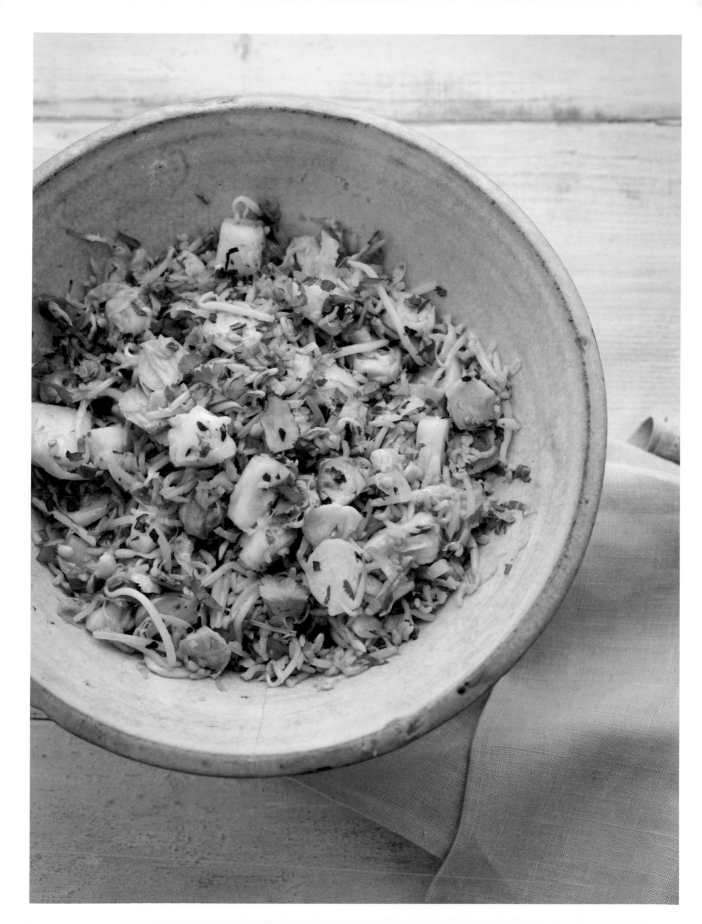

Middle-Eastern minestrone

This is in no sense an authentically Middle-Eastern recipe, but a fancy of mine. To elucidate: it is a vegetable soup that is imbued with Middle-Eastern flavours and, in place of the pasta that you'd cook for a traditional Italian minestrone, I use bulgur wheat.

Like many such soups, it thickens on standing, in which case you can either add more liquid, or eat it as a stew. Either way, it is fragrant and filling, and is fast becoming one of my favourite recipes.

2 x 15ml tablespoons regular olive oil

1 red onion, peeled and chopped

sea salt flakes to taste

1 butternut squash (just under 1kg), peeled, de-seeded and chopped into 2cm cubes

1 clove garlic, peeled and finely grated or minced

2 teaspoons cumin seeds

2 teaspoons coriander seeds

2–3 preserved lemons (depending on size), finely chopped

250g home-cooked chickpeas or drained weight from a jar or can (400g) of chickpeas

1.5 litres mild vegetable stock

100g bulgur wheat

chopped fresh coriander, to serve (optional)

- Heat the olive oil in a heavy-based saucepan that comes with a lid, and sauté the chopped onion sprinkled with a little salt for about 3 minutes until softened.

- Add the chopped butternut squash, the garlic and the cumin and coriander seeds and stir around, letting everything cook for about 10 minutes.

- Tip in the chopped preserved lemons and the drained chickpeas, then pour in the vegetable stock and partially cover with the lid to keep the liquid from evaporating too much. Simmer for about 20 minutes, by which time the butternut should be just cooked.

- Add the bulgur wheat, then re-cover the pan and cook gently for another 10 minutes, by which time the vegetables should be tender and the bulgur wheat soft but still nutty. Sprinkle with chopped coriander on serving, if so desired.

STORE NOTE	FREEZE NOTE
Cool leftovers, then cover and refrigerate within 2 hours of making. Will keep in fridge for up to 3 days. To reheat, pour the soup into a saucepan, adding extra water or stock if needed, then heat gently, stirring occasionally, until piping hot.	Cooled soup can be frozen, in an airtight container, for up to 3 months. Defrost overnight in fridge and reheat as Store Note.

Split pea soup with chilli, ginger and lime

This is one of those thick, wintry soups made spiky and fresh with chilli, ginger and lime. It has the hit of a hot and sour soup, but the nubbliness of the split peas gives those clear, piercing flavours an unfamiliar edge, while adding cosiness at the same time.

SERVES 6–8, MAKES APPROX. 2 LITRES

500g yellow split peas

6 spring onions, trimmed and thinly sliced

3 fresh red chillies, finely chopped (with or without seeds)

2 cloves garlic, peeled and finely grated or minced

2 litres water

2 teaspoons vegetable stock powder, or to taste

5cm piece (25g) fresh ginger, peeled and finely grated

zest and juice of 2 limes, preferably unwaxed

salt to taste (optional)

TO SERVE:

chopped fresh coriander, or sliced spring onions, or chopped fresh chilli, or all 3

○ Put the split peas, spring onions, chillies and garlic into a large casserole or heavy-based saucepan that comes with a lid, and pour in the water. Bring to the boil, and once it's bubbling, clamp on the lid, lower the heat slightly and cook for 40–60 minutes, stirring occasionally, until the split peas are cooked and breaking up in the liquid. You may well have to add more water if the soup gets too thick, although there is a school of thought that holds that this soup should be thick, a positively biblical mess of potage.

○ Once the split peas are cooked and soft, you will need to season with the stock powder. Go gently, adding just a little, as specified, at first, as you have fierce flavourings to come. Add the ginger to the soup, then grate in the zest of the limes and squeeze in the juice. Taste for seasoning – you may need to add a little more stock powder, or salt if you prefer – and immediately pour into bowls, topping with chopped coriander or some more sliced spring onions or red chilli if wished, or all of them.

STORE NOTE	FREEZE NOTE
Cool leftover soup (without toppings), then cover and refrigerate within 2 hours of making. Will keep in fridge for up to 3 days. Reheat gently in a saucepan, stirring occasionally and adding extra water if needed, until piping hot.	Cooled soup can be frozen, in an airtight container, for up to 3 months. Defrost overnight in fridge and reheat as Store Note.

Spiced parsnip and spinach soup

Spiced parsnip soups were the staple of my childhood and teens – those of my vintage and over will most definitely remember the popularity of the curried parsnip soup – but this, while inspired by that memory, is very different. It's rich (though without the butter that was the hallmark of the time), sweet and a glorious snooker-baize green. The spinach improves the texture and taste, adding a robust earthiness, and which, once added, seems the obvious partner to the more mutedly earthy parsnips.

I keep frozen organic leaf spinach (which comes in cubes, and unfurls into leaves as it thaws and cooks in the soup) in the freezer at all times. Someone once told me that spinach draws its nutrients deep from the soil, and it's one of those vegetables where it makes a real difference if it's organic. I don't know if it's true, but somehow this message has gone deep into my consciousness and now I have to obey.

500g parsnips	150g frozen organic leaf spinach
1 fat clove garlic, peeled	lots of freshly ground nutmeg
1 litre chicken or vegetable stock	salt and pepper to taste
1 teaspoon garam masala	

○ Peel the parsnips and cut them into equal-sized pieces that will cook in about the same time: that's to say, leave the skinny twigs as they are, and cut the wider bits into smaller pieces. Cut the garlic into 3, then drop these and the prepared parsnips into a large saucepan (with a lid). Cover with stock, bring to the boil, then reduce the heat slightly, put the lid on and leave to simmer with a certain amount of brio for 15 minutes, or until the parsnips are soft.

○ Stir in the garam masala, add the frozen spinach, then put the lid back on and cook for 5 minutes, by which time the spinach should be thawed and hot.

○ Take the pan off the heat to cool slightly and, using a stick blender, carefully blend the soup until smooth. Add a generous amount of freshly ground nutmeg and season to taste. You may need to add water as this soup does tend to thicken as it stands.

STORE NOTE	FREEZE NOTE
Cool leftovers, then cover and refrigerate within 2 hours of making. Will keep in fridge for up to 3 days. Reheat gently in a saucepan, stirring occasionally and adding extra water if needed, until piping hot.	Cooled soup can be frozen, in an airtight container, for up to 3 months. Defrost overnight in fridge and reheat as Store Note.

Sweet potato, ginger and orange soup

I have this regularly for supper, and I tend to make life easier for myself by always having a stash of baked sweet potatoes in the fridge. If you don't, I advise baking the potatoes the night before, so that when you come to make this soup the next or another night, you are about 3 minutes away from a soothing, comforting, gutsily-flavoured big bowlful. But even if you do roast the sweet potatoes to order, as it were, you need do nothing while they're in the oven, and not much after.

SERVES 2–4, MAKES APPROX. 1 LITRE

2 medium-sized sweet potatoes (approx. 500g total)	zest of ½ orange, preferably unwaxed, and 2 teaspoons juice
750ml vegetable stock	1 teaspoon lime juice
2 teaspoons finely grated fresh ginger	¼ teaspoon cayenne pepper
	salt to taste

○ Preheat the oven to 220°C/gas mark 7. Put the sweet potatoes in a small oven tray, lined with kitchen foil, or a throwaway foil one (the scorched syrup that oozes out of the sweet potatoes as they cook is hell to wash up), and prick them a few times with the tip of a sharp knife or the tines of a fork. Then bake for 1 hour, or until the potatoes are soft within their skins. Remove from the oven and leave to cool. I like to do this the day before, or any time I've got the oven on, and space to spare in it.

○ Get out a saucepan (one with a lid) and, holding one of the sweet potatoes over it, rip open the skin and let the cooked sweet orange flesh drop into the pan. Repeat with the second potato. Pour in the stock, add the grated ginger, the zest of ½ an orange and 2 tablespoons of orange juice, along with the lime juice and the cayenne pepper. Then stir to mix, before clamping on the lid, turning on the heat, and bringing the soup to a boil.

○ Taste for seasoning, leave to cool slightly and then use a stick blender to whizz it smooth, although you could just beat it with a fork if you want a rougher-textured soup.

MAKE AHEAD NOTE	STORE NOTE	FREEZE NOTE
The potatoes can be baked up to 2 days ahead. Transfer to a suitable container, leave to cool, then cover and refrigerate until needed.	Cool leftovers, then cover and refrigerate within 2 hours of making. Will keep in fridge for up to 3 days. Reheat gently in a saucepan, stirring occasionally and adding extra water if needed, until piping hot.	Cooled soup can be frozen, in an airtight container, for up to 3 months. Defrost overnight in fridge and reheat as Store Note.

Pea and broccoli soup

You can never have too many pea soups for my family and, indeed, previous books have been rich in pea soups, all of which I still cook. Not for nothing does the great Nigel Slater call me "the queen of the frozen pea" (an accolade I am most proud of) and this is my latest version, which I've been cooking for the past couple of years, and am more than happy to unveil now.

Along with the frozen peas, you could easily use frozen broccoli and, what with these 2 ingredients in the freezer, and the mint teabag, this makes for a great storecupboard supper. This is not the soup's chief virtue: the sweetness of the peas and the brassic boldness of the broccoli hold each other in check; and the merest touch of mint in its hinterland gives this a certain delicate grace.

I don't quite remember what induced me to use a mint teabag as stock for the soup, but very pleased I am too with my innovation. Please do, though, use pure mint tea and not some fancy mixture. Or rather, by all means try whatever fancy mixture you have in the house, only bear in mind it was your addition should you be less than pleased with it.

It occurs to me only now, that this soup is most virtuous in its ingredients, but, believe me, it tastes nothing of restraint. It was devised to give pleasure, not to deprive – and I'm glad to say it delivers – and with speedy ease.

SERVES 4–6, MAKES APPROX. 1.5 LITRES, OR 6 CUPFULS

5 cups (approx. 1.25 litres) hot water, from a recently boiled kettle

1 pure mint teabag

2 teaspoons sea salt flakes

2 fat or 4 small cloves garlic, peeled

300g frozen peas

300g fresh or frozen broccoli florets

° Pour the water into a saucepan, one that comes with a lid and that is also large enough to take all the ingredients later, then drop in the teabag, stir in the salt, and leave to infuse for 5 minutes.

° Take out the mint teabag, squeezing out all its minty juices as you do so, then put the lid on the saucepan and bring the mint-water to the boil.

° Once the mint-water is boiling, add the garlic and frozen peas, and then let the pan come back to the boil with the lid on.

○ Now add the broccoli and cook, this time with the pan only partially covered, for about 10 minutes, or until the broccoli is soft. You do not have to alter this procedure should you be using frozen broccoli rather than fresh.

○ Let the soup cool just a little before blitzing with a stick blender until smooth, then season to taste and serve.

STORE NOTE	FREEZE NOTE
Cool leftovers, then cover and refrigerate within 2 hours of making. Will keep in fridge for up to 3 days. Reheat gently in a saucepan, stirring occasionally and adding extra water if needed, until piping hot.	Cooled soup can be frozen, in an airtight container, for up to 3 months. Defrost overnight in fridge and reheat as Store Note.

DINE

DINE

This chapter may sound a bit Silver Service, but relax – I don't throw dinner parties, and don't suggest that you do. So, this is not some encomium to any Stepford Wife life, but an attempt to Redefine Dine. I have learnt something about myself, and it's this: I can't invite people over to eat if I wouldn't be comfortable were I in my pyjamas and no make-up. This is not to say I *have* to be in pyjamas and no make-up but, as friends can testify, that is often the case.

But then, I've always been relaxed about the way I feed people: the perfectionist drive makes life hell for host and guest alike. An informal atmosphere is not only the most welcoming one, but – for me – the only way to ensure that I don't regret inviting people over in the first place. I don't do starters; I don't lay the table properly, but leave canisters of cutlery about for people to help themselves; and my food never, ever emulates restaurant service. I don't do smart, I do cosy. You know all those magazine "entertaining" articles, studded with their cook-to-impress checklists? This chapter is the antithesis of all that.

Not all the food I make when cooking for friends is collected here: the Breathe chapter is another trusted resource, and, perhaps self-evidently, the Sweet chapter provides dessert. But here you will find the picky bits I serve, sofa-side, to have with drinks, and those recipes that I rely on for lunch, dinner, or a low-key party, when I want to feed people but, most importantly, want to make my friends feel welcome, and all of us to feel happy.

As for drink, while I generally just offer Prosecco, beer and red or white wine, along with a lot of water, there are times when it makes life easier to have something you can pour out of a jug. In which case, I suggest 3 cocktails: the first, a zingy grapefruit number, is nothing harder to mix up than combining a 75cl bottle of (preferably) pink, sweet, fizzy Muscat (or other sweet, fizzy wine) and 1 cup (250ml) of freshly squeezed, sharp white grapefruit juice, which is about 2 grapefruits' worth. The second, a heady Cosmopolitan Cup, is made by adding, to each 75cl bottle of Prosecco or other dry, fizzy wine, 2 cups (500ml) of cranberry juice from a carton, ¼ cup (4 tablespoons) of vodka, and 1–2 tablespoons of freshly squeezed lime juice to taste, so ½–1 lime. The third is my Saketini, which is made much as a vodka martini, but using sake in place of vermouth, in the ratio 2 parts vodka to 1 part sake, shaken over a lot of ice and poured from a cocktail shaker. I agree this last suggestion is not the pitcher-cocktail I promised, but is too good to leave out, and if you can get someone else to shake up the saketinis, then so much the better. I generally like to put someone else on drinks duty, anyway.

The recipes that follow, bolstered, too, by those in Breathe, in which the focus is on slow-cooked, make-ahead dishes – and, indeed all the recipes in this book – are really just a record of the food I've made for friends as I've settled into my new life and new home. And now I'm happy to share them with you.

Caramelized garlic hummus

While I am quite happy to have a tub of good-quality hummus in the fridge for family fridge-foraging, I don't tend to bring it out for eating out loud, as it were, without some zhuzhing up. Making your own from scratch, I have concluded, is scarcely any harder, and much more satisfying. I am aided in this enterprise by the fact that I cook chickpeas, unsoaked, in my slow-cooker (see **p.211**) and sometimes even freeze them (see Freeze Note, overleaf), plus I always have a couple of jars of fabulous pre-cooked Spanish chickpeas in the cupboard; and I am a compulsive garlic-caramelizer. I cannot stop wrapping bulbs of garlic in foil and baking them in the oven, until the cloves are sweet and soft. I always store some in the fridge (where they keep, in an airtight container or wrapped in foil, for up to 1 week), ready to have this rich, heady purée squeezed into baked potatoes, soups, stews, yogurt – you name it – without any notice. I have given instructions overleaf, should you choose not to follow suit, but what you should know is that I wouldn't fire up the oven specially for them: I just cook them at whatever heat the oven's on at the time; thus, you will see for the Spiced Lamb Stew on **p.197**, I cook the bulbs of garlic, prepared as overleaf, for 2 hours at 170°C/gas mark 3, because that's what the oven's on for the lamb.

As for the chickpeas, I have specified home-cooked ones or those out of a jar, as they are so much better than the canned ones, which can make the hummus too bitty. True, the canned chickpeas are much cheaper, but I go for the least expensive option (dried, which I then cook myself) or the most expensive (Spanish ones from a jar) and miss out the middle path, which has none of the virtues of either of the others. However, 2 x 400g – drained – cans of chickpeas can be used in place of those specified. The seed-sprinkled shards of crisp bread you see alongside the hummus here are simple to make: I split open some wholemeal flatbreads, bought from a nearby Middle-Eastern shop, pour some olive oil on them, sprinkle them with sesame seeds and bake them, on a rack, in a 220°C/gas mark 7 oven for 5 minutes, then break them up when they are handle-able. True, they are too delicate to dip, so you have to spoon the hummus on, but they are very good. Otherwise, grissini, toasted pitta torn into bits, or crudités make the perfect accompaniment for greedy dippage.

1 large bulb garlic, whole and unpeeled

500g cooked chickpeas (from dried) or
1 x 660g jar chickpeas or 2 x 400g cans
chickpeas, drained

zest and juice of 1 unwaxed lemon

4 x 15ml tablespoons tahini

4 x 15ml tablespoons extra-virgin olive oil,
plus more to drizzle on top

4 x 15ml tablespoons cold water

1 teaspoon sea salt flakes, or to taste

good grinding of white pepper

○ Preheat the oven to 220°C/gas mark 7. Cut the top off the bulb of garlic, so that you can just see the tops of the cloves peeking through, discard the top, then sit the bulb on a piece of kitchen foil and seal the ends tightly, while leaving the parcel slightly baggy. Sit it on a small foil tray (or similar) and bake in the oven for 45 minutes. Let it cool in the foil wrapping.

○ Drain and rinse the chickpeas (if using canned or jarred), then tip into a food processor.

○ Add the lemon zest and juice, and squeeze in the soft flesh from the caramelized garlic.

○ Spoon in the tahini and the 4 tablespoons of olive oil and then blitz to a smooth purée.

○ Tip in enough, or all, of the cold water to get the right consistency, adding and blitzing as you go, then add the salt and pepper and check the seasoning. Decant into a bowl and drizzle, if wished, with some more olive oil.

MAKE AHEAD NOTE	STORE NOTE	FREEZE NOTE
Can be made up to 2 days ahead and kept, covered, in fridge. If using frozen and thawed chickpeas, best eaten within 24 hours of making.	Cooked chickpeas should be cooled and refrigerated as quickly as possible and used within 2 days.	The cooked and cooled chickpeas can be frozen, in airtight containers or resealable bags, for up to 3 months. Defrost overnight in fridge.

Miso mayonnaise

I am forever indebted to Yotam Ottolenghi for his mother's mayonnaise recipe, in which she uses a whole egg rather than just the yolk – for all that my late mother would definitely not approve. When I was in New York recently, I ate a miso mayonnaise alongside a black-and-blue steak on a wooden board (we were in hipster territory), but I felt that had the egg been a bit less dominant, I'd have seen the point of the miso more. And I do love miso. So this is my version, and even though fresh coriander certainly adds pungency, it works, matching the miso tonally as well as adding a leafy freshness at the same time.

Should you want to roast some sweet potato wedges to eat with this, I wouldn't try to dissuade you, but I love it just with some herbal, crunchy fennel and sweet, crisp sugar snaps to dip in.

1 egg

375ml sunflower oil

2 x 15ml tablespoons cider vinegar or white wine vinegar

3 x 15ml tablespoons sweet white miso

leaves from large bunch coriander

- Crack the egg into the small bowl of a food processor – these days, most processors come with a smaller bowl that can be clipped on top of the big bowl. (If you don't have a processor, you could use a bowl and a stick blender, or make this – as I was taught by my mother when I was so young I had to stand on a chair to reach the table – by hand with a bowl and whisk.)

- With the motor running, slowly and patiently pour in the oil and then – still with the motor running – slowly pour in the vinegar. You should have a thick, pale mayonnaise in front of you.

- Take off the lid, scrape down, add the miso and the coriander, put the lid back on and process again until the coriander leaves are chopped into small pieces in the mayonnaise. Take off the lid, scrape down to catch any straggling whole coriander leaves, then put the lid back on and give it a final pulse or two before decanting into a bowl and serving with the accompaniment of your choice.

STORE NOTE

The mayonnaise will keep in fridge for up to 4 days from day of making. Transfer to a container, cover and refrigerate as soon as possible. (Do not leave out of fridge for more than 2 hours.)

Note: since this recipe contains raw egg, you should not serve it to anyone with a weak or compromised immune system, such as pregnant women, young children or the elderly.

Sweet potato and chickpea dip

I cooked my first Thanksgiving dinner last year, which felt both significant and pleasurable, and this was the dish I presented with drinks before the great feast. I adore its harvest-festival colours and sweet earthiness and, bejewelled with pomegranate seeds at the end, it is simple but resplendent.

The making of it also happens to rely on two of my favourite cooking tricks, the pre-roasting of whole sweet potatoes and garlic. Baking a batch of sweet potatoes for plundering later will make your cooking life much easier, and never is this more useful than on big occasions. But I should add that, just because this made its first public appearance at Thanksgiving, it certainly doesn't need to be limited to that. It inspires immense gratitude in me throughout the year, and isn't the attitude of gratitude meant to be one of the great happiness indicators?

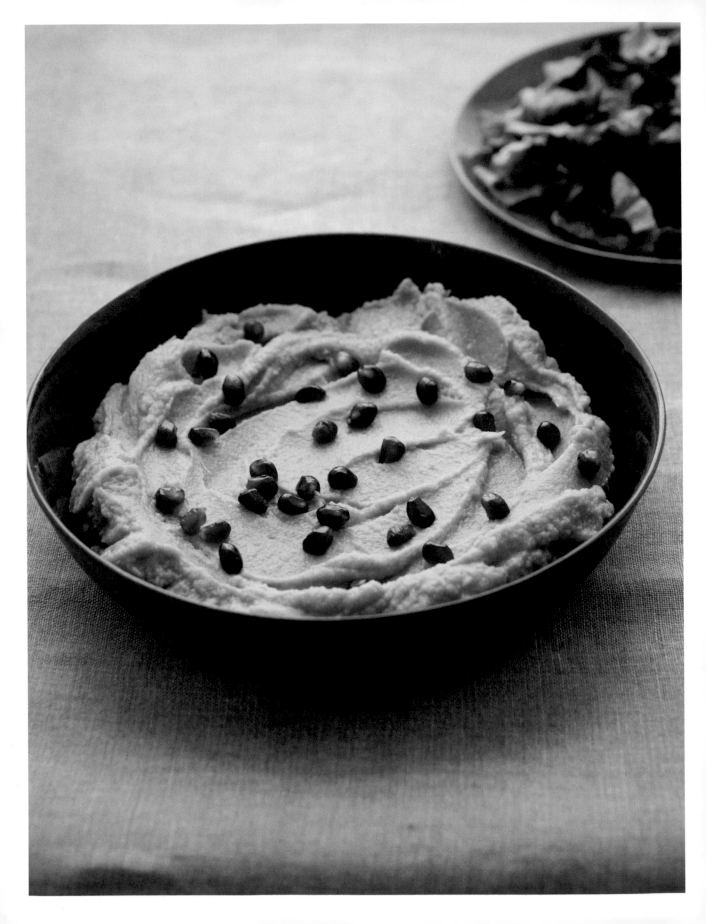

750g sweet potatoes

1 bulb garlic, whole and unpeeled

2 limes, preferably unwaxed

2 teaspoons smoked sea salt flakes (though regular sea salt flakes will do), or to taste

½ teaspoon pimentón dulce or paprika

225g cooked and drained chickpeas (from dried or out of a jar) or 1 x 400g can chickpeas, drained

4cm piece (20g) fresh ginger, peeled and finely grated

2 x 15ml tablespoons pomegranate seeds

- Preheat the oven to 220°C/gas mark 7, and prick the sweet potatoes before placing them on a baking tray and cooking them whole for about 1 hour, depending on their size. You want the flesh inside to be very soft, and no doubt the skin will be burnt in parts by the hot-roast syrup that can dribble out as they cook. This is good.

- The minute the sweet potatoes are in the oven, cut the stalk end off the garlic, leaving the tips of the cloves exposed, and then wrap loosely in foil, sealing the ends tightly to form a baggy parcel, and roast with the sweet potatoes. This should probably be ready in 45 minutes, but I leave it for the hour with the sweet potatoes.

- Let the soft and tender sweet potato and garlic cool; you can do this ahead of time (see Make Ahead Note, below).

- When you are ready to prepare the dip, peel the skin gently away from the sweet potatoes and scoop out the orange pulpy flesh, leaving behind any of the scorched bits. Tip it all into a bowl and then squeeze in the soft, caramelized garlic purée from the exposed cloves.

- Add the finely grated zest from both limes, and the juice from one, the smoked salt, pimentón dulce (or paprika), chickpeas and finely grated ginger, and then blitz with a stick blender (or use a food processor) to make your dip.

- Check the seasoning as well as acidity – you may want more lime juice – and serve, for beauty's sake, sprinkled with pomegranate seeds. I couldn't resist the autumnally-hued vegetable crisps alongside, but I actually serve golden corn chips and crudités, as these last two are, indeed, rather more robust as a dipping vehicle.

MAKE AHEAD NOTE	STORE NOTE
The sweet potato and garlic can be made up to 3 days ahead and kept, wrapped in foil or in a covered container, in fridge.	Leftover dip can be stored, in a covered container, in fridge for up to 2 days from making.

A simple salsa

As far as I'm concerned, you can never go wrong with a simple, spiky salsa and a bowlful of tortilla chips. True, this is on the fiery side – those who want a little less heat should de-seed the chillies – but that, for me, is the whole point. I also make it, as a matter of course, to go with the Oven-Baked Egg Hash on **p.390**, but I am sure you won't have any difficulties finding a wide application for this in your daily life.

I think it's important to treat the salsa with respect and serve only proper corn tortilla chips alongside. If you can get blue corn chips, I'd go for those; otherwise plain, unsalted, yellow corn chips, and no funny flavours, please.

MAKES ENOUGH FOR 6–8 PEOPLE, TO DIP INTO OVER DRINKS

1–2 x 15ml tablespoons regular olive oil

1 small red onion, peeled and finely chopped

2 fat cloves garlic, peeled and finely grated or minced

1 teaspoon cumin seeds

1 teaspoon sea salt flakes

3 fresh jalapeño peppers, finely chopped with seeds intact

2 x 400g cans good-quality chopped tomatoes

- Heat 1 tablespoonful of oil in a medium, heavy-based saucepan over a medium heat, and cook the finely chopped red onion, stirring every now and again, until it's soft but not coloured (beyond its natural hue) in any way, about 5 minutes, adding more oil if necessary – it rather depends on the diameter of your saucepan. Add the garlic to the pan, and give it a good stir before adding the cumin, salt and jalapeños.

- Cook, stirring, for another minute, with the heat a little higher, making sure nothing catches, then tip in the canned tomatoes, stir well, and when it comes to a bubble, lower the heat slightly and simmer for about 15 minutes. You want the sauce to thicken and gain in richness.

- Check for seasoning, and pour into a bowl to cool before serving with the tortilla chips of your choice.

STORE NOTE	FREEZE NOTE
Cool leftovers, then cover and refrigerate within 2 hours of making. Will keep, covered, in fridge for up to 3 days.	The cooled salsa can be frozen, in an airtight container, for up to 3 months. Thaw overnight in fridge and use within 2 days.

Brazilian cheese bread

I have a wonderful Brazilian friend, Helio, mentioned elsewhere in this book and, indeed, other of my books, who has been plying me with *pão de quiejo* for years, but it wasn't until I went to Brazil that I realized what a statement of national identity it is. That's to say, I don't think I ever went into any Brazilian's house without a warm bowl of these cheese breads being forced upon me (in the loveliest way) the minute I stepped through the door. I've tried a number of recipes, but this amalgam of a few of them is the best I've come up with for those outside Brazil, and Helio has given me the nod of approval (it was he who suggested the ready-grated Parmesan, by the way). And now I have found myself pressing these upon anyone who comes to my house. I recommend you do what they do in Brazil, which is to make the dough, form it into balls and then freeze it so that you can always be ready to serve up a warm batch. Alas, I am not always so organized myself.

But before we proceed, I feel I do need to explain what these are like, because cheese bread doesn't quite convey their unfamiliar gooey chewiness. At first you may find them underwhelming: shortly, you will find them addictive; this, a friend tells me, is the working definition of "more-ish". They are rather like cheese-scented choux buns, but with a more papery outside and a softer inside. And they look rather like golf balls, lit up from within. None of this sounds great, I know, but I can't get enough of them, and nor can anyone I give them to.

They are made from manioc flour (sometimes called cassava flour or yucca starch) but you can use tapioca starch, which I found online and is, so far as I can tell, the same thing. You can otherwise find manioc or tapioca flour wherever Brazilians shop or, indeed, in Asian and Middle-Eastern stores, too.

And it is worth mentioning, I feel, that tapioca starch is gluten-free.

300g tapioca starch (see Intro)	125ml sunflower oil
1 teaspoon fine sea salt	2 large eggs, beaten
250ml full-fat milk	100g ready-grated Parmesan

○ Preheat your oven to 220°C/gas mark 7 and line 2 large baking sheets with baking parchment, or use 1 sheet and bake in batches.

○ In a freestanding mixer, using the flat beater, or with a hand-held electric whisk and bowl, combine the tapioca starch and salt.

○ In a saucepan, heat the milk and oil, bringing gently to the boil, and once it's bubbling, take the pan off the heat before it becomes a full rolling boil. Pour immediately into the starch mixture and turn on the motor, though not too fast at first, beating until it forms a sticky batter.

○ Carry on beating the dough for at least 5 minutes (as you want it to cool down before you add the eggs) then scrape down and check with your fingers to see if it is still hot to the touch. You need it to cool to about body temperature, which could take up to 10 minutes of beating.

○ Once you have reached this point, duly whisk in the beaten eggs, spooning them in very gradually, about a tablespoon or so at a time, and make sure that the egg is fully amalgamated before you add the next spoonful.

○ Finally, add – still beating – the Parmesan cheese in 2 batches, and continue to beat until all ingredients are, again, well combined.

○ Scoop teaspoon-sized balls onto the lined baking sheets, or use 1 sheet and bake in batches. If you are baking in batches then refrigerate the unused batter as it waits. I use a rounded measuring spoon and, if needed, dip the spoon in water every couple of scoops, as the dough then drops out of the spoon more easily.

○ Put in the oven, then immediately turn the heat down to 190°C/gas mark 5, and bake for 12–15 minutes, until puffed and with a golden tinge. Let the cheese breads cool a little before serving.

MAKE AHEAD NOTE	FREEZE NOTE
The dough can be made 1 day ahead and kept, covered, in fridge until needed.	The dough can be scooped in balls onto baking sheets lined with baking parchment and frozen. Once solid, transfer to resealable bags or airtight containers and freeze for up to 3 months. Bake directly from frozen, following the directions in recipe, above.

Chicken crackling

The great Simon Hopkinson, author of *Roast Chicken and Other Stories*, gave me – appropriately enough – a bag of chicken crackling as a present, and I pressed him for the recipe. Although I have impatiently cooked my version at a higher heat and for a shorter time than he ordained, I hope he will not be too disapproving.

Since butchers spend a lot of their time skinning chicken for their customers, you shouldn't find it difficult to buy the skin, nor should it cost much; if you're buying other things, they'll probably throw it in for free. And although there is something a bit Hannibal Lecter about the way the raw skin looks, stretched out on the wire rack before it goes into the oven, the finished article is unspookily inviting.

SERVES 4–6, TO PICK AT OVER DRINKS

250g chicken skin

¼ teaspoon fine sea salt

¼ teaspoon cayenne pepper

oil for greasing

- Preheat the oven to 180°C/gas mark 4.

- Oil a large wire rack that can sit over an oven tray or tin, and then stretch the pieces of skin over the rack so that each piece lies flat with none of them overlapping.

- Sprinkle the salt and cayenne over the chicken skin and then place in the oven for 30 minutes. The chicken skin should be golden and crisp, but watch that it doesn't catch too much.

- Take out of the oven and pull the pieces of chicken crackling gently off the rack – you will need a metal spatula to help lift them off – and leave to cool.

- Once cooled, break into nibble-sized pieces and serve with drinks.

MAKE AHEAD NOTE

The crackling can be made up to an hour ahead and left at room temperature. Consume within 2 hours of making.

Sake-sticky drumsticks

I'm always in favour of food that can be eaten by hand: whether over drinks, at the table, or straight from the fridge. But however you eat these, many napkins are called for.

Do consider making the Miso Mayonnaise on **p.115** to go with them, though I'm happy enough with just some limes to spritz over, too. And I know some people are nervous of making party food too spicy (I'm not one of them) so I want to reassure the fire-afeared that none of the gorgeous umami stickiness and savouriness is ruined by leaving out the chilli flakes.

I find the marinade so much more straightforward to make using cups, and, actually, it makes the whole thing feel rather jaunty, too.

MAKES 20 DRUMSTICKS

½ cup (125ml) sake	1 teaspoon toasted sesame oil
¼ cup (4 x 15ml tablespoons) fish sauce	1 teaspoon dried chilli flakes
¼ cup (4 x 15ml tablespoons) soy sauce	20 chicken drumsticks, skin on
¼ cup (4 x 15ml tablespoons) sunflower oil	2 x 15ml tablespoons runny honey

- Mix the sake, fish sauce, soy sauce, sunflower oil, sesame oil and dried chilli flakes together in a measuring jug. Put the chicken drumsticks into a large freezer bag, pour over the contents of the jug, seal the bag, place it in something like a lasagne dish (just in case the bag leaks), and leave in a cool place for 40 minutes or in the fridge for up to 1 day.

- When you are ready to cook, preheat the oven to 200°C/gas mark 6 and line a large, shallow oven tin (I use a roasting tin that measures 46 x 34cm, with a small lip of 1.5cm) with foil and, being careful not to let the bag spill out its precious juices, place the drumsticks, curved-side up, on it. If they've been in the fridge, let them come up to room temperature. Pour off ½ a cupful (125ml) of the marinade, reserving it, pouring the scant remaining marinade onto the drumsticks. Cook in the oven for 45 minutes.

- While the chicken's in the oven, pour the reserved 125ml of marinade into a small saucepan, add the honey and boil until it's reduced to a sticky glaze. This will take 5–7 minutes.

- When the drumsticks have had their 45 minutes, test to see if they're more or less cooked through, then carefully pour the juices that have collected in the tin into the glaze. Stir and pour over the chicken drumsticks, then place back in the oven for 10 minutes. After which, spoon the sticky juices over the drumsticks and roast for another 10 minutes.

- Remove from the oven, then spoon any glaze from the bottom of the tin over the drumsticks, and let them stand until cool enough to be eaten by hand.

MAKE AHEAD NOTE	STORE NOTE	FREEZE NOTE
The drumsticks can be marinated 1 day ahead. It is also possible to freeze the drumsticks in the marinade for up to 3 months (as long as the meat has not been previously frozen); thaw overnight in fridge before cooking.	Cool leftovers, then cover and refrigerate within 2 hours of making. Will keep in fridge for up to 3 days.	Cooled leftovers can be frozen, in an airtight container, for up to 1 month. Defrost overnight in fridge before using.

Lamb ribs with nigella and cumin seeds

Stop what you're doing: I bring you important news. Lamb ribs, almost unknown over here, are one of the most delicious ways of eating lamb, and certainly the least expensive. I'd love to see them more widely available (without the hike in price that so often follows), but until then you will need to find a compliant butcher and ask for them.

Incidentally, in the US they're known as "Denver ribs", since Denver is the largest producer of lamb in America, although one could argue that even there these are not exactly widely known. I feel now's the time for them to garner a little more universal appreciation. I'm certainly evangelical about spreading the word.

Actually, I used to buy breast of lamb (which is where the ribs come from) when I was an undergraduate for 25p per breast (I was cooking on a student budget, after all). I'd braise it, slowly, with spices, in one piece, and it was considered a pretty odd thing to do back then, too. The breast and, consequently, the ribs do cost a bit more now, I concede, but they're still a gratifying good buy. Not that they taste bargain-basement: everyone who's eaten these has said they're the best spare ribs they've ever had.

I like to keep the flavour of the meat to the fore, so don't coat them in a glaze, but give them the scantest covering before they go into the oven. And while it might seem unnecessary to use oil, it does help the spices to stick and the ribs to crisp; anyway, so much of the fat drips off into the pan under the rack. Even so, they are, without question, a fatty cut, but for those of us who love the flavour and the lip-smacking stickiness that this gives, it's a bonus, not a warning. If you're a lean-cut kind of a person, these are not for you. Commiserations.

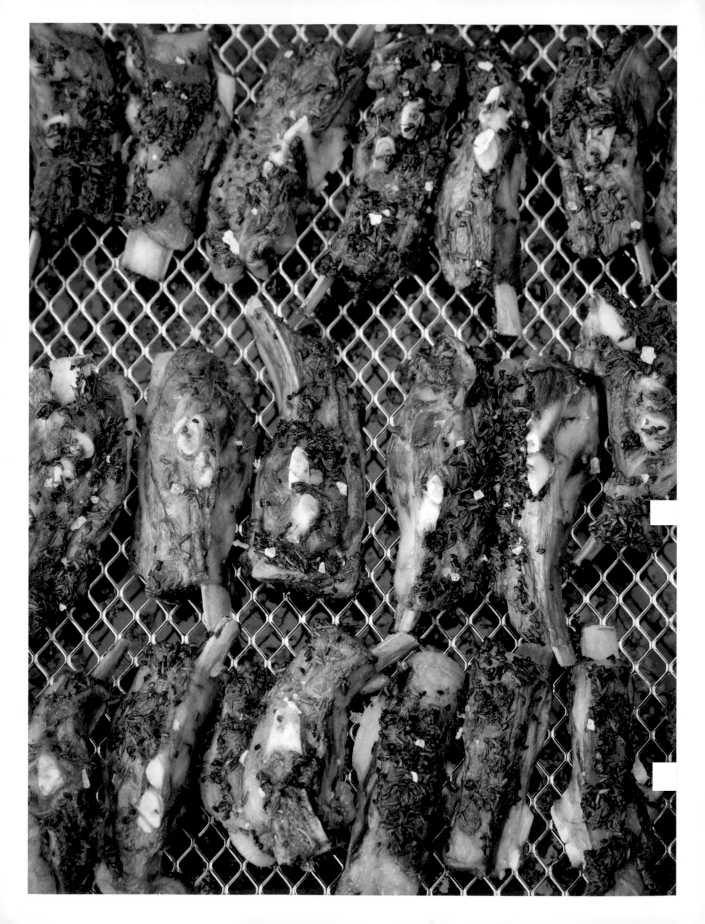

4 teaspoons nigella seeds

4 teaspoons cumin seeds

4 teaspoons regular olive oil

¼ cup (4 x 15ml tablespoons) soy sauce

4 cloves garlic, peeled and finely grated
or minced

24 lamb ribs, cut from 3 lamb breasts, bones in

○ Preheat the oven to 150°C/gas mark 2. Line a large roasting tin with foil and sit
a rack on top. If you haven't got a large enough tin (the one that came with my
oven measures 45 x 38cm), then use 2 tins, and just swap them over in the oven
halfway through cooking, and be prepared to add a further 10–15 minutes on to
the roasting time.

○ Get out a dish and add the nigella and cumin seeds, pour in the oil and soy and
add the garlic. Stir to combine.

○ Dip and schmoosh the ribs, one by one, in this mixture, so that they are lightly
coated on both sides; you may think this scant amount won't be enough for all the
ribs, but it is – just – and you don't want them wet, merely coloured by the liquid
and with some seeds adhering to them.

○ Arrange them on the rack above the lined baking tin and cook in the oven for
1½–2 hours (they can differ in size), or until the fat on the ribs is crisp and the
meat tender.

○ Arrange on a warmed platter and make sure you have a good supply of napkins
to hand.

STORE NOTE	FREEZE NOTE
Cool leftovers, then cover and refrigerate within 2 hours of making. Will keep in fridge for up to 3 days.	Cooled leftovers can be frozen, in an airtight container, for up to 1 month. Defrost overnight in fridge before using.

Butternut and halloumi burgers

While these are not actually burgers, there is something meaty about a slice of roasted butternut squash that lends itself to this way of eating, and the salty halloumi, welded on by the heat of the oven, is the perfect foil to the squash's densely fleshed sweetness. It's always difficult with squash, just as it is with pumpkin, to tell before cooking whether you have a good, juicy one, or if the flesh is going to be stringy and tasteless. But I have found that sweet Coquina butternut squash seems to be very reliable, plus its long shape, before it bulges into the round seedy bit, is well suited to this recipe. Even if you can't find this particular squash, do choose a butternut that has a long neck, as it is this part that you cut to make the "burgers". The remaining part of the squash can be usefully employed in the Tray of Roast Veg (**p.237**) for another meal.

These, for me, are perfect for Saturday lunch all year round, or for a sunny summer supper – icy cold beers and rosé wine close to hand. But they're quick and simple enough to rustle up whenever you need to feed people without much notice.

MAKES 6–8 BURGERS, DEPENDING ON HOW MANY DISCS YOU CAN SLICE FROM THE
BUTTERNUT SQUASH

1 butternut squash

1 x 15ml tablespoon regular olive oil

1 teaspoon dried oregano

1 x 225g block halloumi cheese

4 pitta breads

TO SERVE:

salad leaves of your choice

2 large tomatoes, thickly sliced

○ Preheat the oven to 200°C/gas mark 6. Slice the long part of the butternut into approximately 1.5cm rounds; if it is a uniform size you can get about 6–8 slices before you hit the bulbous, seeded end. Pour the oil onto a large, shallow baking tray and then put the slices of butternut on top. Sprinkle with half of the oregano, then flip the rounds over and sprinkle on the rest.

○ Put in the oven to roast for 20–30 minutes, or until tender and browning at the edges. Then cut the block of halloumi cheese in half, to give 2 square-ish pieces, and stand each half upright, to make it easier to cut each into 3 or 4 slices, depending on how many slices of butternut you have. Place a slice on each round of butternut.

○ Roast in the oven for another 10 minutes, by which time the cheese should be soft and melting – bearing in mind that halloumi never gets very melty – on top of the butternut.

○ While the butternut and halloumi are getting towards the end of their time in the oven, cut the pittas in half crossways and briefly warm them, too, in the oven.

○ Open the mouths of the pitta halves slightly in order to load them with some salad leaves and slip a cheese-loaded butternut round into each pitta pocket, top the butternut burger with a thick slice of tomato, and eat straightaway.

Fish tacos

I am a broad church: when I'm not craving a bowl of food that delivers the same soothing taste from mouthful to mouthful, I like the sort of meal that involves a table full of bits and pieces, much DIY assembly and a lot of condiments. I certainly think this latter way of eating is one of the most relaxing ways of sitting around a table with friends.

These fish tacos are a case in point (see also the Oven-Cooked Chicken Shawarma on **p.157**), and rest assured that the actual preparation is much more low-effort than you might think. For one, I roast the fish that goes in the tacos rather than, as is more traditional, fry it; the quick-pickled onions involve no more than cutting a small red onion into half-moons and steeping them in lime juice; the sweetcorn relish is mainly made out of a can (for which, no apologies) and the spicy sauce comes simply by adding some Korean gochujang into some shop-bought mayo. Yes, I know there is a little cultural melding going on here, but if you have the gochujang for the Slow-Cooker Korean Beef and Rice Pot on **p.218** (much advised) then you will long to find other uses for it. Otherwise, any shop-bought hot sauce of your choice will do or, if you're feeling like getting a little more stuck in, then please, *please* try the Chilli, Ginger and Garlic Sauce on **p.254**, which I eat with practically everything.

SERVES 4–6, AS A MAIN COURSE

FOR THE QUICK-PICKLED ONION:

1 small red onion

juice of 2 limes

FOR THE HOT SAUCE:

½ cup (125g) mayonnaise

2 teaspoons gochujang paste, or other hot sauce, to taste

FOR THE CORN RELISH:

1 x 198g can sweetcorn, drained

1 fresh red chilli

3 x 15ml tablespoons chopped fresh coriander

salt to taste

FOR THE FISH TACOS:

4 skinless fillets of firm white fish, such as hake or haddock (750–900g total), from the thicker loin end

1 teaspoon ground cumin

½ teaspoon paprika

1 teaspoon sea salt flakes

1 clove garlic, peeled and finely grated or minced

2 x 15ml tablespoons regular olive oil

8 soft corn tortillas

FOR THE AVOCADO:

2 ripe avocados

juice of 1 lime

TO SERVE:

salad leaves of your choice

1–2 x 15ml tablespoons chopped fresh coriander

2 limes, cut into wedges

- Preheat the oven to 220°C/gas mark 7 for the fish, and begin by preparing the sides for your tacos. Peel and halve the red onion, then thinly slice into half-moons. Put the red onion slices into a bowl and cover with the lime juice. Stir with a fork to mix the onion well in the juice. Actually, if you can get this done ahead of time (up to 1 day), so much the better, but even 20 minutes is fine.

- Make the hot sauce by mixing together the mayonnaise and the gochujang paste (or other hot sauce) in a small bowl. Set aside.

- For the corn relish, put the canned sweetcorn into a bowl. Finely dice the chilli (de-seed if you don't like too much heat) and add to the sweetcorn, along with the chopped coriander and some salt to taste. Give it all a good stir, and set aside.

- Cut the fish fillets in half lengthways, so you have long fingers, and arrange in a shallow roasting tin. Mix together the cumin, paprika and salt, and sprinkle over the fish fillets.

- Mix the garlic and the oil in a small bowl. Drizzle the fish with the garlicky oil, and roast in the oven for 8–10 minutes, depending on the thickness of your fillets. Check to see if the fish is cooked through (though only just) before taking out of the oven.

- Once you've taken the fish out (though don't let it get cold) turn off the oven and warm the tortillas in the fading heat. Meanwhile, peel, stone and slice the avocados, then spritz with the juice of the lime, ready to serve with the other accompaniments.

- Arrange the fish on a plate (lined with salad leaves, if so desired), sprinkle with some chopped fresh coriander, and take to the table along with the warmed tortillas. If you don't want to add any salad to the fish directly, you may want to put a bowl of shredded iceberg or some other crisp leaves nearby.

- Put the bowls of soused, but drained, red onions, the corn relish, hot sauce and a plate of sliced avocados on the table so that everyone can load their tortillas. A plate of lime wedges and a pile of napkins are both good ideas, too.

MAKE AHEAD NOTE

The pickled onions, hot sauce and relish (minus the coriander) can be made 1 day ahead. Cover and refrigerate until needed. Stir the chopped coriander into the corn relish just before serving.

Greek squid and orzo

The aniseed flavour that underscores this fabulously-easy baked squid and orzo pasta dish is gentle enough not to frighten away any but hardcore fennelphobes and, even then, I have surprised those who profess aniseed-antagonism with just how well it goes down. And it's joyously simple to make, too: all it takes is a little desultory chopping and stirring, and then it cooks itself in the oven, until the squid is so tender that the lightest touch of a spoon cuts through it.

Thank you to Alex Andreou for showing me how to cook this, along with the Strapatsada on **p.49** and Old Rag Pie on **p.318**. I feel the Greek kitchen has been given a fine showing in these pages, and I'm grateful to have been able to do so, not least because learning new recipes that you know will become part of your own trusted repertoire, is one of the great joys of cooking.

SERVES 4–6, AS A MAIN COURSE

2 banana shallots or 1 small red onion	1 x 400g can chopped tomatoes
½ bulb fennel	1 x 15ml tablespoon tomato purée
2 cloves garlic	2 x 15ml tablespoons ouzo
¼ cup (4 x 15ml tablespoons) extra-virgin olive oil, plus a little more for later	large bunch (approx. 100g) fresh dill
	250ml hot water, from a recently boiled kettle
600g squid (cleaned weight)	salt and pepper to taste
300g orzo pasta	

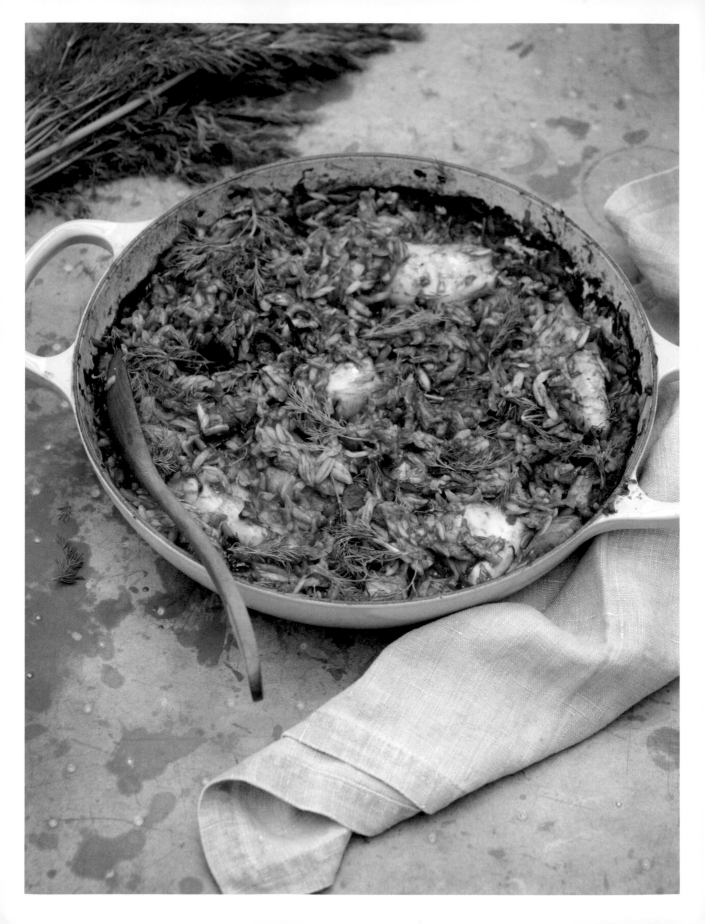

- Preheat the oven to 160°C/gas mark 3. Get out a large casserole or pan (one with a tight-fitting lid) that's big enough to take everything, and that can go on the hob and into the oven later. The shallow casserole you can see in the picture is 30cm in diameter, and the one I always use.

- Peel and halve the banana shallots (or small red onion), then cut into chunky half-moons. Cut the core out of the fennel, and discard it, then slice the fennel, including the tubey parts, into rough chunks. Don't discard the fronds. Press down on the garlic cloves with the side of a heavy knife to bruise them, then peel off the skins.

- Pour the olive oil into the pan, put it over a low heat and add the sliced shallots (or onion), chopped fennel and bruised garlic, along with the squid, left just as it is, and cook it all, stirring every now and again, for 10 minutes. The squid (and the fennel) will give out quite a bit of liquid, so you won't be frying so much as braising.

- Stir in the orzo pasta and the chopped tomatoes. Add the tomato purée to the empty tomato tin, then fill it up with cold water and give it a good stir, before pouring this into the pan. Now pour in the ouzo and give the pan another stir. Do not season at this stage. Turn up the heat, and once it comes to a bubble, clamp on the lid, then transfer the pan to the oven and cook for 1 hour and 20 minutes. When you're near the end of the cooking time, finely chop the dill and boil the kettle.

- When time's up, take the pan out of the oven and remove the lid. The orzo will have absorbed all the liquid and the squid should be tender enough to be cut into with a wooden spoon. Add the hot water and stir well to scrape up any bits stuck to the bottom (these are the bits full of flavour). Add salt and pepper to taste and most of the chopped dill, then stir before putting the pan back in the oven, with the lid off, for 10 minutes.

- Remove from the oven, sprinkle with the remaining dill, and eat with no more than a crisp green salad alongside. And if you wish to grate Parmesan over it as you eat, despite the Italian no-cheese-with-fish-pasta rule, I will not try to put you off. The Greeks do eat this with grated cheese after all.

STORE NOTE

Cool leftovers, then cover and refrigerate within 2 hours of making. Will keep in fridge for up to 2 days. Leftovers are best served cold, with a spritz of lemon juice.

Chicken traybake with bitter orange and fennel

I don't think I could say how often I've made this since settling into my new kitchen. Not that I'm ashamed of being repetitive – I find that comforting – but I've simply cooked it too often to count. It will always, no matter wherever and whenever I cook it, be the taste of my new home, evoking the strength and robust sense of cosiness that emanates from that.

I never quite feel that a house is a home until a chicken has been roasted in it (with apologies to all vegetarians and, indeed, chickens) and this, as it cooks, fills your kitchen with its gentle anise and citrus scent, working as well in midwinter with in-season Seville oranges as it does in summer with eating oranges, their sweetness soured by lemon. Apropos of this, although I normally consider not using the zest of a lemon a culinary hanging offence, here I don't use it, as it would flagrantly, if fragrantly, overpower the essential orange.

I always get the chicken in its marinade a day ahead, but if you don't have time, an hour would be fine (out of the fridge, but in a cool place) so long as you start off with good chicken. If you can afford good organic chicken, buy it. It is this chicken that provides a strong natural "gravy", and the other reasons to do so are even more compelling.

The fennel I've been finding lately has been large but no less full of herbal flavour for all that; if you find only smaller bulbs of fennel, maybe use 3, and just quarter them.

As for what to serve alongside, depending on the time of year, I'd say a pile of mashed potatoes or steamed new potatoes and perhaps some just-blanched sugar snaps, glossed with butter or oil, for crunch.

SERVES 6

2 large bulbs fennel (approx. 1kg total, though less wouldn't matter)

100ml cold-pressed rapeseed oil or extra-virgin olive oil, plus 1 x 15ml tablespoon or so for drizzling on the chicken when cooking

zest and juice of 2 Seville oranges (about 100ml juice), or zest and juice of 1 eating orange and juice of 1 lemon

2 teaspoons sea salt flakes

4 teaspoons fennel seeds

4 teaspoons Dijon mustard

12 chicken thighs, skin on and bone in, preferably organic

- Remove the fronds from the fennel and put them in a resealable bag in the fridge for serving. I discard (that's to say, eat) the tubey bits of the fennel, but if you have a roasting tin big enough, use everything. Cut the bulbs of fennel into quarters and then cut each quarter, lengthways, into 3. Leave on the chopping board while you get on with the marinade.

- Placing a large freezer bag in position inside a wide-necked measuring jug or similar, pour in the oil, add the orange zest and juice (and lemon juice, if using), and spoon in the salt, fennel seeds and mustard. Stir briefly to mix.

- Remove the bag from the jug and, holding it up, add a quarter of the chicken pieces, followed by a quarter of the fennel pieces, and so on until everything's been used up.

- Seal the bag tightly at the top, lay the bag in something like a lasagne dish and squelch it about so that you make the small amount of marinade cover as much of the chicken as possible. It will look as if it isn't enough, but it is, I promise. Leave in the fridge overnight or up to 1 day.

- When you want to cook, remove the marinating chicken and fennel from the fridge and tip the contents of the bag – marinade and all – into a large shallow roasting tin (I use a tin that measures 46 x 34cm with a lip of 1.5cm). Using tongs, or whatever implement(s) you prefer, arrange the chicken pieces so that they are sitting, skin-side up, on top of the fennel. Leave it for 30 minutes or so, to come up to room temperature while you preheat the oven to 200°C/gas mark 6.

- Drizzle some more golden oil onto the chicken, and cook in the oven for 1 hour, by which time the fennel will be soft and the chicken cooked through and bronzed on top.

- Put the chicken and fennel onto a warmed serving plate and put the pan over a medium heat (use a saucepan if your tin isn't hob-friendly) and boil the juices, stirring as you watch it turn syrupy; this should take about 1½–2 minutes in the tin, and about 5 in a saucepan.

- Pour the reduced sauce over the chicken and fennel, and then tear over the reserved fennel fronds.

MAKE AHEAD NOTE	STORE NOTE
The chicken can be marinated 1 day ahead. Store in fridge until needed.	Cool leftovers, then cover and refrigerate within 2 hours of making. Will keep in fridge for up to 3 days.

Roast chicken with lemon, rosemary, garlic and potatoes

I am back to familiar territory with this: the smell of chicken roasting with lemon, rosemary and garlic has always seemed to me the essence of all that is comforting. But this version is so sprightly and robust that I feel it uplifts as it soothes: it is good-mood food, and good-mood cooking, too. You just throw everything in the pan with brio and let it roast away merrily.

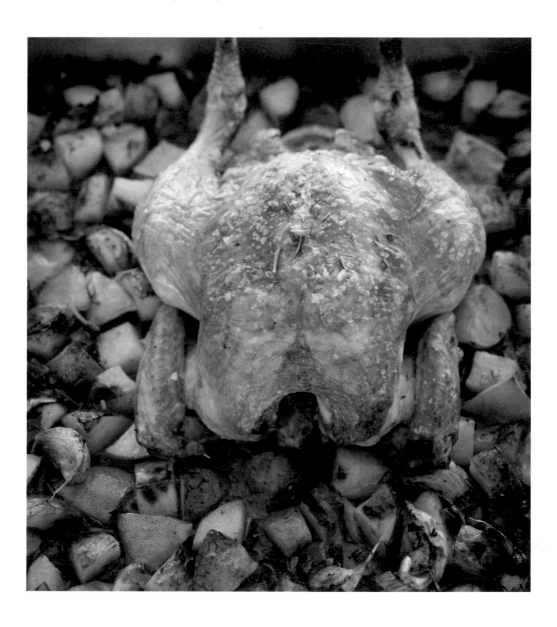

¼ cup (4 x 15ml tablespoons) regular olive oil

2 teaspoons finely chopped rosemary needles, plus more to serve

1 bulb garlic, separated into (unpeeled) cloves

2 leeks

1kg waxy potatoes, such as Cyprus, washed if necessary, but unpeeled

2 unwaxed lemons

1 medium chicken (approx. 1.4kg), preferably organic

sea salt flakes to taste

- Preheat the oven to 220°C/gas mark 7. Get out the biggest roasting tin you have, and pour all but a teaspoon or so of the oil into it. Throw in the chopped rosemary needles and the garlic cloves.

- Trim the leeks and cut each in half lengthways, then slice into half-moons and drop these leek curls into the tin, too.

- Cut the potatoes into 1.5cm slices, then cut each slice into 4, or just halve them if the potatoes are small, and add these to the tin.

- Quarter the lemons, then cut each quarter in half, take out as many pips as you can without exerting yourself unduly and toss the lemon quarters into the pan. Now schmoosh everything to mix, and then make a space in the middle of the tin for the chicken to sit in.

- Untruss the chicken, place it in the reserved parking space, pour the tiny bit of remaining oil on top of it and sprinkle sea salt flakes on top of the chicken only. Place in the oven for 1 hour and 10 minutes, and if the juices of the chicken run clear when you push the tip of a knife into the joint where the thigh meets the body, remove the chicken to a board to sit, letting the juices from its cavity spill back in to the tin as you do so, then put the potato mixture back in the oven for 10 minutes until soft and golden. If the chicken needs longer, keep everything in the oven until the chicken's cooked.

- When it's ready, and the chicken has rested, either carve it or cut into joints as wished – I find the chicken goes further if carved. If you don't want to serve the lemony, garlicky potatoes from their tin (I never mind), transfer them to a serving plate or dish and sprinkle with ½ a teaspoon or so of finely chopped rosemary needles and sea salt flakes to taste.

STORE NOTE	FREEZE NOTE
Transfer leftover cooked chicken to a container, then cover and refrigerate within 2 hours. Will keep in fridge for up to 3 days.	Cooked and cooled chicken can be frozen, in airtight containers or resealable bags, for up to 2 months. Defrost overnight in fridge before using.

Chicken Cosima

I am smiling as I'm writing this, as it is what I cooked for my daughter to celebrate her 21st birthday, not long after we'd moved into our new home. Actually, I cooked huge vats of it, in a pan so big that both the children could fit into it together when they were little – and have the lid put on, too. Not that I was in the habit of squeezing them into saucepans.

I made this for the momentous event, as I wanted to create something that had all my daughter's favourite ingredients in it, that would be easy to make, and amenable once made. It sits comfortably on a low heat or in a low oven if you need to wait before serving, and it doesn't require anything more than to be ladled out into shallow bowls. The Leek Pasta Bake on **p.208** was also presented, for non-meat-eaters, and both are great for a party and can be scaled up or down easily.

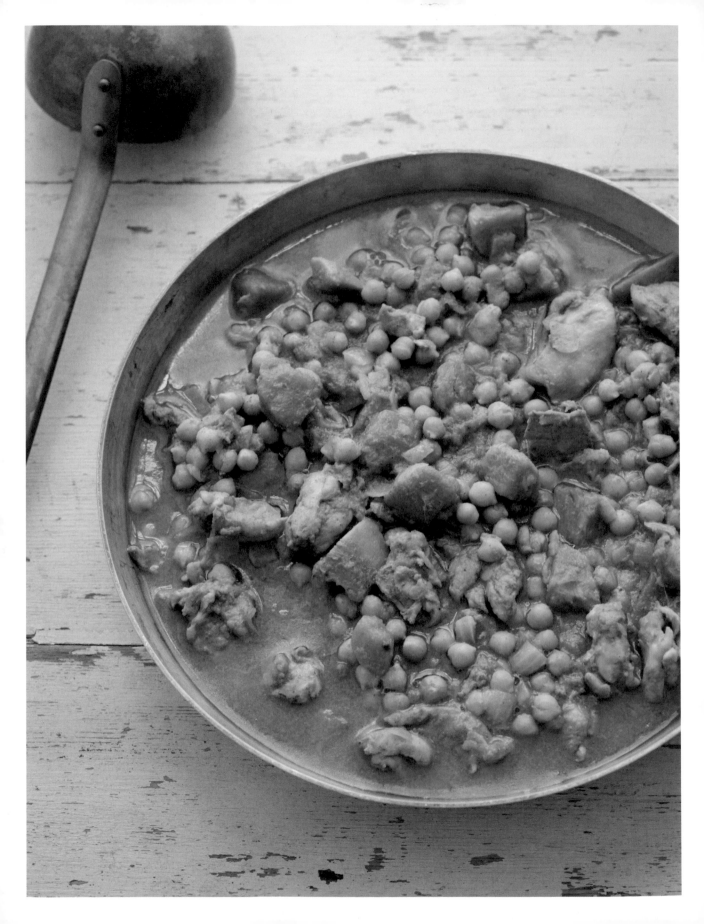

SERVES 6

2½–3 x 15ml tablespoons plain flour

1 teaspoon ground coriander

1 teaspoon ground cumin

½ teaspoon ground turmeric

½ teaspoon paprika

½ teaspoon sea salt flakes

6 large skinless and boneless chicken thighs, cut into bite-sized chunks

1 x 15ml tablespoon cold-pressed coconut oil or regular olive oil

1 onion, peeled and chopped

500g sweet potatoes, peeled and cut into 2–3cm chunks

500ml hot chicken stock

500g cooked chickpeas (from dried) or 1 x 660g jar chickpeas or 2 x 400g cans chickpeas, drained

chopped fresh coriander, to serve

- Preheat the oven to 200°C/gas mark 6.

- Measure the flour, spices and salt into a freezer bag and then tip in the chicken. Shake the bag around to coat the chicken with the floury spice.

- Heat the oil in a wide casserole or pan (with a lid), and then fry the onion until softened but not really coloured.

- Add the chicken and all the contents of the bag to the pan, and stir around for a minute or so, then add the peeled and chopped sweet potatoes and stir again.

- Pour in the hot stock, then bring the pan up to the boil and tip in the drained chickpeas. Give it another good stir, then clamp on the lid and put in the oven for 25 minutes.

- Check that the chicken is cooked through and the sweet potatoes are tender, then take out of the oven and leave with the lid on to stand for about 10 minutes.

- Ladle into bowls, sprinkling each with chopped coriander.

STORE NOTE

Transfer leftover chicken to a container, then cool, cover and refrigerate within 2 hours of making. Will keep in fridge for up to 3 days. Reheat leftovers gently in a saucepan until piping hot. Stir occasionally, adding a splash of water or chicken stock if needed.

Tequila and lime chicken

Someone once said to me on Twitter that Mother Hens must use me as a warning to frighten their chicks when they were misbehaving. There's no denying it, I do cook an awful lot of chicken. But you cannot have too many chicken recipes in my book and this is, after all, my book.

This is relatively new to my repertoire but firmly established for all that. True, the tequila doesn't exactly convey flavour, or not so that you could name it, but it sure brings fire – augmented by the chilli flakes – and tenderizes the chicken beautifully.

If you want to bulk it out, then look no further than the Cuban Black Beans on **p.214** or simply chop up some sweet potatoes and roast them in cold-pressed coconut oil and cumin in the oven at the same time. But when I want something lighter, a simple green salad does me. At all times, some avocado mashed with salt then sprinkled with fresh coriander and a few more chilli flakes, to be dolloped on the plate, is highly desirable.

It was while cooking this, during an extended (work) stay at the Chateau Marmont in LA, that I set off the fire alarm. Somehow that feels entirely appropriate.

1 medium chicken (approx. 1.4kg), preferably organic, jointed into 8 pieces

75ml tequila blanco

zest and juice of 2 limes, preferably unwaxed

½ teaspoon dried chilli flakes, plus more to sprinkle on at the end

2 teaspoons sea salt flakes

2 x 15ml tablespoons regular olive oil

TO SERVE:

chopped fresh coriander

lime wedges

○ First, put the jointed chicken pieces into a freezer bag.

○ Mix together the tequila, zest and juice of the limes, the chilli flakes, salt and olive oil, and then tip this into the freezer bag with the chicken. Seal or tie tightly (letting out the air first) and place it (on a tray or in a dish) in the fridge to marinate for 6 hours or overnight, or up to 2 days, or leave outside the fridge, but in a cool place, for 40 minutes if you're short of time.

○ Preheat the oven to 220°C/gas mark 7. If the chicken is in the fridge, take it out and remove the chicken pieces from the bag, reserving the marinade. Sit the chicken pieces on a smallish, shallow baking tray for about 30 minutes to allow them to come to room temperature. It's important that the chicken pieces sit on the tray without a lot of room to spare, or else the marinade will immediately evaporate in the hot oven. When you are ready to put it into the oven, pour half of the marinade over the chicken pieces and transfer to the hot oven for 25 minutes.

○ Take the chicken out of the oven, pour the other half of the reserved marinade over it, then put the chicken back in for another 25–30 minutes. Check it is cooked through before removing from the oven.

○ Put the chicken pieces on a serving plate. Then add a little boiling water to the pan to help get every last bit of flavour-sticky juice out, and pour it over the chicken on its plate. Scatter with chopped coriander and – if you like it hot – some more dried chilli flakes, and serve with some lime wedges alongside.

MAKE AHEAD NOTE	STORE NOTE	FREEZE NOTE
The chicken can be marinated up to 2 days ahead. Store in fridge until needed.	Transfer leftover cooked chicken to a container, then cool, cover and refrigerate within 2 hours. Will keep in fridge for up to 3 days.	The chicken can be frozen in its marinade – as long as the meat has not been previously frozen – for up to 3 months. Defrost overnight in fridge before using. Leftover cooked and cooled chicken can also be frozen, in airtight containers or resealable bags, for up to 2 months. Defrost overnight in fridge before using.

Chicken and wild rice

I've been cooking this, or a version of it, for years, but it wasn't until I returned to it recently for this book – having found a scribbled recipe in an old notepad – that I realized that it was really a version of my newly learnt squid and orzo dish; the cooking method is virtually identical. Everything is linked: Only Connect.

Of course, the flavours are very different, and so, therefore, is the finished dish. And I love the mellow depth of the spices against the sour-sweet cranberries and glistening spikiness of the wild rice. The strange thing is, when I first cooked this, I hadn't planned it out at all, but simply raided my fridge and cupboards and set to, scribbling down what I'd cobbled together only afterwards. But then, I am a person guided so much more by instinct than strategy. And it's a reminder that in cooking, as in life, without risk there is no reward.

2 x 15ml tablespoons regular olive oil	8 skinless and boneless chicken thighs, each chopped into 4 pieces
1 onion, peeled and chopped	
1 clove garlic, peeled and finely grated or minced	250g wild rice
	75g dried cranberries
1 teaspoon ground turmeric	1 litre chicken stock
2 teaspoons coriander seeds	salt and pepper to taste
2 teaspoons cumin seeds	handful finely chopped fresh coriander

○ Preheat the oven to 180°C/gas mark 4. Put a wide, flameproof casserole, that will take all the ingredients snugly, and that comes with a lid, on the hob. Add the oil, and cook the onion for 5–10 minutes, stirring once or twice, on a low to medium heat, until just softened. Since we have turmeric a-coming, I'd advise against using a wooden spoon or spatula.

○ Add the garlic to the oniony pan and then stir in the spices.

○ Turn the heat to high and add the chicken pieces, stirring for 3 minutes until sealed, although they will not colour much.

○ Add the rice and stir for 1 minute, followed by the cranberries and the chicken stock, and bring to the boil. Clamp on the lid and transfer to the oven, and cook for 1 hour.

○ Remove from the oven, check the rice is cooked – the grains will be swollen and starting to split open but still have bite to them – and season with salt and pepper, then put back in the oven for another 15 minutes without the lid on this time. Because the wild rice (actually a grass, not a rice) doesn't absorb all of the liquid, this isn't dry like a regular pilaf, but makes a scant, rich yet runny sauce. And it's wonderfully dramatic looking: the chicken and cranberries now golden against the blackly gleaming spikes of wild rice.

○ Stir in half the coriander and then sprinkle the rest over the top. That's if you're serving straight from the pan you've cooked it in, as I have here; otherwise, stir in half the coriander, transfer to a serving dish and scatter the remaining coriander over the top.

STORE NOTE

Cool leftovers, then cover and refrigerate within 2 hours of making. Will keep in fridge for up to 2 days. Reheat in a saucepan, with a little extra liquid, stirring occasionally until piping hot all the way through.

Oven-cooked chicken shawarma

Chicken shawarma is usually cooked on a spit, but I saw a recipe by the excellent Sam Sifton (a home cook, therefore eminently trustworthy) in the *New York Times* (where he is the food editor) for roasting it in the oven, and felt it was therefore safe to give it a go. Though I should say that, while my recipe is inspired by him, it is not his recipe. And though I was delighted with it, for me the crucial test was my son's approval. For a while, we lived on what I could loosely call London's Shawarma Strip, and my son went out nightly – after dinner, if you please – for at least one shawarma. I proffered my version tentatively, and he pronounced in its favour.

Here, I've served it modestly, on a pile of shredded iceberg, with some warmed (proper) pitta, lemon wedges and a tahini sauce, as made below. Although here my son dissented, and said that only lamb shawarma should be served with tahini sauce. When I make this for friends, or for a family lunch or supper, I certainly also include my Caramelized Garlic Yogurt Sauce (**p.256**) and slice up some fresh tomatoes sprinkled with mint, and bring out my Quick-Pickled Carrots (**p.262**) and Quick Gherkins (**p.258**), or I just cut some cucumbers into wedged slices, and macerate some red onions, cut into half-moons, with red wine vinegar or lime.

SERVES 6–10, DEPENDING ON HOW YOU CHOOSE TO SERVE IT

12 skinless and boneless chicken thighs

2 unwaxed lemons

100ml regular olive oil

4 fat or 6 smaller cloves garlic, peeled and finely grated or minced

2 dried or fresh bay leaves

2 teaspoons paprika

2 teaspoons ground cumin

1 teaspoon ground coriander

1 teaspoon dried chilli flakes

¼ teaspoon ground cinnamon

¼ teaspoon freshly grated nutmeg

2 teaspoons sea salt flakes

lettuce leaves, to serve

FOR THE SHAWARMA SAUCE:

1 cup (250g) plain yogurt

4 x 15ml tablespoons tahini

1 fat or 2 smaller cloves garlic, peeled and finely grated or minced

fat pinch salt, or to taste

1 tablepoon pomegranate seeds

- Take a large resealable freezer bag and put the chicken thighs in it.

- Using a fine microplane grater (for choice), grate in the lemon zest, then squeeze the lemons and add the juice. Pour in the olive oil and add the garlic, then add all the remaining ingredients, except for those for the sauce.

- Squish everything about together, then seal the bag, place it on a plate or in a dish, and refrigerate for at least 6 hours, or up to 1 day.

- When you're ready to cook, preheat the oven to 220°C/gas mark 7, remove the chicken from the fridge and allow it to reach room temperature.

- Tip the contents of the freezer bag into a shallow roasting tin – mine measures 44 x 34 x 1.5cm – and make sure all the chicken thighs are lying flat and not on top of one another (if possible) before roasting in the hot oven for 30 minutes, by which time they should be cooked through (though obviously you must check) and golden on top.

- When the chicken's more or less cooked, make the sauce simply by combining the yogurt with the tahini and garlic, stir and salt to taste, and sprinkle with a few pomegranate seeds.

- Line a platter or a couple of plates with crisp lettuce, shredded or torn into pieces, and then top with the piping hot chicken, pouring the oily juices over them, unless you are, for some inexplicable reason, anti-oily-juices. If you wanted to make the chicken go further, you could cut the thighs into chunky slices rather than leaving them whole. And please do add any of the suggested accompaniments, itemized in my Introduction.

MAKE AHEAD NOTE	STORE NOTE	FREEZE NOTE
The chicken can be marinated 1 day ahead. Store in fridge until needed.	Transfer leftover cooked chicken to a container, then cool, cover and refrigerate within 2 hours. Will keep in fridge for up to 3 days.	The chicken can be frozen in its marinade – as long as the meat has not been previously frozen – for up to 3 months. Leftover chicken can also be frozen, in airtight containers or resealable bags, for up to 2 months. Defrost overnight in fridge before using.

Tamarind-marinated bavette steak

Skirt or flank steak is eaten a lot in America, and in France, but hardly at all here in the UK. This is madness, as it is so much cheaper than any other sort of steak and so rich in flavour. I think what has put people off in the past is that, in Britain, it has been cooked in low and slow braises, which turns it into shoe leather. Bavette is the external part of the skirt (onglet being the internal connecting tissue) and all you need to do to cook it is, as my butcher puts it, "sear the hell out of it and serve it rare". I find 2 minutes a side on a very hot, ridged griddle optimum, but this does mean it's only for those who like their steak blue. The other key point is how you carve it: it must be sliced against the grain. That holds true with all steak, but with a cut like bavette, it will be inedibly chewy if you disobey. Luckily, the grain is very distinct (as you can see to the left of the picture) so it's very easy to identify and then cut across it.

You don't have to get the whole piece. I don't like cooking individually cut steaks, as it's all in the fine slicing as far as I'm concerned, but a 500g piece will be plenty to feed 4, and is the size I often go for, cooking it for exactly the same amount of time as overleaf.

The tamarind and soy marinade tenderizes the meat, but also gives such a glorious tanginess (I have a sour tooth). I keep Thai tamarind paste, which is condensed almost into a brick, in my fridge, and that's why I proceed as below. But if you are using tamarind paste out of a jar (and which tends to be runny), then use 75ml and simply add it to the rest of the marinade ingredients, without cooking it or adding water. Either is fine, but it just so happens that the genuine article is better, and less expensive.

I serve this thinly sliced, as if it were a joint of beef, but it would also make for fantastic beef tacos, and is wonderful cold, stuffed into a baguette or tossed into a salad, so leftovers are a real boon.

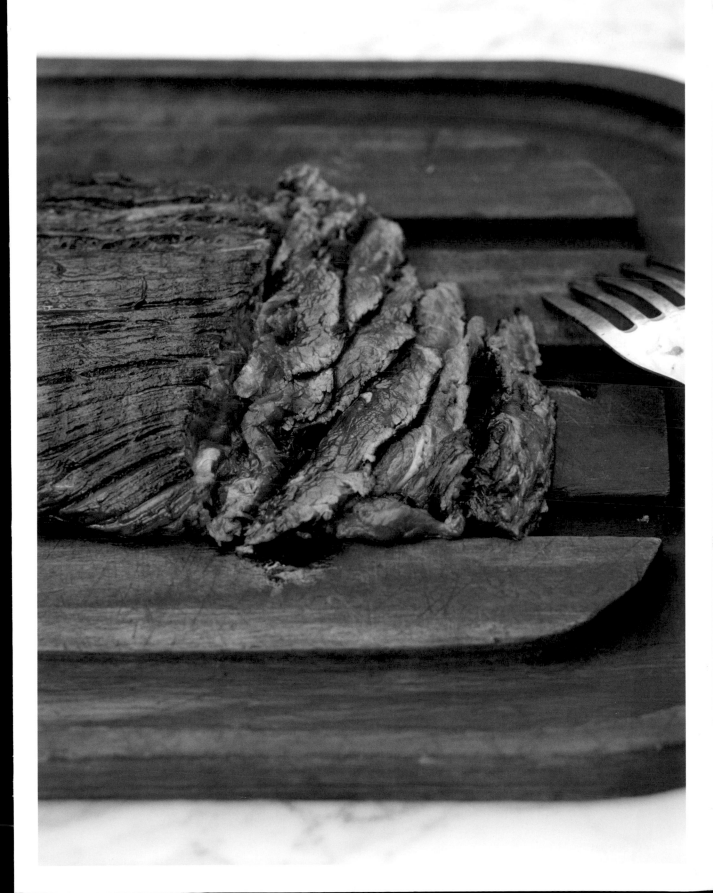

SERVES 6

50g tamarind paste	2 x 15ml tablespoons sunflower oil
¼ cup (4 x 15ml tablespoons) soy sauce	1 x 15ml tablespoon runny honey
¼ cup (4 x 15ml tablespoons) hot water, from a recently boiled kettle	750g (whole piece) bavette steak

○ Put the tamarind paste, soy and hot water into the smallest saucepan you have, and stir over a low heat to dissolve the tamarind. When it's as smooth as you think you can get it – the tamarind paste I use says it's without stones, but I do find the odd one, and I don't bother to get rid of them – remove to a bowl or jug, whisk in the oil and honey, and leave to cool. Do not use until it is cold.

○ Put the bavette steak into a resealable freezer bag, pour in the cold marinade and squelch it about so that the thin steak is covered on both sides, then seal, lay on a plate and put in the fridge overnight or for 1 day.

○ Bring it back to room temperature, prepare a large piece of kitchen foil, then heat a ridged griddle till very, very hot. Lift the steak out of its marinade, letting any excess (and there will be a lot) drip back into the bag and then slap the meat on the griddle and cook for 2 minutes a side.

○ Immediately (I use tongs for all this) transfer the steak to the piece of foil and make a tightly sealed but baggy parcel, and let the meat rest, on a chopping board, or any surface that is not too cold, for 5 minutes. Then unwrap the foil, transfer the steak to a board, and carve in thin slices against the grain.

MAKE AHEAD NOTE	STORE NOTE	FREEZE NOTE
The steak can be marinated 1 day ahead. Store in fridge until needed.	Transfer leftover cooked steak to a container, then cool, cover and refrigerate within 2 hours. Will keep in fridge for up to 3 days.	Leftover cooked and cooled steak can be frozen, in airtight containers or resealable bags, for up to 2 months. Defrost overnight in fridge before using.

Butterflied leg of lamb

So long as you don't have to butterfly it yourself, this is the quickest way to cook a joint of lamb, and the easiest way of carving it. And although lamb has become the most expensive of meats now, serving it this way at least means it goes further.

In this recipe, I've brought together a favourite cut and a long-beloved flavour combination: anchovies bring out the sweet richness of lamb quite extraordinarily. There is nothing original about the pairing, just as it is hardly novel to cook lamb with thyme and garlic, but the gloriousness of home cooking is that it relies on the comforting rituals of familiar flavours rather than losing itself in a mad pursuit of novelty.

I have specified an approximate weight for the lamb, but the reality is, a leg of lamb will weigh as much as it does, according to season. Whatever the weight, I give the lamb its half-an-hour blast in the oven – any less and the skin won't brown. It is the amount of time you let it rest *out* of the oven that will determine how pink it is.

1.5kg (approx.) boned and butterflied leg of lamb

1 x 15ml tablespoon fresh thyme leaves, plus more to sprinkle on at the end

6 anchovy fillets (the sort packed in oil)

4 fat cloves garlic, peeled

2 x 15ml tablespoons extra-virgin olive oil

1 teaspoon sea salt flakes

- Preheat the oven to 220°C/gas mark 7. Get out a large, shallow tin and put the butterflied leg of lamb in, skin-side down. If there is any thick part still not very "butterflied" or flattened, then put another slit in with a knife.

- Put the tablespoonful of thyme leaves on a chopping board and place the anchovy fillets on top. Cut the garlic cloves in half lengthways, then add to the thyme and anchovy fillets on the board.

- Roughly chop all these ingredients together to make a paste to spread on the lamb.

- Rub this paste into the slashes in the butterflied lamb, and then spread the remainder on top of the meat, smearing all you can onto it.

- Drizzle the extra-virgin olive oil over and then leave the lamb to come to room temperature (this could take up to 30 minutes).

- When you are ready, carefully turn the lamb over, still on its tray, and rub some of the oil in the tin onto the skin, then sprinkle with the salt.

- Put in the oven for 30 minutes, then take it out and tent with foil, leaving it to rest for 10–15 minutes if you want the meat pink. If you prefer your lamb less pink, leave it to stand for 30 minutes.

- Transfer the meat to a board and cut it into very thin slices across. Pour the cooking juices into a small pan and heat on the hob. Pour some over the sliced meat. Sprinkle with some chopped thyme leaves and serve with the remaining juices.

STORE NOTE	FREEZE NOTE
Transfer leftover cooked lamb to a container, then cool, cover – or wrap tightly in foil – and refrigerate within 2 hours of making. Will keep in fridge for up to 2 days.	Cooked and cooled lamb can be frozen, in airtight containers or resealable bags, for up to 2 months. Defrost overnight in fridge before using.

BREATHE

BREATHE

Most of our lives are spent rushing about, scrabbling for time and having to cook in snatched moments, with scarcely a minute to catch our breath. This chapter sets a different, slower, pace and yet the recipes in it couldn't suit our modern, frenzied life better.

It is essential to realize that slow-cooking isn't about a dream of olden-days farm-house living: it makes your life easier in the here and now. These are the recipes I rely on when I have friends over midweek and no time to get anything together on the evening itself, and this is the food we eat together as a family. I try to keep a stash of everyday-supper portions in the freezer – money in the bank. These recipes really cook themselves, needing no more than to be left in a low oven, with no interference from me. All I have to do is reheat them later. Strictly speaking, you have to be there only to throw everything into a pot and bung said pot in the oven, though I know there are those who are anxious about leaving the house with the oven left on. Since I work from home, that isn't a factor for me, but anyway, that is where the slow cooker comes in.

I have grown to love my slow cooker, not least because I've found one that suits my way of cooking. The bowl itself is made of cast iron and is removable, so if I want to brown anything on the hob first, I don't need to add to the washing-up by using a frying pan. And I can serve straight from the pot itself when the food's ready. I have professed my deep and elemental love for cooking with cast iron earlier (see my encomium on p.xiii), and even when I am not actually doing the cooking, but leaving the food to cook itself, I feel it makes a difference, bringing that old-fashioned, cooked-at-the-fireside depth of flavour that synthetic materials, however efficient, cannot replicate.

Similarly, I use enamelled cast-iron casseroles for slow-cooking stews in the oven. The heat is much more evenly generated, so you don't get hot spots, and the flavour really does seem better. They are expensive, I know, but as I said in *Kitchen*, they last for ever (one of mine was a wedding present to my parents in 1956), which also means you don't have to buy them new – and I always like an excuse to go eBaying. But much as cooking is about practicality, we also form emotional attachments to old, loved and trusted pots and pans, and those heavy-duty casseroles that have been with me so much of my adult life make cooking part of an important continuum. The slow-cooked stews that are ushered out of them form a thread of cooking and eating that runs through my life, and my children's. Though that's not to say I don't enjoy adding to my collection, but I do so knowing that one day my son and daughter, and maybe even their children, will be cooking out of them.

This sense of continuum is at the heart, too, of why I so love this way of cooking. It buys me breathing space, and this is space I can relax into, in the secure and happy knowledge that food will be on the table later. And, for me, it's a boon that the recipes that follow are better if left for a couple of days before being reheated. In fact, I insist upon it. The happy knowledge that the food is there and, furthermore, that I don't have to worry or fuss about it, makes me breathe easier.

Malaysian red-cooked chicken

Yasmin Othman is my patient teacher in the arts of Malaysian cooking, and I am grateful to her. This, properly called *ayam masak merah*, gets its red colour as much from the fiery chilli paste at its base as from the tomatoes. In fact, when I posted a picture of my first attempt online, I was strictly enjoined by a chorus of Malaysians to add more chillies. They could tell my error just by the colour. Yes, it is hot, but not frighteningly so, yet what is more unfamiliar is the desirably dry texture of the curry. Dry, in the context of curries, and more particularly here, simply means that the chicken mustn't swim in a sauce, but be thickly coated by it. I require nothing more alongside it than plain rice.

SERVES 4–6

6 long dried red chillies (not the small dried bird's eye chillies)

1 large red onion, peeled and roughly chopped

3 cloves garlic, peeled and roughly chopped

5cm piece (25g) fresh ginger, peeled and sliced

3 fresh red chillies, roughly chopped with seeds intact

2 x 15ml tablespoons sunflower oil

2 sticks lemongrass, trimmed and bruised

3 x 15ml tablespoons tomato purée

12 chicken thighs, bone in and skin removed

1 x 400g can chopped tomatoes

200ml coconut milk

½ teaspoon sea salt flakes

TO SERVE:

2 shallots, peeled and thinly sliced

3–4 x 15ml tablespoons sunflower oil

- Soak the dried chillies in hot water for 5 minutes to soften; many will float rather than be submerged by the water. Remove them from the water, tearing into pieces – best to use disposable vinyl CSI gloves for this – and shake out as many seeds as possible.

- Blitz the onion, garlic and ginger into a paste with the fresh red chillies and soaked dried chillies in a bowl with a stick blender.

- In a large wok (that comes with a lid), heat the oil, then add the just-blitzed-up chilli paste and bruised lemongrass to the wok and fry for 5 minutes over a medium heat, stirring every now and again.

- Add the tomato purée and fry for 1 minute, then add the chicken thighs to the pan, stirring to coat them well in the mixture.

- Add the canned tomatoes, then add water from the cold tap to the empty can so that it is quarter-filled, then swill the can and pour the water into the wok, followed by the coconut milk, stir well and add the salt.

- Bring to the boil, then cover with the lid, turn down the heat and leave to simmer for 30 minutes, lifting the lid every so often to stir the chicken in the sauce.

- Remove the lid, turn the heat up a little and cook, uncovered, at a bold simmer for 30 minutes; the sauce will start to thicken and become a deeper red. Transfer to a dish to cool, and refrigerate, covered, for at least 1 day and up to 3 days (see Note, below).

- To reheat, put the chicken in its sauce back in the wok, put on the lid, and cook over a medium to low heat until the chicken is hot all the way through, about 20 minutes, lifting the lid to stir every so often to make sure the heat is evenly distributed. Remove the lid, turn up the heat and let the sauce bubble away for for about 15 minutes, so it becomes more like a thick paste that sticks to the chicken thighs. Once the sauce is the right consistency, taste and add more salt if you wish.

- You don't have to sprinkle crisp shallot rings over the top, but you will be glad if you do. Heat the oil in a cast-iron or heavy-based frying pan and fry the sliced shallots until they are golden and crisp. As soon as they are cooked, carefully transfer to some kitchen roll and leave to cool. Indeed, you can cook these at any time while the chicken's cooking, or even before. Sprinkle over the red-cooked chicken on serving.

MAKE AHEAD NOTE	FREEZE NOTE
The shallots can be fried up to 4 hours ahead. Leave at cool room temperature until needed. The curry paste can be made 2 days ahead then covered and stored in fridge until needed. The chicken curry (without shallots) can be made up to 3 days ahead. Cool, cover and refrigerate within 2 hours of making. Will keep in fridge for up to 3 days. Reheat as per recipe, above.	Freeze in an airtight container for up to 2 months. Defrost overnight in fridge and reheat as Make Ahead Note.

Note: the chicken should be reheated once only.

Massaman beef curry

This is another recipe inspired by my Thai travels and I have cooked it many, many times since. It is essentially a beef and potato stew, with all the comfort that this implies, but the rich mellow flavours bring a vibrancy not immediately conveyed by that description. A massaman curry is a relatively mild curry, so don't feel that the amount of paste I use will blow you away. I do feel strongly, though, that unless you use authentic Thai pastes, you will not get a curry that truly delivers on flavour. Anyway, I buy my coconut milk, tamarind paste and all my curry pastes from a Thai provisioner online and not only is the quality much better, but the prices are much lower than the supermarket varieties.

As for the coconut, you will see that I add the cream from the top first, but I can't tell you how often I open the tin upside down, and so can't then follow my own instructions. In other words, relax: with good pastes and coconut milk, this cannot go wrong.

I like to blanch some green beans, chopped into short lengths, which I then refresh in cold water and mix with some thinly sliced shallots to sprinkle on top, or – for the family supper version – I just serve a bowl of plain-cooked green beans alongside.

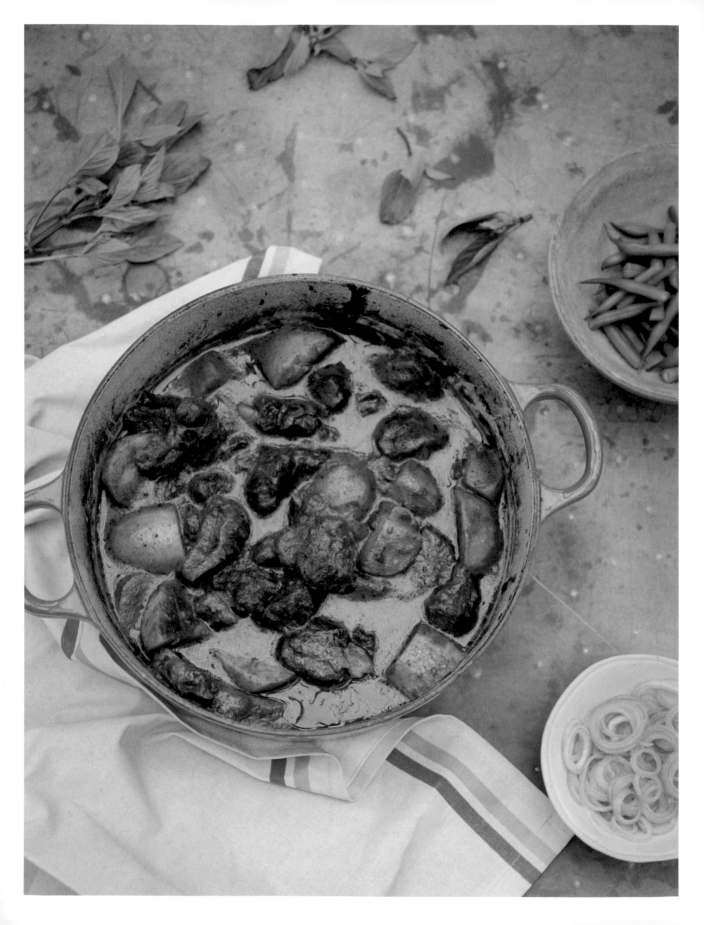

2½ teaspoons tamarind paste

25g palm sugar or soft light brown sugar

500ml hot water, from a recently boiled kettle

1 x 400ml can coconut milk

½ cup (125ml/140g) massaman curry paste, or to taste

1 teaspoon sea salt flakes

1kg beef shin off the bone, cut into 4–5cm cubes

750g waxy potatoes, peeled

small bunch Thai basil or coriander, to serve

- Preheat the oven to 170°C/gas mark 3. Put the tamarind paste and the sugar in a measuring jug and add boiling water to the 250ml mark. Stir with a fork to help dissolve the paste and sugar.

- In a large, heavy-based pan or casserole that has a tight-fitting lid – I use one of 24cm diameter – spoon in the cream from the top of the coconut can. Add the curry paste and then heat, stirring every now and again, until bubbling (some of the oil may separate out at this stage, but that's fine). Add the contents of the jug – with its water, tamarind and sugar – and the rest of the coconut milk, along with the salt, and stir to combine, before adding the beef. Stir well, and let it come to a bubble. As soon as it does, clamp on the lid, turn off the heat and transfer to the oven to cook for 2 hours.

- Once it's out of the oven, leave to cool, then refrigerate for at least 1 day, or up to 3 days, to allow the beef to get tender and the flavours in the sauce to develop.

- About half an hour before you want to eat, preheat the oven to 200°C/gas mark 6, and cut the potatoes into similar-sized chunks as the beef, then add them to the pot of curry. Place on the hob, add 250ml of boiling water and bring to a bubble, then clamp on the lid and transfer to the oven for 30 minutes, or until the stew is bubbling and hot and the potatoes are tender. Sprinkle with some shredded Thai basil leaves, should you be able to get hold of them, or scatter with chopped coriander, and bring to the table immediately.

MAKE AHEAD NOTE	FREEZE NOTE
Cook curry for 2 hours as per recipe, above, then cool, cover and refrigerate within 2 hours of making. Will keep in fridge for up to 3 days.	Freeze cooled curry in an airtight container for up to 3 months, defrost overnight in fridge before reheating as per recipe, above.

Note: the curry should be reheated once only.

Oxtail on toast

Sometimes I get obsessed with a recipe, and this is such a one. I first ate the most divine oxtail on toast at a restaurant called Hubbard & Bell, and could talk of nothing else for days. Some months later, I came across a recipe for Oxtail Marmalade in Jody Williams' *Buvette* cookbook and knew I had to have a go myself. My recipe is much simpler than either version, but I am grateful for the inspiration from both.

It is quite extraordinary how much mileage you get from this: it makes enough to spread on 6–8 pieces of toast, and you'll still be able to conjure up a sauce with what's left to eat with wide egg noodles, or over polenta. Just make sure to reheat only as much as you need for each outing. I freeze mine in portions – enough to spread on 4 pieces of toast – for much comfort and joy at later dates.

MAKES 2 LITRES, ENOUGH FOR 6–8 PIECES OF TOAST, PLUS A STEW FOR 4 OR A SAUCE TO POUR OVER 500G PASTA (DRIED WEIGHT) FOR 4–6

1 onion, peeled and roughly chopped

1 clove garlic, peeled and roughly chopped

1 carrot, peeled and roughly chopped

1 stick celery

small handful fresh parsley

1 x 15ml tablespoon (15g) duck, goose or bacon fat

zest and juice of 1 clementine or ½ orange, preferably unwaxed

2 teaspoons dried thyme, or 1 x 15ml tablespoon fresh thyme leaves

2 teaspoons ground allspice

2 teaspoons cocoa

4 x 15ml tablespoons red vermouth or ruby port

500ml beef stock (the sort that comes "fresh" in tubs is fine)

2 x 15ml tablespoons Worcestershire sauce

2 teaspoons sea salt flakes

1.25kg oxtail, cut into 5–6cm slices

2 bay leaves

fresh thyme, to serve (optional)

○ Preheat the oven to 170°C/gas mark 3.

○ Put the chopped onion, garlic and carrot into the bowl of a food processor fitted with the steel blade. Tear the celery stick into 2 or 3 pieces and drop that in too, along with the parsley, and blitz till finely chopped. Or you can simply do this by hand.

○ Melt the duck (or other) fat over a medium heat in a heavy-based casserole (with a tight-fitting lid), and when hot, grate in the zest of the clementine (or orange), stirring it in the warm fat and letting the scent waft up, before adding the mixture from the processor. Cook, stirring every now and again, for 5 minutes.

○ Add the dried thyme (or fresh thyme leaves), ground allspice and cocoa and stir together before pouring in the vermouth (or port). Let it bubble up, then pour in the beef stock and Worcestershire sauce, squeeze in the juice of the clementine or orange (don't worry if you get a bit of pulp) and sprinkle in the salt. Give it a stir, then add the oxtail to the liquid in the pan, bring to a bubble, add the bay leaves, clamp on the lid and transfer to the oven to cook for 3½ hours.

○ You'll know the oxtail is ready when it's falling off the bone. Using 2 forks, start pulling the meat off and shredding it. If you want to wait until it's a little cooler, by all means do. Cool the stew, remove the bones, then keep in the fridge in a covered container for at least 1 day, or up to 3 days.

○ When you're ready to reheat the oxtail, remove the fat, which will have risen to the surface in a solid disc, and add as much oxtail as you need to a pan that's big enough for the portion size you've settled on. It will seem dry, but this is just because the juices have jellied – you do not need to add water, however much you itch to. But you must make sure the heat under the pan is low, and the lid is tightly clamped on, to preserve the liquid you do have, and make sure it is piping hot before serving.

○ Spread on toast made with good bread – I find a cupful of stew, in its cold jellied state, is enough for 3 pieces of toast, maybe 4 – and strew with some fresh thyme leaves, should you have some.

MAKE AHEAD NOTE	CONVERSION NOTE TO SLOW COOKER	FREEZE NOTE
The oxtail can be made up to 3 days ahead. Cool, cover and refrigerate within 2 hours of making.	Halve the stock and cook on low for 8 hours, until the oxtail is tender enough to shred, before adding the dried or fresh thyme, ground allspice and cocoa and continuing as per recipe, above.	Freeze cooled oxtail in an airtight container for up to 3 months. Defrost overnight in fridge before reheating.

Note: the oxtail should be reheated once only.

Asian-flavoured short ribs

Since America is such a big beef country, short ribs are found easily and every-where. Unfortunately, they are – outside of trendy gastropubs, which have irritatingly forced the price up a bit – virtually unknown in Britain. This has to change. The meat is luscious and sweet, and if that weren't inducement enough, they are poetically known in the butchery business as Jacob's Ladder.

I make this stew – which is almost embarrassingly easy – when I want full-on gorgeousness but nothing much to do when people actually turn up. You might need to ask a butcher for the ribs in advance, and you will also need to ask for them to be cut into 4–5cm cubes. You'll need a large pan (with a lid) to cook them in – I use one of 35cm diameter – as, unless you can more or less fit the ribs into one layer, the liquid they cook in won't cover them sufficiently. If you don't have a pot big enough, then use a large roasting tin and cover tightly with foil.

I like to eat this with some short grain brown rice cooked with a few cardamom pods, and the Roast Radishes on **p.227** or some crunchy green beans.

2.5kg beef short ribs, cut into 4–5cm squares

1 cup (250ml) hoisin sauce, from a jar

2 cups (500ml) water

¼ cup (4 x 15ml tablespoons) soy sauce

½ cup (125ml) Chinese (Shaoxing) rice wine

2 x 15ml tablespoons Chinese 5-spice powder

1 x 15ml tablespoon dried chilli flakes

1 x 15ml tablespoon toasted sesame oil

4 fat cloves garlic, peeled and finely grated or minced

TO SERVE:

1 fresh red chilli, finely chopped

2–3 x 15ml tablespoons chopped fresh coriander

3–4 limes, cut into wedges

- Preheat the oven to 150°C/gas mark 2. Clatter the chunks of short ribs into a large pan, and read the Introduction for pointers here, if you haven't done so already.

- Mix together all the remaining ingredients and pour over the ribs.

- Cover with a layer of baking parchment or greaseproof paper, tucking it in tightly to seal as best you can, before putting on a lid, or cover the top of the pan with foil and seal the edges securely. Cook in the oven for 4–4½ hours: the meat should be tender and starting to come away from the bones.

- Transfer the ribs to a vessel that will fit in the fridge later to cool, and then tenderly remove as many of the bones as possible, before covering and refrigerating for at least 1 day, or up to 3 days.

- Before you reheat them, remove the hard layer of fat that will have formed on the top (I do this with my hands, encased in a pair of disposable vinyl gloves, CSI-style), transfer to a large ovenproof dish that you can also serve the ribs in – I use a ceramic dish measuring 28 x 26 x 8cm just because I like the way its shape mirrors the cubes of meat – and reheat, covered with foil or a lid, depending on what you're cooking in, at 200°C/gas mark 6 for 1 hour, or until piping hot.

- Scatter some finely chopped chilli and chopped fresh coriander over the ribs on serving, and put some lime wedges on the table so that everyone can squeeze this sour juice into their rich, sweet stew, to taste, on eating.

MAKE AHEAD NOTE	FREEZE NOTE
The ribs can be made up to 3 days ahead. Cool, cover and refrigerate within 2 hours of making.	Freeze in an airtight container for up to 3 months. Defrost overnight in fridge before reheating as per recipe, above.

Note: the ribs should be reheated once only.

Beef chilli with bourbon, beer and black beans

I refer to this at home as The Texas Chilli Massacre, as my recipe is far from being authentic in the eyes of Americans serious about their chilli. My offences are double: the inclusion of beans is not considered proper Stateside, and my addition of maple syrup is a further heresy in the South. But while I apologize to anyone I may offend, I do not, *cannot*, apologize for this. It is everything I dream of in a chilli: deeply flavoured and resonantly fiery but not burning. But you have seen my casual disregard for rules, so feel free to reduce the chilli quotient if you wish.

As for the chillies, I find ancho chillies in the spice aisle at my supermarket, but if you can't get them easily, then just add another 2 teaspoons of dried chilli flakes. You won't have the smokiness, but you will have the intense heat. Also, you could blister the fresh chillies over a flame to compensate. One last note: if you are a contact lens wearer, as I am, you must wear disposable vinyl gloves for the chilli wrangling.

I haven't made a mistake with the beans, by the way: they don't need pre-soaking; indeed they — and the eventual chilli — are much better for not being soaked.

There's nothing wrong in eating this with no more than some hunks of good bread, but my accompaniment of choice would be baked potatoes and coconut-milk yogurt (such as CoYo) that's had some chopped fresh coriander stirred into it. Sour cream is also an option. And some salving slices of avocado atop your bowlful of chilli is always a good way to go.

2 dried ancho chillies (approx. 30g total)

250ml hot water, from a recently boiled kettle

2 x 15ml tablespoons sunflower oil

1 large onion, peeled and chopped

4 fresh jalapeño peppers or other chilli peppers, chopped but not de-seeded

3 fat cloves garlic, peeled and finely grated or minced

2½ teaspoons ground cumin

2½ teaspoons ground coriander

1 teaspoon dried chilli flakes

1.75kg boneless shin of beef, cut into cubes

150ml bourbon whiskey

1 x 33cl bottle Mexican beer, or other lager

500g dried black turtle beans

1 litre cold water

2 teaspoons sea salt flakes

2 x 15ml tablespoons maple syrup

- Preheat the oven to 150°C/gas mark 2.

- Put the ancho chillies in a measuring jug and add boiling water to the 250ml mark.

- Heat the oil in a large, heavy-based pan – bearing in mind, you have many good things to go in it – then add the onion and cook, stirring every now and again to make sure it isn't catching, for about 5 minutes, or until beginning to soften. Add the chopped jalapeños and cook, stirring, for another 3 or so minutes, before adding the garlic, followed by the cumin, coriander and chilli flakes. Stir well.

- Add the cubes of beef, followed by the bourbon and let it bubble up in the hot pan before pouring in the beer.

- Add the black beans, and – wearing disposable vinyl gloves – tear the soaked ancho chillies into pieces (discarding the tough stalks) and drop them into the pan, then pour in the soaking liquid, followed by the litre of cold water, and the salt and maple syrup. Bring to a bubble, then clamp on a lid and transfer to the oven to cook for 4 hours, by which time the meat will be meltingly tender. My children won't let me wait when I make this and want to eat it immediately, but this dark, rich, heat-packed stew is even better if left to cool, then reheated in a day or two.

MAKE AHEAD NOTE	CONVERSION TO SLOW COOKER	FREEZE NOTE
The chilli can be made up to 3 days ahead. Cool, cover and refrigerate within 2 hours of making.	Reduce the litre of cold water in recipe to 200ml. Cook on low for 8–10 hours, until the beans have softened and the meat is tender. After 6 hours, check on the chilli and, if the beans have absorbed most of the liquid, add a little water from a freshly boiled kettle.	Freeze cooled chilli in an airtight container for up to 3 months. Defrost overnight in fridge before reheating. Reheat gently, stirring occasionally, until piping hot.

Note: the chilli should be reheated once only.

Italian veal shank stew

Perhaps this is a bad thing for someone who writes cookery books to admit, but I do find myself, when I come across a recipe I love, cooking it over and over again whenever people come for supper. This is a case in point, and I actually have to find a reason *not* to cook it. I first ate it years ago, made by the most generous and talented cook I know, Helio Fenerich of Helio's Kitchen, and this is my version of the recipe he was kind enough to give me.

I need at this point to repeat a small lecture I gave in *Nigellissima*: I know there is widespread revulsion at the idea of eating veal, but it is crucial to know that both the RSPCA and Compassion in World Farming are urging us to eat veal, so long as it is labelled "rose veal" (which is humanely reared), otherwise countless animals are needlessly destroyed. It is time to rethink our prejudices. Lecture over.

SERVES 8–10

2 carrots, peeled and roughly chopped

1 large onion, peeled and roughly chopped

4 cloves garlic, peeled and roughly chopped

4 sticks celery, torn into pieces

small bunch fresh thyme

3 x 15ml tablespoons sunflower oil

2 whole veal shins (ask butcher to cut the ends off to reveal the marrow)

½ x 400g can chopped tomatoes

250ml dry white vermouth or white wine

1 teaspoon sea salt flakes

good grinding of pepper

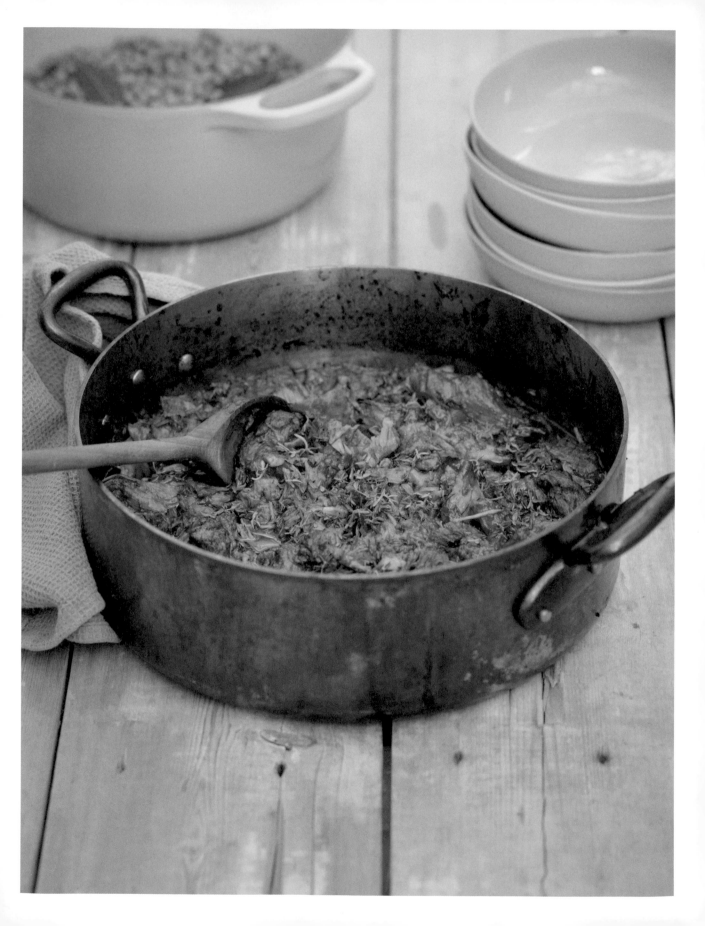

- Preheat the oven to 180°C/gas mark 4. Put all the vegetables, along with 2 tablespoons of thyme leaves – reserving the rest for later – into the bowl of a food processor and blitz until finely chopped. You can also do this by hand.

- In a large roasting tin that will go on the hob, heat the oil over a medium to high heat, and brown the veal shins. They are quite big, and this does involve a bit of comedy wrangling to get them brown on all sides, but you do not have to be fanatical about it. Remove the meat once it's browned.

- Add the finely chopped vegetables – your soffrito – and cook over a medium heat, stirring, for 10–15 minutes, or until the mixture has softened.

- Add the canned tomatoes (if you can't bear having half a can of tomatoes roaming free in the fridge afterwards, then nothing too terrible will happen if you chuck the whole can in, but I am restrained, and don't), the vermouth (or wine) and sprinkle with the salt and a good grinding of pepper. Stir well, then return the veal shins to the tin, and turn them in the vegetably juices, spooning a little on top of the shanks. There won't be much liquid, but that's how it's meant to be.

- Turn off the heat, and cover with baking parchment or greaseproof paper, tucking it around the meat in the tin, then cover the whole tin with 2 layers of foil, sealing the edges tightly. Transfer to the oven and cook for 3 hours, or until the meat is beginning to fall off the bone.

- Remove the foil and the parchment or greaseproof paper, and when the meat has cooled down enough to handle, pull the meat off the bones, shredding it with your hands, and discard any gluey bits of rind. Actually, I eat them then and there, as my treat, but not everyone has a taste for the glutinous. Now for the fun part: rap the bones against the inside rim of the tin so that the marrow shoots out into the stew; this is not for the squeamish.

- Transfer the rich stew to a dish that will fit in the fridge to cool, then cover it and refrigerate for at least 1 day, and up to 3 days. When you want to eat it, preheat the oven to 200°C/gas mark 6, transfer the stew to a casserole or ovenproof dish with a lid, stirring in the layer of marrow fat, and let it come to room temperature, then put the lid on and reheat in the oven for 30 minutes, or until piping hot. Taste to see if you wish to add more seasoning, and serve immediately, strewn with the reserved thyme.

MAKE AHEAD NOTE	FREEZE NOTE
The stew can be made up to 3 days ahead. Cool, cover and refrigerate within 2 hours of making.	Freeze cooled stew in an airtight container for up to 3 months. Defrost overnight in fridge before reheating as per recipe, above.

Note: the stew should be reheated once only.

Barbecuey pork butt

It's embarrassingly childish of me to find this name funny, but I do, and that's why I'm keeping it. Pork butt is what Americans call pork shoulder, although my butcher says that it is more properly the blade bone part, which is why I have specified so in the ingredients. What I've made below, though, is essentially pulled pork, and I'm sure any part of the shoulder would do just fine.

The real treat about this – apart from the ease of preparation and the joy of eating – is that you cook it for such a long time in a low oven, that not only does your house smell magnificent (I put this in late at night, and come down at breakfast to be heralded by it), but you don't need to do anything when the hungry hordes arrive, except shred it. But I have also given an option for a shorter cooking time, should that make life easier.

If you have a double oven, ask the butcher to give you the scored rind too, snip it into pieces with kitchen scissors and roast in an oven preheated to 220°C/gas mark 7 for 25 minutes, then turn them over for a final 5 minutes. Serve alongside the pork.

This is very, very good squidged into baps, or eaten alongside the Cuban Black Beans (**p.214**) or the Sweet and Sour Slaw (**p.240**), or both.

2kg boneless and rindless pork shoulder from blade end, with a good layer of fat remaining, rolled and tied

2 x 15ml tablespoons soft light brown sugar

2 x 15ml tablespoons Dijon mustard

2 x 15ml tablespoons sherry vinegar

2 teaspoons sea salt flakes

2 teaspoons Chinese 5-spice powder

2 teaspoons hot chilli powder

4 cloves garlic, peeled and finely grated or minced

- Line the base and sides of a small roasting tin, just large enough to take the pork, with a double layer of foil, sit the pork in it, fat-side up, and let it come to room temperature, which takes about 40–60 minutes, depending on your fridge and the weather. When it's almost there, heat the oven to 250°C/gas mark 9.

- Mix the sugar, mustard and vinegar in a bowl, stir in the salt, 5-spice and hot chilli powder, then add the garlic.

- When the pork is ready to go into the oven, mix the rub ingredients together again (I use a rubber spatula for this, and for smearing the pork joint) and cover the pork joint with as much as you can. The barbecuey rub may not look very appealing at this stage, but that need be of no concern. Put the smeared pork into the very hot oven and leave for 10 minutes – by which time the top will be beginning to burn in parts – and turn down the oven to 100°C/gas mark ¼ and cook for at least 12 hours, or up to 18, tenting with foil after 14–15 hours.

- Alternatively, after the 10 minute blast at 250°C/gas mark 9, turn the heat down to 150°C/gas mark 2 and cook for 5½–6 hours, tenting with foil after 3 hours.

- Remove from the oven, untie, discard any bits that are too blackened to eat (though the burnt bits are my favourite) and pull to pieces with a couple of forks. Pour over some of the juice (though you might want to spoon off a little of the fat first) and serve immediately.

STORE NOTE	FREEZE NOTE
Cool leftovers, then cover and refrigerate within 2 hours of making. Will keep in fridge for up to 3 days. Reheat in an ovenproof dish, covered with foil – or wrap pork in foil, if small portions – in an oven preheated to 150°C/gas mark 2 for about 30 minutes (timing will depend on quantity) until piping hot. Add a splash of water, if needed, to prevent it from becoming too dry.	Freeze in an airtight container for up to 2 months. Defrost overnight in fridge before reheating as Store Note.

Note: the pork should be reheated once only.

Pork buns

Where do I start? I know: in New York, in Momofuku Noodle Bar in the East Village, to be precise. The name of the restaurant is Japanese; David Chang, the owner and head chef, is Korean-American; the slow-braised pork belly, squished into their steamed buns, definitely have Chinese heritage, though they are not to be confused with those other — *char sui* — pork buns. These are more like sandwiches, or belly-pork burgers, and within the steamed bun that holds the slices, can be placed all manner of deliciousness. For me, that means the Chilli, Ginger and Garlic Sauce on **p.254**, the Thai Pickled Peppers on **p.261**, or just freshly chopped chillies, some coriander leaves simply torn from their stalks, plus some shredded spring onions and slender cucumber batons, and, if in the mood, some crisp, fried shallot rings, but the game-changer here is the pork belly.

In the West we eat pork belly roasted, so that the skin goes crisp, making for soft meat with a roof of crackling. But there is another way, though it's not for fatphobes. When the meat is softly braised, the fat remains and is, indeed, essential to the dish. It is all succulence: every bit of it.

While it's a time-consuming recipe, it is a very simple one. And if it makes your life even easier, you can cook the pork ahead of time, and reheat it quickly when you want to eat it. Here's the thing: the pork looks much more beautiful to serve if you slice to order, but it is actually much easier to slice the meat if you do it once it's cold. And the buns do taste rather more Momofuku-like that way too.

You will need to go to a Chinese supermarket to get the steamed buns although I suppose you could use regular soft bread buns, but bear in mind that these juicy slices of meat can be eaten with rice or noodles, or however you please.

MAKES ENOUGH TO FILL 14–28 PORK BUNS

½ cup (70g) sea salt flakes

½ cup (100g) caster sugar

1.25kg boneless and rindless pork belly (though still with some fat covering), cut in half lengthways to make 2 pieces

¼ cup (4 x 15ml tablespoons) hoisin sauce, plus more to serve

14–28 Chinese soft "bao" buns (see Intro), or soft bread buns to serve

TO ACCOMPANY:

1–2 banana shallots, thinly sliced

3—4 x 15ml tablespoons sunflower oil for frying

½ large cucumber

4 spring onions, trimmed

large bunch coriander

Chilli, Ginger and Garlic Sauce (see p.254) or any hot sauce

- Fill a measuring jug with 1 litre of cold water from the tap. Add the salt and sugar, and stir to dissolve. Put the 2 pieces of pork belly into a large resealable freezer bag and pour in the brining liquid. Seal the bag, sit it in a dish and leave in the fridge for at least 8 hours, and up to 24.

- When you are ready to cook, remove the pork from the fridge to let it come to room temperature, and preheat the oven to 250°C/gas mark 9. Pour a cupful (250ml) of cold tap water into a measuring jug, add the hoisin and stir to mix well. Take the pork out of its brine (over the sink), pat it dry and put the 2 slabs, fat-side up, into a roasting tin in which they will sit snugly; I used one measuring 28 x 24 x 6.5cm. Moisten the top of each slab with 1 tablespoonful of the hoisin mixture and cook in the oven for 30 minutes, by which time the fat will have coloured and scorched in parts.

- Take it out of the oven, turn the heat down to 150°C/gas mark 2, and pour the remainder of the hoisin jug into the roasting tin, avoiding the top of the meat. Cover the tin tightly (and carefully – it will be hot) with a layer of thick foil (or 2 layers of regular foil) and put back in the oven for 2 hours, by which time the meat will be cooked through and tender. While the pork's cooking, you could always fry your sliced banana shallots in hot oil till crisp, and leave them to cool on a double layer of kitchen roll, to be sprinkled on later.

- Remove the cooked pork from the oven and onto a carving board. If you are serving straightaway, leave it to stand for a few minutes while you microwave or steam the buns, then carve each slab of pork into 1cm slices – I get 14 slices out of each piece. If the pork falls to pieces slightly as you carve, do not worry, as it tastes as good shredded and, indeed, is often served in the buns this way.

- Cut the cucumber and spring onions into thirds, crosswise, then slice both into fine strips, lengthways, tear some coriander leaves from the stalks, and transfer these to small dishes to go alongside the pork, along with the chilli sauce and some hoisin.

- If I've made this ahead and reheated the slices, I make up the buns and hand them round myself, filling each bun with 2 slices (though if you want this to go further, just 1) of pork belly, along with the strips of spring onion and cucumber, coriander, hoisin and fried shallot if wanted, and the chilli sauce. If I'm slicing the pork there and then, I let everyone make up their buns themselves.

MAKE AHEAD NOTE	FREEZE NOTE
Leave the pork to cool out of its cooking liquid (and pour the liquid into a bowl or jug, to be refrigerated), then wrap each slab tightly in foil and refrigerate for up to 3 days. To reheat, remove the solid disc of fat from the pork's cooking liquid, then add ¼ cup (4 tablespoons) of the jellied stock to a shallow baking tin, smoosh it around to cover the base, then slice the pork. Sit these slices in a single layer in the tin, cover with foil, and cook for 15 minutes in an oven preheated to 200°C/gas mark 6 until piping hot. Turn the slices in the liquid before serving.	Cooled, cooked pork can be tightly wrapped in a double layer of foil and frozen for up to 3 months. Defrost overnight in fridge, and slice and reheat as Make Ahead Note.

Note: the pork should be reheated once only.

Lamb shank and black garlic stew

This is a very lazy take – with some additions of my own – on a wonderful lamb tagine in Sabrina Ghayour's gloriously inspiring *Persiana* cookbook. The first time I made it, I followed standard procedure and provided a shank per person, but it occurred to me that actually, no one needs a whole shank, so I now shred the sweet meat (making sure I extract every little bit of marrow from the shank bones) which makes it go much further. Couscous might seem the obvious accompaniment, and it's a good one, but I prefer to produce a pile of proper pitta or good bread and the Chickpeas with Cumin and Spinach (**p.211**). If you haven't come across black garlic, you must try to find it: it has a flavour that tastes somehow caramelized and fermented at the same time, and adds a fabulous musky richness. It's much easier to get now, as it is being produced in the UK, but if this eludes you, or doesn't appeal, then use 2 bulbs of home-caramelized garlic in its place (see Caramelized Garlic Hummus, **p.113**, for instructions). If you're using this rather than black garlic, then just chop the onions by hand and squeeze the garlic pulp into the pan once the tomatoes have gone in.

SERVES 10–12

2 large onions (450–500g total), peeled and quartered

2 bulbs black garlic (see Intro), broken into cloves and peeled

3 x 15ml tablespoons (45g) goose or duck fat

2 teaspoons cumin seeds

2 teaspoons ground allspice

2 teaspoons ground cinnamon

250ml red vermouth or full-bodied red wine

2 x 400g cans chopped tomatoes

2 teaspoons sea salt flakes

6 lamb shanks

○ Preheat the oven to 150°C/gas mark 2. Put the onions and black garlic cloves into the bowl of a food processor and chop finely. You could also do this by hand, but the black garlic is very sticky. It also disperses better in the stew if it is blitzed to a near-pulp.

○ In a large pan, big enough to take everything later (I used one of 30cm diameter and 15cm deep) and that comes with a lid, melt the goose or duck fat, then add the contents of the food processor, scraping with a spatula to get every last bit. Cook, stirring frequently, for 3 minutes over a medium heat, or until the onion starts to soften, and then stir in the cumin seeds, ground allspice and cinnamon.

○ Turn the heat up to high, and then pour in the red vermouth or wine. Let this bubble up before adding the contents of the 2 cans of tomatoes, then fill each can with cold water from the tap, and pour that in, too.

○ Stir in the salt and add the lamb shanks, bring again to a bubble, then clamp on the lid and transfer to the oven to cook for 4 hours, by which time the sauce will be rich and the meat will begin to fall off the bone.

○ Leave in a cool place with the lid off and when the shanks are not too hot to handle (you might need to leave this for 1 hour, depending on the sensitivity of your hands; I plough in after 30 minutes), strip the meat from the shanks, and knock each shank bone against the inside rim of the pan to make sure the marrow and any juices in the bone go into the stew. This can be messy. Discard the bones, and shred the lamb a little more, using 2 forks. I then pour this into the pan I'm going to reheat and serve this in later – a pan of 28cm diameter and 10cm deep, or one with a 6-litre capacity, should be fine – as being in the cold pan will help the lamb cool faster. Once cooled, cover and stash in the fridge for at least 1 day, or up to 3 days. Or, if this is easier for your fridge, decant when cool into airtight containers or a dish of fridge-friendly size.

○ Before reheating the stew, take it out of the fridge, remove any fat from the surface and leave for 1 hour (less if in airtight containers) to come to room temperature, and preheat the oven to 200°C/gas mark 6. Cook for 1–1¼ hours, until piping hot, and if everyone's not ready to eat, just switch off the oven, and let the pan sit there for up to 30 minutes.

MAKE AHEAD NOTE	FREEZE NOTE
The shanks can be made up to 3 days ahead. Shred and cool as quickly as possible, then cover and refrigerate within 2 hours of making.	Freeze in an airtight container for up to 3 months. Defrost overnight in fridge before reheating as per recipe, above.

Note: the shanks should be reheated once only.

Spiced lamb stew with a goat's cheese and thyme cobbler topping

A mellow, aromatic stew, this has established itself as a Sunday stalwart in my house, and although there is nothing wrong in serving the stew just as it is, for me it achieves everything it ought when topped with scone-like, tender biscuits, tangy with goat's cheese and fragrant with thyme. It also saves you making any potatoes or other starch to serve alongside. And if you whizz over to the instructions for the cobbler topping, you will see how dreamily easy they are to make. As, indeed, is this.

Caramelized garlic has become a leitmotif in my cooking life, and here is where it all started.

SERVES 8

2 bulbs garlic, whole and unpeeled

2 x 15ml tablespoons regular olive oil

2 onions, peeled and roughly chopped

1½ teaspoons dried thyme

2½ teaspoons ground cinnamon

1.25kg lamb neck fillet (or use shoulder), chopped into chunks as for a stew

250ml red vermouth or full-bodied red wine

4 carrots (350g), peeled, quartered lengthways (halved if they're skinny carrots) and sliced into 3cm chunks

2 aubergines (500g), chopped into roughly 4–6cm chunks

375ml hot water, from a recently boiled kettle

2 teaspoons sea salt flakes

3 star anise

- Cut the tops off the garlic bulbs, so that you can see the tops of the cloves peeking through. Discard the tops, and sit each bulb on a separate piece of foil, then seal the ends tightly to form a slightly baggy parcel. Sit these on a small foil tray or dish that will go in the oven. Preheat the oven to 170°C/gas mark 3.

- In a large – wide rather than tall – casserole or pan (one that has a tight-fitting lid and will go in the oven), heat the olive oil and add the chopped onions. Cook over a medium to low heat for about 10 minutes, stirring frequently to make sure that they soften without burning. If they go golden, that's fine, you just don't want them to go any further than that. Stir in the dried thyme and cinnamon.

- Turn the heat up under the pan, then add the chunks of lamb, and stir well, though don't expect the lamb to sear.

- Pour in the vermouth or wine, stirring to try and pick up some of the bits sticking to the bottom of the pan, then add the carrots, aubergines, hot water, salt and star anise, stir again and let the panful of stew come to a bubble.

- Clamp on the lid, then transfer to the oven, putting the prepared garlic in at the same time, and cook for 2 hours. Once out of the oven, let the stew cool, with the lid off, and as soon as you can handle the garlic, squish the caramelized cloves into the stew, stir and let it cool. Then transfer to a suitable container, cover and keep in the fridge for at least 1 day, or up to 3 days, before reheating.

- To reheat, remove any fat from the surface, then transfer the stew to a dish that will fit both it and the cobbler topping – I use a wide, shallow casserole of 30cm diameter and 8cm deep – and bring to a bubble on the hob. Let it simmer for 30 minutes.

- If you're making the cobbler topping, preheat the oven to 220°C/gas mark 7 while the stew is simmering, and see next recipe. Or, if you want to serve the stew unadorned, then make sure the meat is piping hot on the stove before taking to the table.

MAKE AHEAD NOTE	FREEZE NOTE
The stew can be made up to 3 days ahead. Cool, cover and refrigerate within 2 hours of making.	Freeze in an airtight container for up to 3 months. Defrost overnight in fridge before reheating as per recipe, above.

Note: the stew should be reheated once only.

Goat's cheese and thyme cobbler topping

I first made this to go on top of the Spiced Lamb Stew in the previous recipe, but please don't feel you have to restrict its usage to this. I certainly don't. Regard it, rather, as a helpful blueprint. You can change the goat's cheese to Cheddar, use all butter, add other spices, or vary the herbs. Any stews, adorned with this gorgeously golden topping, are most highly recommended contenders for a cosy Sunday lunch, and I also often top a regular meat sauce with a cobbler, made with half Red Leicester, half butter (both grated) and a ¼ teaspoon each of English mustard powder and ground mace in place of the turmeric, and do without the herbs altogether. As the cobbler topping cooks in the oven, with a hot stew beneath it, the little scones both bake and steam, becoming light and tender as they rise in the oven with their tops crisp and golden, while the underside fuses with the sauce below.

These are really a doddle to make. I love the feel of the soft dough under my hands, and the quiet mood that descends on me as I pat and roll them into being. Indeed, the very act of making them reduces rather than adds to any stress.

125ml full-fat milk, plus 2 teaspoons	½ teaspoon ground turmeric
1 teaspoon lemon juice	1 x 15ml tablespoon fresh thyme leaves, plus a few sprigs for later
175g plain flour, plus more for rolling and cutting	50g crumbled goat's cheese
2 teaspoons baking powder	50g fridge-cold unsalted butter
¼ teaspoon bicarbonate of soda	1 egg
½ teaspoon fine sea salt, plus a pinch	

○ Pour the 125ml milk into a cup or small jug, stir in the lemon juice and let it stand while you get on with the rest.

○ Mix the flour, baking powder, bicarb, ½ teaspoon of salt, turmeric and thyme leaves in a mixing bowl. Crumble in the goat's cheese, and grate in the butter. I use a microplane ribbon grater, the sort you might use for shaving chocolate. Stir together lightly with a fork.

○ Now, as if you were making a crumble, rub the butter and goat's cheese into the spiced flour with your fingers. In other words, work the fats into the dry ingredients by – using a flutteringly light movement, like a butterfly's wings – rubbing the pads of your thumbs against the middle 3 fingers of each hand, catching the mixture as you go. When you have a flaky, porridge or oat-like texture, pour in 100ml of the lemon-soured milk and mix together with a wooden spoon until you have a slightly damp, squidgy dough. If you find you don't need the remaining 25ml of lemon-soured milk, then don't use it.

○ Lightly flour a surface you can roll out on, then tear off a large piece of baking parchment and place it nearby. Form the soft dough into a ball, press it down into a fat disc and sit this on the floured surface, then immediately turn the dough the other way up. Roll or pat it into a thickness of just under 1cm, dip a 6cm round cutter – or the rim of a glass will do – into a little extra flour and start cutting out discs, sitting them on the sheet of baking parchment. Gather up the remaining dough, and start again by making a ball, flattening it into a fat disc, and continue rolling and re-rolling like this, until you have used up all the dough. You should have approximately 20 "biscuits" or cobbler-scones.

○ When the stew you want to cover is warmed through, and the oven is preheated to 220°C/gas mark 7, you can top it with these little scone-like biscuits. First, though, make an egg wash by whisking together the egg, 2 teaspoons of milk and a pinch of salt. With the hot stew in front of you, arrange the soft shallow scones on top and, moving quickly but calmly, brush the egg wash onto the biscuits and place back in the oven for a further 15 minutes until the biscuits are risen and golden and the stew is bubbling.

Slow-cooked black treacle ham

Nothing will ever take the place of my Ham in Coca-Cola from *Bites* – in my heart or on my table – but this slow-baked ham is a revelation of a different sort. Instead of being boiled and then transferred to a hot oven to be glazed, I cook it so, so slowly, in the oven, draped with black treacle, then wrapped in foil, so that it steams sweetly in the low heat. I then remove the ham from the oven and its foil, take off the rind, stud the layer of fat on top with cloves and cover with a mustardy black treacle glaze, and put the joint briefly back in a very hot oven. Cooked like this, the meat is astonishingly tender and carves into thin slices with ease; there is also very little shrinkage, and no wrangling with large joints of meat in boiling liquid.

I always like a ham on Christmas Eve, which means that there is cold ham as well as cold turkey for Boxing Day (and general sandwich duty), and this is the way to cook it to make your life easier. And if the 12–15 hours' cooking doesn't suit you, you can cook it for 5 hours in a 180°C/gas mark 4 oven instead, before proceeding with the glaze.

The juices that collect from the first step of cooking are gorgeously flavoured, but very intense. I pour a little of them over the cut slices of meat, but go sparingly.

You will notice that I don't soak the gammon joint first: this is because I no longer find that the gammon I buy is salty enough to require soaking, but obviously you can, if you or your butcher feel it necessary. Whether you choose a smoked or "green" gammon is entirely a matter of your own taste.

By the way, when you measure out your treacle, it'll make life a lot easier if you oil your receptacle first.

SERVES 10–12, WITH LEFTOVERS

3.5kg joint boneless gammon, rind on
150g black treacle

FOR THE GLAZE:

approx. 1 x 15ml tablespoon whole cloves

¼ cup (4 x 15ml tablespoons) black treacle

¼ cup (4 x 15ml tablespoons) demerara sugar

1 x 15ml tablespoon Dijon mustard

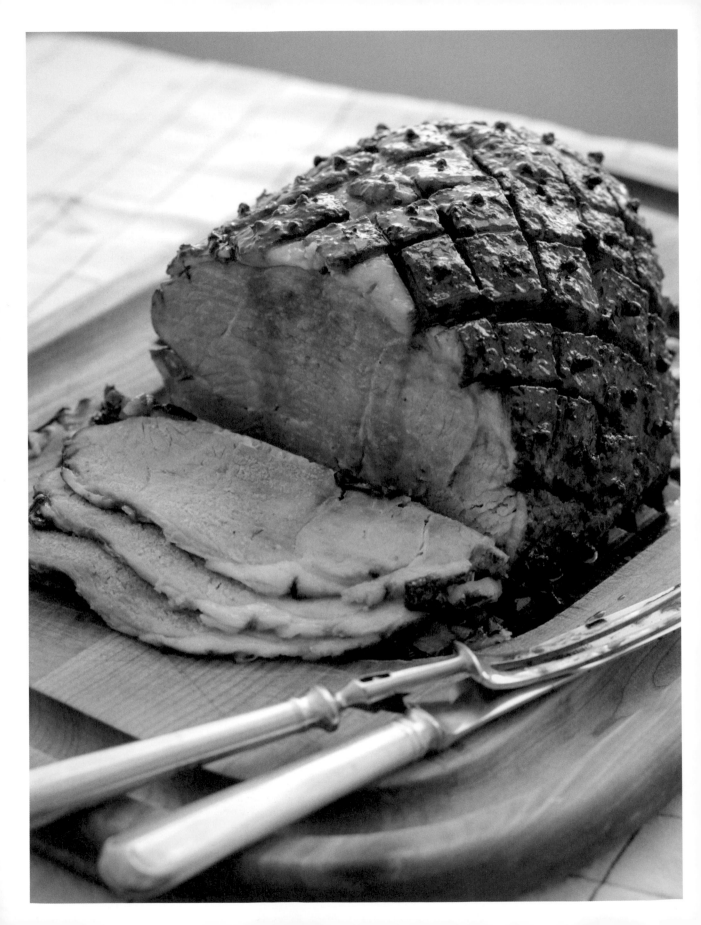

- Preheat the oven to 250°C/gas mark 9, and let your gammon come to room temperature.

- Line a large roasting tin with a layer of foil, and then sit a wire rack on top of this foil. Tear off a large piece of foil (big enough to wrap around the ham) and place this over the rack on the roasting tin. Tear off a second, large piece of foil and place on top, but in the opposite way to the first, so you have 4 corners of foil ready to wrap your ham in.

- Sit the gammon on the foil and then pour the black treacle over it, straight onto the rind, letting it run down both sides. Don't worry too much about spreading it over the ham, as once it's in the heat of the oven, it will coat the ham well enough.

- Now lift up the sides and ends of the first layer of foil and make a seal at the top, leaving some room around the gammon, then seal the ends. Then take up the other piece of foil and do the same: you are trying to create a good seal around the gammon, so pinch together any open gaps that remain. Finally, tear off another piece of foil and put over the top of the whole parcel, making sure it's well sealed.

- Put carefully into the oven and let it cook for 30 minutes, then turn the oven down to 100°C/gas mark ¼ and leave for a further 15–24 hours.

- The following day, take the gammon out of the oven and open up the foil seal. It will have made some liquid, which you can reserve to moisten the carved meat later. Carefully lift the gammon out onto a board and peel off the rind to leave a good layer of fat.

- Increase the oven temperature to 200°C/gas mark 6. Using a sharp knife, cut a diamond pattern in the fat layer, drawing lines one way and then the opposite way, about 2cm apart.

- Stud the centre of each diamond with a clove, then mix together the black treacle, demerara sugar and Dijon mustard in a bowl and spread over the fat on the ham. It will dribble off a bit, so just spoon it back over the gammon before putting back in the oven for 20 minutes, by which time the glaze will be burnished and blistered in the heat. Remove from the oven, and transfer to a board. Let it rest for 10–20 minutes before carving into thin slices.

STORE NOTE	FREEZE NOTE
Cool leftovers as quickly as possible, then cover (or wrap tightly in foil) and refrigerate within 2 hours of making. Will keep in fridge for up to 3 days.	Freeze in an airtight container (or wrapped in foil, and then put in a resealable bag) for up to 2 months. Defrost overnight in fridge before using.

Make-ahead mash

No one is doubting the glory of mashed potatoes, and while they are not difficult to make, they can be quite a faff in large quantities at the last minute. This is the answer: a tangy, subtly cheesy mash, with a crunchy topping, that has revolutionized my cooking life. I made them for the first time last year for Thanksgiving, and they have happily appeared on my table several times since. They come heartily recommended with the ham on the previous page, and any time you want to spread the load when you have people coming over.

SERVES 12

2.5kg potatoes for mashing, such as Maris Piper

salt for potato water to taste

175g soft unsalted butter

250ml sour cream

good grinding of nutmeg

good grinding of pepper

35g grated Parmesan

sea salt flakes to taste

FOR THE TOPPING:

75g dried breadcrumbs

75g soft unsalted butter

50g grated Parmesan

- Peel the potatoes, then cut each one roughly into quarters, put into a large pan of salted water and bring to the boil. Lower the heat slightly and cook until the potatoes are tender and soft but not disintegrating. The timing will depend on the size of your pan, but allow about 30 minutes once the water has come to the boil.

- Before you drain the potatoes, reserve 2 cupfuls (500ml) of the cooking water, then drain the potatoes and put them back in the hot, and now dry, pan with the lid on, but off the heat.

- Melt the butter and sour cream in a saucepan, then pour this over the cooked and drained potatoes in their warm pot, and mash them while slowly adding some of the reserved potato cooking water to get the right softness and consistency. I keep this a fairly loose mixture, since it will thicken on standing and reheating. Add the nutmeg, pepper, Parmesan and sea salt to taste.

- Once you are happy with your mash, spoon it into a wide, shallow ovenproof dish and smooth the top. You can let this cool and then refrigerate it, covered with clingfilm, for up to 3 days, although if you want, you can, of course, proceed to the next stage immediately.

- When you're ready to reheat, preheat the oven to 200°C/gas mark 6 and take the dish of potatoes out of the fridge to come to room temperature.

- Tip the breadcrumbs into a bowl, then add the butter, a teaspoonful at a time, and mix together to form a lumpy crumble. Dot over the top of the potatoes, and then sprinkle with the Parmesan. Bake for 30 minutes, or until piping hot all the way through.

MAKE AHEAD NOTE

The potatoes, without the topping, can be made up to 3 days ahead. Cool, cover and refrigerate within 2 hours of making. Allow to come to room temperature (about 30 minutes) before adding the topping ingredients and baking.

Note: the potatoes should be reheated once only.

Leek pasta bake

This had its first outing, together with the Chicken Cosima on **p.149**, for my daughter's 21st birthday, as a dish made for non-meat-eaters, and to provide ballast later on in the night. I have since found out that Parmesan is not vegetarian; it is fine to do without it, and use 350g of a vegetarian-friendly Cheddar. Indeed, feel free to use whatever cheese you have to hand.

SERVES 8, AS A MAIN DISH

500g leeks (trimmed and cleaned weight)	2 teaspoons Dijon mustard
250ml dry white vermouth or white wine	50g Parmesan, grated
500ml cold water	300g strong Cheddar, grated
2 teaspoons sea salt flakes	grinding of pepper
500ml full-fat milk	500g tortiglioni or rigatoni pasta
75g soft unsalted butter	salt for pasta water to taste
75g plain flour	

° Cut the leeks into 1cm slices before putting them into a wide, heavy-based saucepan, one that has a tight-fitting lid. Add the vermouth (or wine) and water and salt – the leeks should be just covered – then put on the lid and bring to the boil. Once they are bubbling, keep them covered – you will need the cooking liquid later, so you don't want it to evaporate – and cook until soft and no longer squeaky, about 10 minutes. About 5 minutes in, it's a good idea to take the lid off briefly and give a robust stir or two to help the rounds of leek unfurl a bit.

° Drain the leeks and set aside, reserving their cooking water. I do this by sitting a large sieve over a wide-necked measuring jug; you should have about 500ml-worth. Add the milk to this leek-cooking-liquor, and if it doesn't make the liquid come up to the 1-litre mark, just top it up with a little more milk. This might be a good moment to put the pasta water on to boil.

° Make sure there isn't any stray leek left in the pan, and then melt the butter in it over a medium heat. Add the flour and mustard, and whisk to form a roux, then cook, whisking, for 1–2 minutes or so until the bubbling mixture thickens a bit.

° Take the pan off the heat, and then gradually pour in the milky-leek liquor, making sure you keep whisking to incorporate the liquid and to get rid of any lumps.

- Once all the liquid is added, put the pan back on a medium heat, and – swapping your whisk for a wooden spoon or spatula – cook it, stirring all the while with the spoon or spatula, until the sauce is thick, smooth and has lost its floury taste. This will take about 10 minutes.

- Once the white sauce is thickened, turn the flame off under the pan (or, if you're cooking on electric, remove the pan from the stove) and, using your wooden spoon or spatula, beat in the Parmesan and 225g of the Cheddar, seasoning with pepper to taste, making sure the cheeses are fully incorporated, before stirring in the leeks. Take off the heat and cover.

- When your pan of pasta water has come to the boil, salt to taste, then add the pasta and cook until rather more al dente than you'd normally want it. Reserve a couple of cups of the pasta water before you drain it.

- Beat half a cupful (125ml) of the pasta cooking water into the sauce and then pour half of the sauce into a lasagne dish of about 27 x 37cm or a roasting tin, or receptacle of your choice. Tip in the drained pasta, then pour the remaining sauce over this and stir gently to make sure all is mixed together. Add more pasta water if needed; you'll want this quite runny as it will thicken both on standing and baking. Let this stand for 10 minutes (or leave to cool and then refrigerate for up to 3 days, making sure it comes back to room temperature before baking).

- When you're ready to bake, preheat the oven to 220°C/gas mark 7. Sprinkle the remaining 75g grated Cheddar over the top of the pasta and bake in the hot oven for about 20–25 minutes, or until bubbly and golden on top. Check it is hot all the way through by inserting the tip of a knife into the centre. It should come out feeling hot. If you want the top crusty and burnished, place under a hot grill for a couple of minutes, keeping a careful eye on it. Or just leave it for longer in the hot oven. Let it stand out of the oven for 10–20 minutes before serving.

MAKE AHEAD NOTE

The pasta bake can be made up to 3 days ahead. Cool, cover and refrigerate within 2 hours of making. Allow to come to room temperature (about 30 minutes) before baking.

Note: the pasta bake should be reheated once only.

Slow-cooker chickpeas with cumin and spinach

I am very proud to say that with this recipe I have converted someone who claimed never to eat chickpeas. And I had something of a revelation myself in the process. Hitherto, I had made a rule for myself only to buy chickpeas from Asian or Middle-Eastern shops, having been terribly disappointed with supermarket chickpeas, which, however long I soak them and cook them, seem to stay mean, small and resistant. But without soaking, any chickpeas cooked by this method in a slow cooker seem to grow plumptious and tender. Because of the bicarbonate of soda, you do have to throw away the water they're cooked in, so you don't gain a flavoursome stock in the process, but for me this is a trade-off I am happy to make. But do taste the liquid: it may be that the bicarb doesn't offend you.

I like this as a meal in itself, which can be gorgeously bolstered by having some feta crumbled over as you eat, but I make it very often in place of potatoes to accompany roast chicken or stews, or whenever the fancy takes me.

SERVES 6–8

500g dried chickpeas	4 teaspoons cumin seeds
½ teaspoon bicarbonate of soda	1 cup (250ml) vegetable stock
500g spinach	sea salt flakes to taste
2–3 x 15ml tablespoons extra-virgin olive oil	
1 clove garlic, peeled and finely grated or minced	

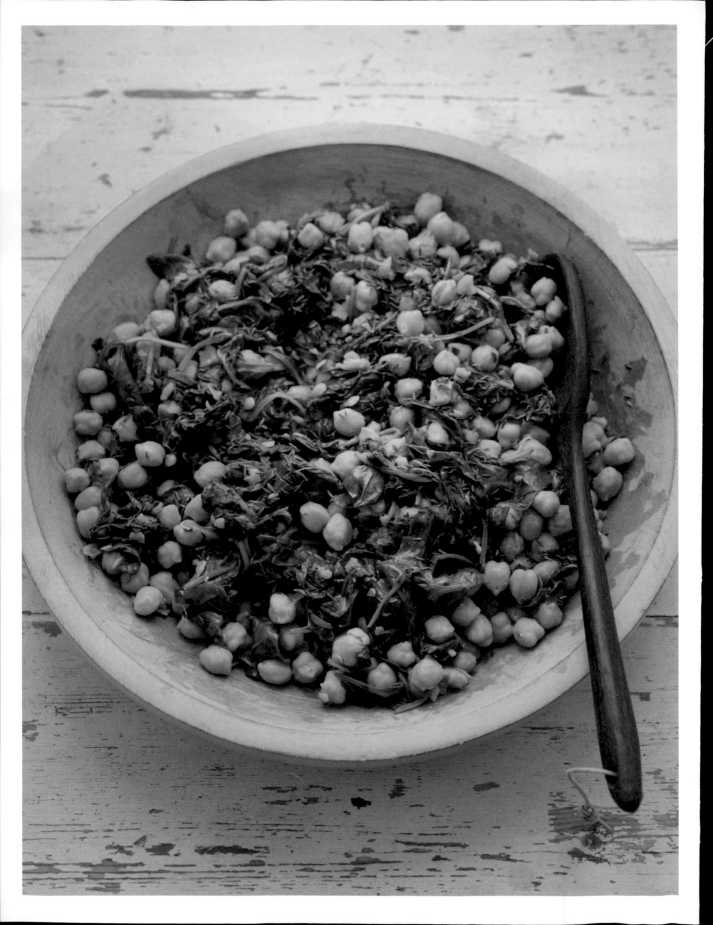

- Put the chickpeas into the slow cooker and cover with enough cold water to come 4–5cm above the chickpeas. Add the bicarbonate of soda and cook on low for 6–8 hours. Generally, 6 hours is fine, but you can keep them in there for longer without their getting too soft and starting to disintegrate.

- Drain the chickpeas and rinse the spinach. In the bowl of the slow cooker, if it is one that can go on the hob – otherwise use a big casserole or pan that comes with a lid – pour in the oil and add the garlic, then put on the heat, but do not let the garlic burn. Stir 3 teaspoons of the cumin seeds into the hot garlicky oil, then add half of the spinach, which will still have some water clinging to the leaves, and a quarter of the stock. Clamp on the lid and let the spinach wilt in the heat for about 3 minutes. Give it a stir, then add the rest of the wet spinach and another quarter of the stock, stir again, and put the lid on again to allow this to wilt.

- Tumble in the drained chickpeas and tenderly stir to mix, adding as much stock as you need to facilitate this. Salt to taste, and take off the heat.

- Toast the remaining teaspoonful of cumin seeds in a hot, dry, pan and sprinkle over the top of the chickpeas before serving.

STORE NOTE	CONVERSION TO OVEN	FREEZE NOTE
Cool leftovers, then cover and refrigerate within 2 hours of making. Keep refrigerated for up to 2 days. Reheat in a saucepan over a low heat, adding a splash of extra stock if needed, and stirring occasionally, until piping hot.	Preheat the oven to 150°C/gas mark 2. Put the chickpeas into a large heavy-based pot and add enough cold water to cover by 5cm, then bring to the boil on the hob. When bubbling, lower the heat, add ½ teaspoon of bicarbonate of soda, then clamp on the lid and cook in the oven for 2 hours, by which time the chickpeas should be soft, if not as plump as by the slow-cooker method.	Freeze leftovers in an airtight container for up to 3 months. Defrost overnight in fridge before reheating as Store Note.

Note: the chickpeas should be reheated once only.

Slow-cooker Cuban black beans

I had always taken it for granted that all dried beans needed to be soaked before cooking, but no, this is not the case. Furthermore, black beans lose so much of their intensity if you soak them. Cooked from dry, all their dark and oozing "gravy" stays in the pot and doesn't get thrown away with the soaking water.

When I've eaten black beans in Cuba or Miami, the peppers in this dish were always green, but I cannot bring myself to use green peppers, so use the sweeter, juicier red ones instead. This recipe won't work with other beans, however.

SERVES 6–8

2 onions, peeled and finely chopped	2 x 15ml tablespoons cumin seeds
2 red peppers, de-seeded and finely chopped	good grinding of pepper
6 cloves garlic, peeled and chopped	1 litre water
500g black turtle beans	2 bay leaves
1 fresh red chilli, chopped but not de-seeded	salt to taste

○ Put all the ingredients into the slow cooker and cook on low for 6–8 hours. Once the beans are cooked, salt to taste, then remove from the heat and let stand for at least 30 minutes, so that the liquid thickens. Better still, leave them to cool completely so that the flavour develops, and then reheat gently.

○ Eat warm with rice and some freshly chopped coriander, or wrap into burritos and serve with avocado, grated cheese and sour cream. They're also very good cold, eaten – albeit messily – with tortilla chips.

STORE NOTE	CONVERSION TO OVEN	FREEZE NOTE
Cool leftovers, then cover and refrigerate within 2 hours of making. Will keep in fridge for up to 2 days.	Put all of the ingredients in a heavy-based casserole and cover with 3cm cold water. Bring to the boil on the hob and then clamp on the lid, and put in an oven preheated to 150°C/gas mark 2 for 2 hours until the beans are cooked and have produced a dark gravy. Let it cool, and leave for a day before reheating. The beans will be tender, but the sauce will not be as thick as the slow-cooker method.	Freeze in an airtight container for up to 3 months. Defrost overnight in fridge before using. Reheat in a saucepan over a low heat, adding a splash of extra water if needed, and stirring occasionally, until piping hot.

Note: the beans should be reheated once only.

Slow-cooker beef and Guinness stew with prunes and black treacle

This, with its black stout, black treacle and glistening prunes, is a dark beauty, with a deep and intense flavour to match. Its rich sweetness makes it a perfect companion piece to my ever-growing collection of pickles (and see **pp.258–264**), but if you haven't succumbed to pickle-making as I have, then I suggest you buy a jar each of pickled walnuts and pickled red cabbage as a tangy accompaniment. Some baked potatoes with sour cream are just gorgeous with this, too.

The "good beef stock" that I mention in the ingredients list is the sort that comes "fresh" in tubs from the supermarket, by the way.

1.75kg boneless shin of beef, cut into cubes	⅓ cup (100g) black treacle
250g prunes	1–2 drops sunflower oil, to oil the cup or bowl
500ml good beef stock	1 long or 2 short sticks cinnamon
250ml Guinness or other dark stout	3 bay leaves
1 teaspoon sea salt flakes	

- Put the cubes of beef in the bowl of the slow cooker, add the prunes and mix with your hands.

- Pour the stock and stout into a 1-litre measuring jug and add the salt. Measure the black treacle into an oiled third-cup measure, or oil the bowl you're weighing it in, and add to the stock and stout, stir to mix, then pour over the beef and prunes in the slow cooker.

- Add the cinnamon and bay leaves, pushing them under the stock, then take the bowl to the slow cooker base (if yours, like mine, comes in 2 separate parts) and cook on low for 8 hours, by which time the meat should be fork-tender and the prunes plumped and soft. Switch off and, without burning your mouth, check for seasoning.

- You could eat this now – the meat will be tender enough – but I think it is best if you leave it for 1 day, or up to 3 days, so that the flavours deepen and meld together, before reheating, from room temperature, in an oven preheated to 200°C/gas mark 6 for 30 minutes, until piping hot all the way through. Or you can reheat on the hob, bringing it up to a bubble and then simmering for 30 minutes.

MAKE AHEAD NOTE	CONVERSION TO OVEN	FREEZE NOTE
The stew can be made up to 3 days ahead. Cool, cover and refrigerate within 2 hours of making.	Cook the stew in a cast-iron casserole dish with a tight-fitting lid in an oven preheated to 150°C/gas mark 2 for 3 hours, or until meat is tender and prunes are plump and soft. Add a little water if the sauce is becoming too dry. Let it rest before serving.	Freeze in an airtight container for up to 3 months. Defrost overnight in fridge before reheating.

Note: the stew should be reheated once only.

Slow-cooker Korean beef and rice pot

The Korean element in this recipe is supplied by the intense chilli paste, gochujang, which has been a staple in my kitchen since, indeed, *Kitchen*. You can buy it in Asian supermarkets or online and once you try it – for those who have yet to discover it – you will find excuses to use it in your cooking over and over again. I have also been inspired, here, by the Korean dish *bibimbap*, although this is a nod to it rather than a version of it. It is certainly very much simpler to make. But if you wanted to top each bowl with a fried egg, I wouldn't stop you…

SERVES 6

500g minced beef, preferably organic	¼ cup (4 x 15ml tablespoons) gochujang paste
1¼ cups (200g) short grain brown rice	¼ cup (4 x 15ml tablespoons) soy sauce
1 x 400g can chopped tomatoes	300g beansprouts

○ Put the beef and the rice in the bowl of the slow cooker.

○ Tip the chopped tomatoes into a jug, then fill the empty can with cold water from the tap, and pour the water, swilling as you go, into the jug. Add the gochujang paste and soy sauce, stir to combine, then pour over the rice and beef in the slow cooker. Now give everything a stir, put on the lid and cook on low for 4 hours. By the end of its cooking time, the beef will be tender, all the liquid will have been absorbed, and it will be thick and sticky.

○ Put the beansprouts into a large bowl, and pour boiling water over, to cover. Let them stand for 1 minute, then drain and stir into the sticky beef and rice. Put the lid back on for 5 minutes, then switch off the slow cooker, and serve.

STORE NOTE	CONVERSION TO OVEN
Cool leftovers, then cover and refrigerate within 2 hours of making. Will keep in fridge for up to 1 day. Reheat in an ovenproof dish, covered with foil, in a 150°C/gas mark 2 oven for about 30 minutes (timing will depend on quantity), or reheat in microwave-safe containers in the microwave, until piping hot all the way through, before serving.	Mix all of the ingredients in a heavy-based or enamelled cast-iron casserole with a tight-fitting lid, adding an extra 125ml water, and cook in an oven preheated to 180°C/gas mark 4 for 2–2½ hours, by which time the rice will be tender, the liquid absorbed, and the mixture thick and almost sticky. Prepare the beansprouts as per recipe, above, and stir them in and leave, with the lid on, out of the oven, for 10 minutes.

Slow-cooker Moroccan chicken stew

My chook-from-the-souk is a lightly fragranced golden stew that gains more succulence from having the bones of the chicken thighs in as well. If you make this in advance (and all stews are better this way), you can easily remove the fat that the skin produces once the stew has sat in the fridge. The skin gives flavour, too, and both skin and bones are removed on serving and the tender meat shredded.

SERVES 6

8 chicken thighs, skin on and bone in

1 onion, peeled and finely chopped

2–3 preserved lemons (depending on size), roughly chopped

2 x 400g cans chickpeas or 1½ x 660g jar chickpeas, drained and rinsed

2 teaspoons cumin seeds

1 teaspoon ground ginger

1 long or 2 short sticks cinnamon

pinch (¼ teaspoon) saffron threads

500ml chicken stock

50g golden sultanas

70g pitted green olives

chopped fresh coriander, to serve

○ Put everything into the slow cooker and cook on low for 4 hours.

○ Once the stew's ready, remove the slow cooker from its base and let the stew stand for 10–15 minutes with the lid off, before going in to shred the chicken. Discard the skin and bones. Place in a warm bowl to serve and scatter with coriander.

STORE NOTE	CONVERSION TO OVEN	FREEZE NOTE
Cool leftovers, then cover and refrigerate within 2 hours of making. Will keep in fridge for up to 3 days.	Heat 1 x 15ml tablespoon olive oil in a cast-iron casserole or heavy-based pot (big enough to take the chicken in one layer) and cook the onion for 5 minutes, until softened. Add the remaining ingredients and bring to the boil, then cover with a piece of greaseproof paper and the lid, and cook in an oven preheated to 180°C/ gas mark 4 for 1 hour, or until the chicken is tender and falling off the bone.	Freeze in an airtight container for up to 3 months. Defrost overnight in fridge before using. Reheat in a covered saucepan over a low heat, stirring occasionally, until piping hot.

Note: the stew should be reheated once only.

SIDES

Butternut
waxy potatoes
basil
beetroot
ginger

SIDES

A doctor once told me that I was the only person she had advised to eat fewer vegetables. I am a carnivore who can regularly make a kilo of broccoli, hot with chilli and ginger, for my supper, without fleshy accompaniment and with breezy disregard for my digestive system.

But then, my mother thought nothing of eating an entire cabbage, dressed just with butter and white pepper, in one undistracted sitting. I have inherited that desire to wallow in the splendour of just one bowl of food, and in the singularity of its deliciousness. But I have recently found myself searching, as I cook, for simple side dishes that have the grace to accompany a flesh, fish or fowl recipe without upstaging it and yet, at the same time, having the confidence to hold their own. There is something so aesthetically gratifying about cooking vegetables: their colours make my kitchen sing, and, if only I could, me along with it. I am embarrassed about the number of times I simply roast a chicken for supper, but these are the recipes that combine the comforting rituals of the familiar with the exuberance of the new — something that we all need, both in and out of the kitchen.

They are not the only vegetable recipes in the book, however: many in the preceding chapters provide ideas for side dishes by stealth, in the introductions. Here, though, the admiring focus is on them alone. And, being something of a condiment queen, I have relished the opportunity to throw in a sauce or two. A meal, however pared back it is, feels complete to me only when I have within my reach a jar or bowl of something I can spike my food with as I eat.

This brings me to the new love in my cooking life: I cannot stop pickling things; I have become a toursomaniac. But toursomania — the compulsive need to pickle; the coinage is my own — is not something I see myself being cured of any time soon. As someone who once compiled her Kitchen Gadget Hall of Shame, I should be embarrassed to admit this, but I have recently purchased a Japanese pickle-press.

Don't be alarmed, though, all the pickles here are simple affairs. Along with most of the kitchen contraptions I buy (late at night and online, usually), the pickle-press may well not see the light of day but rather, in the time-honoured fashion, languish in the dusty depths of the cupboard under the stairs. These pickles are unruffling to make, requiring no special skills, equipment or patience, and you can allow yourself a moment of quiet satisfaction, and greedy anticipation, both while you conjure them into existence and as you bring them to the table, too.

Roast radishes

I came across a recipe for roast radishes on thekitchn.com and was immediately prompted to make my own version. The only work lies in halving the radishes in question, and they need hardly any time in the oven. Their peppery crunch is transformed in the heat to a piquant juiciness – and, oh, their pink-cheeked prettiness! I make them nearly every time people come for supper, and they have never failed to charm.

You can also turn them into a salad: for the amount of radishes below (though you may want to halve them) toast 100g hazelnuts while the radishes are in the oven, then chop them, and toss radishes and nuts in a tangle of watercress and a dressing made with orange juice, olive oil and sea salt flakes.

SERVES 8–10

600g radishes

2 x 15ml tablespoons olive oil

1–2 x 15ml tablespoons finely chopped fresh chives or spring onions

1 teaspoon sea salt flakes, or to taste

° Preheat the oven to 220°C/gas mark 7.

° Slice the radishes in half from top to tail: they look beautiful with the green parts left on, though you may want to trim them if they have long tails.

° Put into a bowl and pour in the olive oil, then toss the radishes so they are coated evenly.

° Tip out onto a baking tray, or shallow roasting tin, and turn all the radishes cut-side down, so that you have a sea of pink humps.

° Roast in the hot oven for 10 minutes, then take them out and toss with the chopped chives (or spring onions) and salt, checking the seasoning and adding more of either if you wish. Serve hot, though a stash of these, cold, should you have leftovers, is a rich resource, to be called upon later in the week, added to salads or noodle soups, or simply, pinkly, spooned onto the side of your plate as you eat.

STORE NOTE

Cool leftovers, then cover and refrigerate. Will keep in fridge for up to 5 days. Eat cold.

Purple sprouting broccoli with clementine and chilli

This recipe came about as so many recipes do: I was in a kitchen (my publisher's, in fact) and just seized upon the most immediately available ingredients. It worked so gloriously, and I have stayed true to it, cooking it faithfully and frequently – when the season allows – in my own kitchen. And when purple sprouting broccoli is not available, I simply use leggy tenderstem, or regular broccoli, instead.

SERVES 4–6

500g purple sprouting broccoli

salt for broccoli water

zest and juice of 1 clementine or ½ orange, preferably unwaxed

¼ teaspoon coarse celery salt or ½ teaspoon sea salt flakes, or to taste

1 heaped teaspoon Dijon mustard

2 x 15ml tablespoons cold-pressed rapeseed oil or extra-virgin olive oil

½ teaspoon dried chilli flakes

○ Put a pan of water on to boil for the sprouting broccoli, adding salt to taste once it comes to the boil. Trim any woody ends from the broccoli.

○ Put half of the clementine (or orange) zest into a jar or bowl, and reserve the other half for the time being. Add the clementine (or orange) juice, celery salt (or sea salt flakes), Dijon mustard, oil and a ¼ teaspoon of the chilli flakes to the jar, and give everything a good shake. Or, if making this in a bowl, just whisk together.

○ Cook the sprouting broccoli for about 2 minutes, until just tender, but still with some crunch to it. It's impossible to give a precise timing guide as it really depends where in the season it is. Drain the broccoli and return to the hot but dry pan, add the dressing ingredients and toss gently but thoroughly before transferring to a plate or bowl. Sprinkle with the remaining zest and chilli flakes, and serve.

STORE NOTE

Cool leftovers, then cover and refrigerate as quickly as possible. Will keep in fridge for up to 5 days. Eat cold.

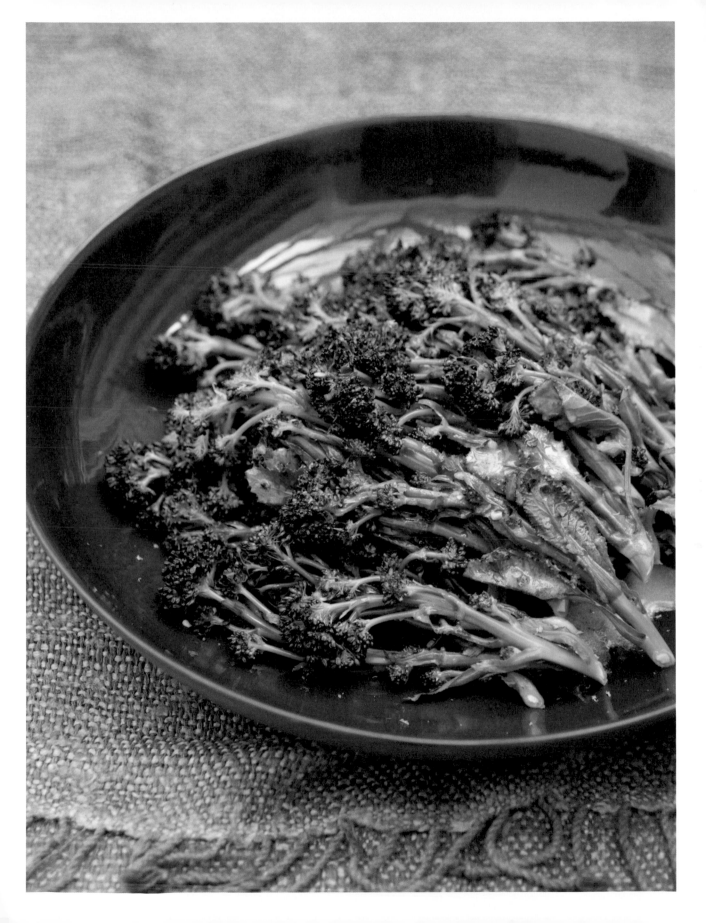

Broccoli two ways, with ginger, chilli, lime and pumpkin seeds

I may be extravagant, but I am never wasteful (something I am called upon to say often) and I can never bear to see the stalk from a head of broccoli go into the bin. Even if I'm cooking a head of broccoli and want just the florets, I now keep the stalk in a freezer bag in the fridge, to be peeled and stir-fried a day or so later.

SERVES 6

3cm piece (15g) fresh ginger, peeled

4 x 15ml tablespoons pumpkin seeds

1 head broccoli (approx. 500g)

salt for broccoli water

2 teaspoons lime juice

pinch salt

½ teaspoon toasted sesame oil

1 x 15ml tablespoon sunflower oil

FOR THE STALK:

1 teaspoon sunflower oil

1 fresh red chilli, de-seeded and chopped

3cm piece (15g) fresh ginger, peeled and cut into matchsticks

1 x 15ml tablespoon water

2 teaspoons lime juice

- Put a pan of water on to boil for the broccoli. Coarsely grate the peeled ginger onto a lipped plate (this should yield about 2 teaspoons of grated ginger). Get out a piece of kitchen roll and spoon the ginger into the centre, then – moving swiftly – bring up the sides of the paper, and twirl the ends to form a mini swag bag and squeeze out the juice (you can squeeze this back onto the plate). This should give you about 1 teaspoon of pungent ginger juice. Now you have performed my new favourite trick, you can move on. You'll need the ginger juice in a minute, though.

- Toast the pumpkin seeds by shaking them about, in a cast-iron or heavy-based frying pan, without oil, over a medium to high heat, until they have coloured and are fragrant. Transfer to a plate, but don't wash up the pan as you'll need it shortly.

- Cut the stalk off the head of broccoli, and set it aside. Break the head into florets. Peel the stalk with a vegetable peeler and then slice into thin strips, rather like bamboo shoots.

- When the broccoli water comes to the boil, add salt to taste, then cook the florets in the boiling water for 2–3 minutes, making sure they still have their bite, drain and put back into the dry pan, now off the heat.

- Make the dressing for the florets by whisking together the lime juice, ginger juice, salt, sesame and sunflower oils in a small bowl until combined. Then pour this dressing, along with half of the toasted pumpkin seeds, over the cooked broccoli florets in the pan, and toss together. Let this stand while you get on with the stalks.

- In the pan you toasted the pumpkin seeds in, heat the sunflower oil, then add the sliced broccoli stalks and stir-fry for 1 minute before adding half the chopped chilli and the ginger matchsticks and frying for another 30–60 seconds. Add the water and lime juice and stir-fry for another scant minute, until the stems are starting to soften slightly but still have some bite.

- Tip the florets into the centre of a platter, scatter most of the stir-fried stalks around, then drop some onto the florets, and sprinkle with the remaining pumpkin seeds and chopped chilli.

STORE NOTE

Cool leftovers, then cover and refrigerate as quickly as possible. Will keep in fridge for up to 5 days. Eat cold.

Braised peas with mustard and vermouth

I am never without a supply of petits pois in the deep freeze: cooked slowly, with a scant amount of flavourful liquid, they are both comforting and elegant. True, they lose their bright green colour, but do not fear the khaki, as what they lack in vividness of hue is more than compensated by the vibrancy of their flavour. And because they can sit for a long time, only improving, they make life very much easier when you have people over for supper, when the less last-minute faffing, the better.

SERVES 8

2 x 15ml tablespoons extra-virgin olive oil	2 teaspoons sea salt flakes
1 x 907g packet frozen petits pois	2 teaspoons Dijon mustard
125ml dry white vermouth or dry white wine	2 bay leaves

° Heat the oil in a heavy-based pan (with a lid) and tumble in the peas, stirring in the heat, then add the vermouth (or wine) and let it come to a bubble.

° Add the salt, mustard and bay leaves. Bring to the boil, put the lid on and simmer for 20–30 minutes, then remove from the heat and leave to stand in a warm place for up to 1 hour with the lid still on. I like these best, however, when they have been left to continue their sweet braising in a 120°C/gas mark ½ oven for 1–2 hours once they've been cooked on the hob.

STORE NOTE	FREEZE NOTE
Cool leftovers, then cover and refrigerate as quickly as possible. Will keep in fridge for up to 5 days. Reheat in a small saucepan over a low heat, stirring occasionally, until piping hot.	Freeze leftovers in an airtight container for up to 3 months. Defrost overnight in fridge before reheating as Store Note.

Quick coconutty dal

This is rather like a spiced pease pudding, though the spicing is delicate rather than shoutily invasive. I wanted coconuttiness, but not the rich heaviness of coconut milk, and the recently (but now less so) modish coconut water proved the perfect solution; but it is the mace that seems to bring everything together.

Although this makes more than you need for 2 people, I make this amount even when there are only 2 eating (and see the Indian-Spiced Cod on **p.27**), and I do this on purpose, for the fabulousness of leftovers. I like recipes that do double-duty, and this makes a wonderful soup on its second outing. I take one cupful, and make soup with it by heating it with a cupful of vegetable stock and a teaspoonful of garam masala. I'll admit the outcome is not a beautiful-looking soup, but it is certainly a beautiful-tasting one.

SERVES 2–4

200g red lentils	200ml water
300ml coconut water	¼ teaspoon ground mace
1 stick cinnamon	salt to taste
2 cardamom pods, bruised	

- Put the lentils into a saucepan that has a lid, and add the coconut water, cinnamon stick, cardamom pods and water.

- Bring to the boil, then put on the lid and simmer for 20 minutes. After this time, check to see if the lentils are soft; they should have absorbed the water and be close to a purée. If the lentils are not tender enough, then add a little more water and simmer for another 5 minutes or so.

- Once they are soft and the water is absorbed, beat in the ground mace and salt with a fork, until you have a mushy-pea-like consistency. It thickens on standing, so if you are making this a little ahead of time – it can be left in the pot with the lid on, retaining its warmth for up to 1 hour – you will need to add more liquid on serving, and do check for spicing again, too.

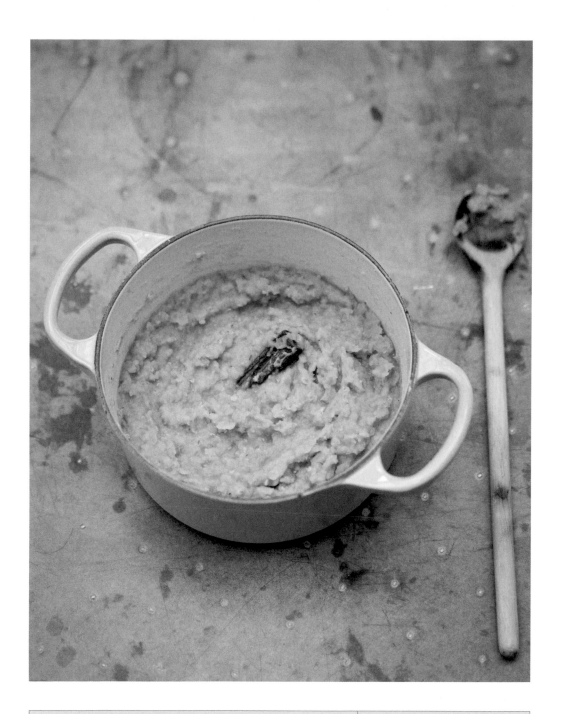

STORE NOTE	FREEZE NOTE
Cool leftovers, then cover and refrigerate within 2 hours of making. Will keep in fridge for up to 2 days. Reheat in a small saucepan over a low heat, stirring occasionally and adding extra liquid as needed, until piping hot, or use for soup.	Freeze in an airtight container for up to 3 months. Defrost overnight in fridge before reheating as Store Note.

Note: the lentils should be reheated once only.

A tray of roast veg

This recipe came about because I had half a butternut squash left over once I'd made the Butternut and Halloumi Burgers on **p.134**, but I am often to be found going through the vegetable drawer in my fridge, picking out odds and ends that are coming towards the end of their life, needing only the fierce heat of the oven to revive them, and me.

In other words, you do not have to replicate exactly the vegetables I have used here, but make good use of whatever you happen to have to hand. Just be sure to cut the vegetables into similar sizes so that they will all cook in the same time. Do not expect, though, the vegetables to emerge fashionably al dente by this process: I think it's time we appreciated the depth of flavour that comes from slow-cooking vegetables, as we already do with meat.

SERVES 8

approx. 500g butternut squash, peeled and de-seeded

2 leeks, trimmed and cleaned

2 red peppers, membranes and seeds removed

1 small cauliflower

4 x 15ml tablespoons cold-pressed rapeseed oil or regular olive oil

1 x 15ml tablespoon fennel seeds

1 teaspoon pimentón picante or paprika

- Preheat the oven to 200°C/gas mark 6. Cut the butternut into approximately 4cm chunks. Tip into a large, shallow roasting tin.

- Slice the leeks into 2–3cm rounds and add to the tin as well. Cut the peppers into 4cm pieces and add these to the tin.

- Cut the florets off the cauliflower, breaking up any large florets, and now add these to the roasting tin, too.

- Pour in the oil, and sprinkle the fennel seeds and pimentón picante or paprika over the vegetables, then mix everything well so that all is evenly covered.

- Roast in the oven for 45 minutes, by which time the vegetables should be tender and cooked through, but give them a little longer if needed.

> **STORE NOTE**
>
> Cool leftovers, then cover and refrigerate as quickly as possible. Will keep in fridge for up to 5 days. Eat cold.

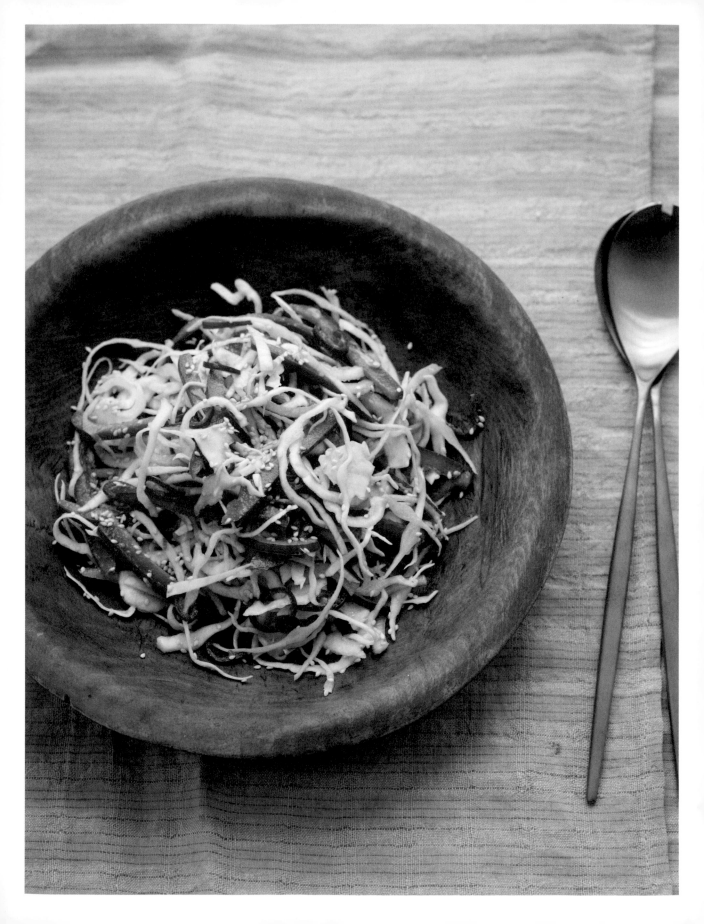

Slaw with miso ginger dressing

While you could use a processor to shred the cabbage, I can't help thinking it is so much simpler just to slice it thinly by hand. You'll have less to wash up and, besides, I love this "chop wood, carry water" aspect of cooking. By which I mean that simple tasks like these allow for that all-important decompression in the kitchen. So chop away, and let everything else recede while you do this.

SERVES 6–8

1 red onion, peeled and sliced into quarter-moons

2 x 15ml tablespoons rice vinegar

2 x 15ml tablespoons sake

2 x 15ml tablespoons sesame seeds

1 small white cabbage

3 small or 2 regular-sized red peppers, membranes and seeds removed

4 fresh red chillies, de-seeded (not too efficiently)

1 fat or 2 thin cloves garlic, peeled and finely grated or minced

2.5cm piece (12g) fresh ginger, peeled and finely grated

2 x 15ml tablespoons sweet white miso

2 x 15ml tablespoons soy sauce

1 teaspoon toasted sesame oil

- Put the sliced red onion into a small bowl with the rice vinegar and sake, and leave for 10 minutes.

- Meanwhile, toast the sesame seeds by heating them in a dry, heavy-based frying pan until fragrant and then decant them to a plate to cool.

- Shred the cabbage, and cut the peppers and chillies into thin slices, putting them into a large bowl as you go. Toss to mix well.

- Add the garlic and ginger to the onions. Add the miso, soy sauce and sesame oil, and mix together.

- Now pour the onions, and their dressing, over the vegetables, and mix again.

- Finally, add the cooled, toasted sesame seeds, then toss to combine, and serve.

> STORE NOTE
>
> Refrigerate leftovers in a covered container straightaway. Will keep in fridge for up to 3 days, though the vegetables will soften as they stand.

Sweet and sour slaw

Here is another exercise in chopping meditation for you! There is much to slice, but you end up with a bright tangle of slaw that feeds a crowd and has enough zing in it to bring a table of cold cuts to life. It's also a fitting partner for the Beef Chilli with Bourbon, Beer and Black Beans (**p.182**) or Barbecuey Pork Butt (**p.188**), and much else besides.

SERVES 10–12

1 red cabbage (approx. 800g), halved

4 fat or 6 skinny spring onions, trimmed

2 red peppers, membranes and seeds removed

1 yellow pepper, membranes and seeds removed

1 orange pepper, membranes and seeds removed

1 fresh red chilli, de-seeded

large bunch (approx. 100g) fresh coriander

250ml pineapple juice, from a carton

2 limes, preferably unwaxed

1½ x 15ml tablespoons sea salt flakes, or to taste

2 teaspoons toasted sesame oil

2 teaspoons maple syrup

○ Shred the cabbage thinly and put into the largest bowl you have. It may be easier to use a huge saucepan as you need to toss all the ingredients together later, and even my largest mixing bowl isn't big enough.

○ Slice the spring onions into batons and then cut each baton into thin slices lengthways, so that you, again, have shreds. Add to the cabbage.

○ Cut the peppers into very thin slices. Add to the cabbage and spring onions.

○ Finely chop the red chilli, and do the same with the coriander – stalks and leaves. Add the chilli and all but a tablespoon of the chopped coriander to the cabbage bowl.

○ In a bowl or measuring jug, mix together the pineapple juice, the zest and juice of 1 lime and the juice of half of the second. Sprinkle in the salt, add the sesame oil and maple syrup, and whisk together before pouring over the prepared vegetables. Toss to mix, then leave to stand for at least 15 minutes, and up to 2 hours, before serving. Sprinkle the reserved tablespoonful of chopped coriander over the finished slaw.

STORE NOTE
Refrigerate leftovers in a covered container straightaway. Will keep in fridge for up to 3 days, though the vegetables will soften as they stand.

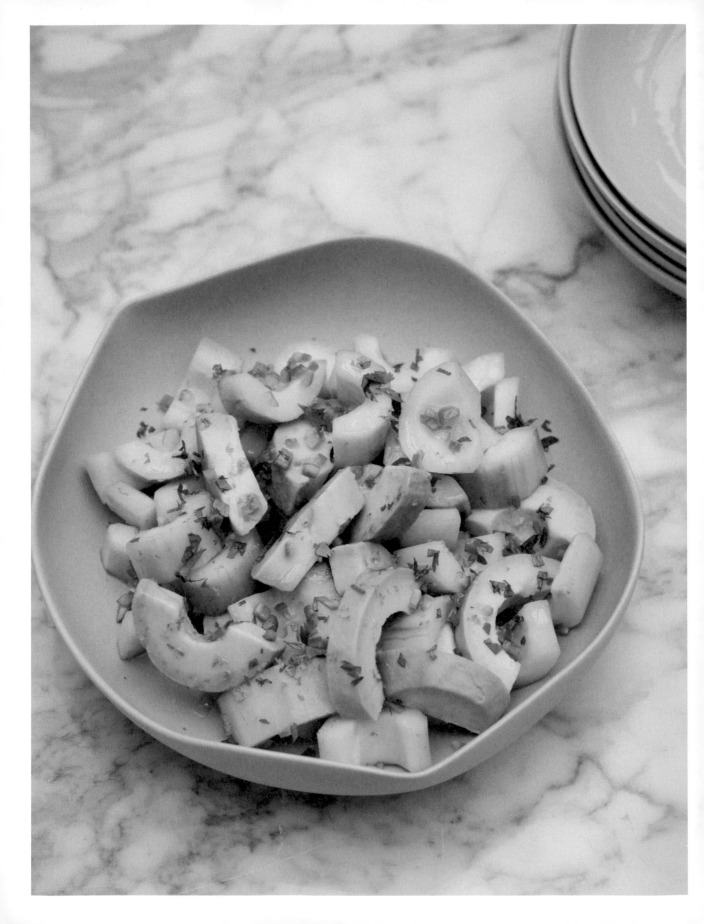

Cucumber, chilli and avocado salad

Like poor Becky Sharp biting into a green chilli thinking it looked so cool and refreshing, it is easy to be lulled by the soothing greenness of this – the salving avocado, the juicy cucumber – but do not overlook the fierce flecks, made even more zingy by the lime's acid rasp.

SERVES 4–6

1 cucumber, peeled

1 ripe avocado, peeled

1 green chilli, de-seeded (if desired) and finely chopped

4 x 15ml tablespoons chopped fresh coriander

zest and juice of 1 lime, preferably unwaxed

2 x 15ml tablespoons extra-virgin olive oil

sea salt flakes to taste

◦ Cut the cucumber in half lengthways and scrape out the seeds with a small spoon. Slice the half-boats into 2cm pieces and tip into a bowl.

◦ Dice the avocado into similar-sized pieces and add to the bowl, along with the chilli, chopped coriander, the lime zest and juice, the oil and the sea salt.

◦ Mix gently but thoroughly, and then tip out onto a serving plate.

Potato and pepper bake

I never feel the need to apologize for using jars of chargrilled peppers, for while I don't eat them just as they are, I find them the most useful ingredient, as has already been demonstrated in these pages, and in previous books. Just make sure that you are using peppers that are preserved in oil rather than brine. The potatoes don't roast in this oil, so much as braise: they will crisp up in parts, but mostly just become softened and rich in the sweet peppery juices.

SERVES 8–10

2kg waxy maincrop potatoes, such as Cyprus

2 x 290g jars chargrilled peppers in oil

2 x 15ml tablespoons coriander seeds

- Preheat the oven to 220°C/gas mark 7.

- Peel the potatoes, cut them into 2.5cm slices, then quarter each slice (halving the smaller end slices) and toss them into a large shallow roasting tin.

- Tip the jars of peppers – they are normally in quite small strips, snip them with scissors if they're not – oil and all over the potatoes. Add the coriander seeds and toss to combine before baking in the oven for 1 hour, by which time the potatoes will be soft on the inside and their outside golden, but not crisp, except at the corners.

- Using a slotted spatula or slotted spoon (let the excess oil drip back into the pan), transfer the potatoes to a large warmed bowl and either serve immediately, or let them stand for 15 minutes, or up to 45 minutes, as they are also excellent warm rather than hot.

MAKE AHEAD NOTE	STORE NOTE
Peel and slice potatoes, submerge in a bowl of cold water, then cover and refrigerate for up to 1 day. Drain and pat dry before using.	Cool leftovers, then cover and refrigerate as quickly as possible. Will keep in fridge for up to 5 days. Reheat on a baking sheet in a 200°C/gas mark 6 oven for about 20 minutes (timing will depend on quantity).

Criss-cross potatoes

I have Hettie Potter to thank for these, and for so much else. I suppose they are a mixture of roast and baked potatoes: the tops crisp and cook to a beautiful gold, but you still have the fluffiness underneath. If you want the skins to be crunchy, then pour a little olive oil into your hand and rub this onto the skins before you bake.

SERVES 4–8

4 baking potatoes	1 teaspoon sea salt flakes, or to taste
2 x 15ml tablespoons regular olive oil	

- Preheat the oven to 220°C/gas mark 7.

- Cut the potatoes lengthways so that you have shallow halves. Cut a diamond pattern of grooves into the flat flesh of each potato (not more than 3mm or so deep, just enough to score them) about 2cm apart.

- Put, cut-side up, on a baking sheet or shallow roasting tray. Drizzle each potato half with a little oil and sprinkle with some sea salt flakes.

- Bake for 45 minutes, or until the tops of the potatoes are golden and the insides soft.

STORE NOTE

Cool leftover potatoes on a plate, then cover and refrigerate as quickly as possible. Will keep in fridge for up to 5 days.

Porcini parsnip purée

There are many reasons I am drawn to this recipe: the partnership of parsnip and porcini is earthy – woodsy but delicate. It requires so few porcini to infuse it with flavour; and this flavour is not only showcased in the purée, but is richly, aromatically present in the cooking liquid, which I keep and use as a broth for noodle soups later on, and insist you do, too. And should you have purée left over as well, mix the two, for a soup all of its own (this is a very generous recipe). I don't like to add butter to the purée, as I want nothing to clutter the purity of the flavours conveyed in the beautiful broth, but feel free to, if you wish.

This is wonderful as a substitute for mash with sausages or, indeed, any strong meats.

SERVES 2–3

3g dried porcini mushrooms	1 teaspoon sea salt flakes, or to taste
750ml hot water, from a recently boiled kettle	good grating of fresh nutmeg
500g parsnips, peeled	few sprigs thyme, to serve (optional)

- Put the dried porcini in a saucepan big enough to take the parsnips later and pour the hot water over them, then clamp on a lid and put over a medium to high heat while you prepare the parsnips.

- Cut the thicker ends of the parsnips into quarters and the twiggy bits into 2 lengthways. Or, if they are very skinny, just cut them in half lengthways and then cut those lengths in half, across, so that they are all the same size. Add the parsnips to the now-bubbling pan, replace the lid and simmer for 15 minutes.

- The parsnips should now be gorgeously tender. Drain them in a large sieve over a bowl or jug, so that you keep all the cooking liquid; you should have about 400ml liquid left. Fork out the porcini pieces and discard as they will have given out all their flavour by now. Then tip the drained parsnips back into the pan on the hot hob (but with the heat off), and mash with a fork, adding some of the cooking liquid to help get the parsnips to a texture you like: I find the parsnips can take 200ml of the liquid while still maintaining enough solidity. The more liquid, the more gorgeously bosky the flavour of the purée will be.

- Season to taste, add some freshly grated nutmeg, and clamp on the lid so it keeps warm. You can adorn the purée with a scattering of thyme sprigs, not just for beauty, but because their fragrance gladly answers the woodsy call of the porcini-scented parsnips.

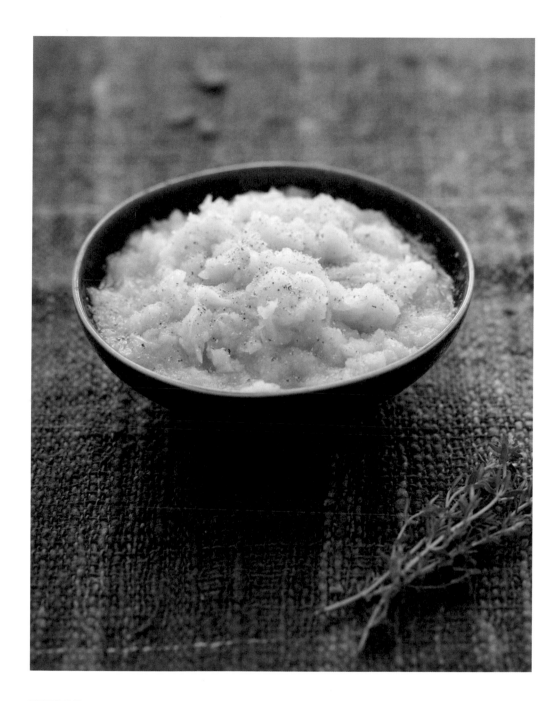

STORE NOTE	FREEZE NOTE
Cool leftovers, then cover and refrigerate as quickly as possible. Will keep in fridge for up to 5 days. Reheat in a small saucepan over a low heat, stirring occasionally, until piping hot.	Freeze in an airtight container for up to 3 months. Defrost overnight in fridge before reheating as Store Note.

Note: the purée should be reheated once only.

Butternut squash with za'atar and green tahini sauce

I find it difficult to let a recipe be; I suspect all cooks do. So this started life as butternut squash with za'atar – that aromatic mixture of thyme, sumac and sesame seeds – but once I'd served it drizzled with the Green Tahini Sauce that follows, I found I was no longer happy with the squash in its near-naked state. Feel free to use pumpkin in place of the squash, when in season. In either case the sweet vegetable flesh against the herby, earthy taste of the tahini dressing is a rapturous pairing.

SERVES 8–10

1 large (approx. 1.5kg) butternut squash, peeled

2 x 15ml tablespoons regular olive oil

2 x 15ml tablespoons za'atar

TO SERVE:

Green Tahini Sauce (see p.253)

○ Preheat the oven to 200°C/gas mark 6. Cut the squash in half, de-seed, then cut each half into half again, lengthways, and cut into vaguely triangular chunks – think large bite-sizes.

○ Pour the oil into a large, shallow roasting tray – I use one measuring 46 x 34cm with a small lip of 1.5cm – and then tip in the squash and schmoosh it about so that the orange butternut chunks are gleaming with oil. Then sprinkle the za'atar over the squash and perform the same pleasing procedure all over again, so that all the pieces are equally seasoned.

○ Roast in the oven for 45 minutes, or until tender. It's always a bit of a lottery with squash. Test after 35 minutes, and be prepared to go for 1 hour if necessary. You can serve just as it is, or let it stand for 10 minutes or so, and then drizzle with some of the Green Tahini Sauce, and put the rest in a bowl with its own serving spoon on the table alongside.

STORE NOTE

Cool leftovers (without sauce), then cover and refrigerate as quickly as possible. Will keep in fridge for up to 5 days.

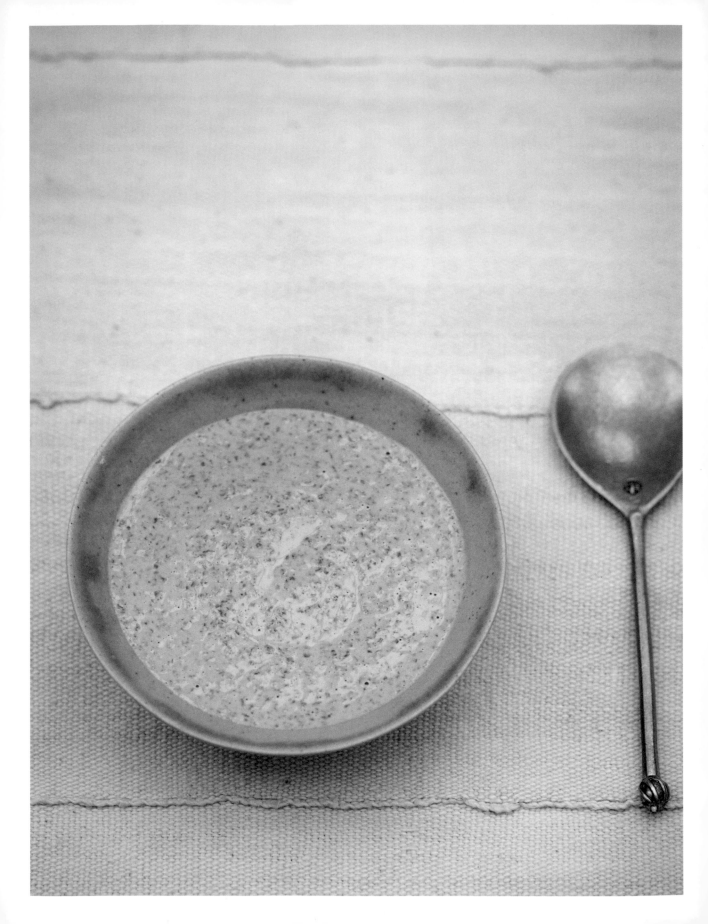

Green tahini sauce

When I'm making this to go with the butternut squash on the preceding pages, I add thyme to echo the za'atar and make the sauce green with parsley. But you can play freely with the herbs you use: I often make this with half parsley and half coriander, and sometimes throw in mint, as well. It's wonderful with any roast vegetables, as well as meat or fish, and is the work of lazy moments.

MAKES APPROX. 500ML

150g tahini

¾ cup (175ml) water

1 clove garlic, peeled and roughly chopped

juice of 1½–2 limes

salt to taste

2 x 15ml tablespoons (4g) thyme leaves

large bunch (approx. 100g) parsley

○ Put the tahini and water into the small bowl of a processor or blender. Add the chopped garlic, then squeeze in the juice of 1½ limes, and add a sprinkle of salt and the thyme leaves.

○ Tear the leaves off the bunch of parsley, discarding the stalks, then put into the blender or processor bowl, and blitz the sauce until smooth.

○ Check the seasoning, adding more salt or lime juice, if you feel it needs it.

STORE NOTE

Store leftover sauce in an airtight container or screw-top jar in fridge for up to 5 days. If needed, stir before using.

Chilli, ginger and garlic sauce

I am that hypocritical person who looks askance at those who somehow need to dollop everything they eat with ketchup, while never myself sitting down at the table without a jar of English mustard by my side. I even travel with tubes of the stuff. But this fierce and brightly coloured sauce is, I rather feel, eclipsing the Colman's for me. I now always have a jar in the fridge, and there's not a foodstuff I leave pure and undaubed. It brings fire and joy in equal parts, and is dangerously addictive.

MAKES APPROX. 200ML

100g fresh red chillies, roughly chopped but not de-seeded

2 cloves garlic, peeled

10cm piece (50g) fresh ginger, peeled and roughly chopped

1 teaspoon fine sea salt, or to taste

4 teaspoons sunflower oil

2 teaspoons sugar

juice of 1 lime

° Put all the ingredients into a bowl and blitz to a purée with a stick blender (or you can use a food processor).

° Leave it to rest for about 15 minutes before serving, as it will be frothy and needs to settle. The flavours seem only to get richer as it stands, a bright beacon, in your fridge.

STORE NOTE	FREEZE NOTE
Store cooled leftover sauce in an airtight container or screw-top jar in fridge for up to 2 weeks.	Freeze in an airtight container for up to 3 months. Defrost overnight in fridge and use within 2 days.

Caramelized garlic yogurt sauce

Maybe it's age, but I find that raw garlic has less and less appeal for me. I find its pungency so much better conveyed when the heat of the oven has muted it and added silky sweetness. And really, how hard is it to wrap a garlic bulb in foil and leave it in the oven to roast?

I'm giving directions here for said garlic to be caramelized for a shorter time at a high heat, but in real life I roast bulbs of garlic whenever I have an oven on, and alter the cooking time according to the temperature, to ensure I have a ready supply in the fridge (where they keep, in an airtight container or wrapped in foil, for up to a week). This doesn't require split-second timing, merely for you to check that the cloves are soft, sweet, scorched and ready, once cooled, to be squeezed into the thick tangy yogurt.

Eat this with the Oven-Cooked Chicken Shawarma on **p.157**, along with, or instead of, the tahini yogurt sauce, or put it on the table whenever you roast lamb or vegetables. It is also mighty fine in a baked potato.

MAKES APPROX. 450ML

1 large bulb garlic, whole and unpeeled	1 teaspoon sea salt flakes, or to taste
400g Greek yogurt	

○ Preheat the oven to 220°C/gas mark 7. Cut off the top of the garlic bulb, just enough so that the cloves are peeking through. Tear off a piece of kitchen foil and sit the garlic on it, then pull up the sides and make a loose but tightly sealed parcel. Bake in the oven for 45 minutes, by which time the little tips of the cloves that peek out should be caramelized and the bulb of garlic will feel soft. Leave to cool.

○ Squeeze the garlic out of their skins into a bowl and a bronze purée will emerge.

○ Spoon in the yogurt and salt, and stir to mix. Nothing's to stop you adding herbs at this point, but I prefer this pale and interesting.

○ Divide between bowls for your table.

STORE NOTE
Store leftover sauce in fridge. Will keep for up to 3 days.

Quick gherkins

Now this is where my pickling obsession started. For all that, it isn't really a pickle, more of a sprightly salad, but I eat these spikily soused cucumbers just as I do gherkins. Indeed, I like them so much better: they taste much fresher (as, indeed, they would), are less mushy and don't have that coruscating acid sting. If you can get Lebanese cucumbers, do, as they have much more crunch and flavour, but I have made these as well with regular cucumbers. And I know it might seem unnecessary to use 2 different vinegars, and I am sure white balsamic vinegar is entirely disreputable (I have it in the house, as my son likes it; that's my excuse) but this combination works, and I'm sticking to it. I dare say if you wanted to, you could use just rice vinegar, in which case up the quantity and add a little sugar.

SERVES 6–8

375–400g Lebanese cucumbers	2 x 15ml tablespoons rice vinegar
1 teaspoon coriander seeds	2 teaspoons white balsamic vinegar
1 teaspoon sea salt flakes	2 x 15ml tablespoons fresh dill leaves, plus more to serve
good grinding of coarse white pepper	

° Using a vegetable peeler, peel lengths of skin off the cucumbers so you end up with striped cucumbers, then cut them into long batons and put into a shallow, non-metallic bowl in which you can fit most of them in one layer. Add the remaining ingredients.

° Cover with clingfilm and swill everything around, so the cucumbers get a good coating. It may not look like there's enough liquid, but the batons will give out more liquid as they sit, and their cucumberiness melds with the spiced vinegar beautifully. Leave for at least 20 minutes before serving.

STORE NOTE
The gherkins will keep in a sealed jar in fridge for up to 1 week.

Thai pickled peppers

When I was in Thailand, a jar of these was offered at every meal. I now do the same, and by that I mean I do not limit their usage to Thai food. As you can see, it is not a difficult recipe: it is simply a matter of slicing chillies and leaving them in vinegar. The rule seems to be 1 part chopped chillies to 2 parts vinegar (and this ratio is about volume not weight), so that those who want the chillified vinegar have enough of that, and those who (like me) prefer to drain the liquid away while spooning out the chillies are both kept happy. There is no need to make as much as below: simply chop the chillies you have, measure them in a cup, and then double that volume to get to the requisite amount of vinegar.

MAKES APPROX. 500ML

¾ cup (75g) fresh red chilli peppers (not bird's eye chillies)

1½ cups (325ml) rice vinegar

1 x 500ml preserving jar or similar-sized resealable jar with vinegar-proof lid

° Thinly slice the chillies and put into your preserving jar (though, in fact, I first made this in an empty, cleaned 400g Nutella jar) and pour the vinegar over them. Seal the jar with its lid, and leave in the fridge for 48 hours before using.

STORE NOTE

The pickled peppers will keep in a sealed jar in fridge for up to 1 month.

Quick-pickled carrots

I look at it like this: if I can summon the patience to cut carrots into julienne strips, then anyone can. I think the trick of making pickling manageable – and the same goes for jam-making – is to deal in small batches only. From experience, when you make masses of jars, you end up pressing them on people in an effort to unload them. If you make one jar, as I do, you will gratefully bring it out for a month, to add crunch and piquancy as you eat, and there is very little that a delicate pickle like this can't enhance.

MAKES APPROX. 500ML

2 large carrots (approx. 250g total), peeled	2 bay leaves
¾ cup (175ml) cider vinegar or white wine vinegar	1 teaspoon mustard seeds
	1 teaspoon fennel seeds
¾ cup (175ml) cold water	4 cardamom pods
2 x 15ml tablespoons runny honey	1 x 500ml preserving jar or any resealable jar with vinegar-proof lid
2 teaspoons sea salt flakes	

- Peel the carrots and cut them into matchsticks, and put them into a non-metallic bowl or jug while you get on with the pickling liquid.

- Put the vinegar, water, honey, salt, bay leaves, mustard and fennel seeds into a saucepan. Crush or crack the cardamom pods and pop them in, too. Bring to the boil, then take the pan off the heat, and stir to make sure that the salt is dissolved. Pour this liquid over the carrots and leave for about 1 hour to reach room temperature, then stash in the fridge for about 1 hour before eating.

STORE NOTE

The pickled carrots will keep in a sealed jar in fridge for up to 1 month.

Quick-pickled beetroot with nigella seeds

I thought until now that the only way I could eat beetroot was raw, but this gentle, ginger-infused pickle is another step in beetroot-rehabilitation for anyone with a school-induced loathing for the stuff. It's sweet and tangy, and the perfect accompaniment to sausages (most excellent in a sausage sandwich) and deep and dark stews. I can also recommend removing the ruby strands from their liquid and tossing them into a generous amount of fresh dill for a sprauncy little salad.

If ginger syrup is not to be found, then do use the syrup from a jar of stem ginger.

MAKES APPROX. 500ML

4 small raw beetroots (approx. 250g total), peeled

¾ cup (175ml) cider vinegar or white wine vinegar

¾ cup (175ml) cold water

3 x 15ml tablespoons ginger syrup or syrup from a jar of preserved ginger

2 teaspoons sea salt flakes

2 bay leaves

2 teaspoons nigella seeds

1 x 500ml preserving jar or any resealable jar with vinegar-proof lid

° Wearing a pair of disposable vinyl gloves – or this your hand will *fo sho* the multitudinous seas incarnadine – cut the beetroot into thin slices, and then cut each slice into matchsticks. This may be boring, but it's not difficult, and there aren't enough beetroots to deal with to make heavy weather of it. Put them into a non-metallic bowl or jug while you get on with the pickling liquid.

° Put the remaining ingredients into a small saucepan, and bring to a boil. Take off the heat, and stir to make sure the salt is dissolved, then pour over the prepared beetroot and leave until it reaches room temperature. Cover and place in the fridge for about 1 hour – or until cold – before eating, or storing in your jar for up to 1 month.

STORE NOTE

The pickled beetroot will keep in a sealed jar in fridge for up to 1 month.

Sushi pickled ginger

Who knew I'd ever turn into the sort of person who makes her own sushi ginger? Given that you could put anything in front of me right now and I'd pickle it, it actually makes sense. After all, I am sure the flavour of these pages indicates how far gone I am on ginger. No matter that I don't make my own sushi – *yet* (anything could change, and often does) – as this fiery stuff is wonderful alongside a piece of grilled fish or chicken, or gorgeously fatty pork.

The beetroot is there just to bring its beautiful tint; it is not evident in the taste. You could leave it out entirely. I, on the other hand, couldn't.

MAKES APPROX. 250ML

125g fresh ginger, peeled

1 teaspoon fine sea salt

½ cup (120ml) rice vinegar

¼ cup (60ml) water

¼ cup (55g) caster sugar

small piece (5g) raw beetroot

1 x 250ml preserving jar or any resealable jar with vinegar-proof lid

° Use a vegetable peeler to slice the ginger into thin strips. Transfer to a bowl, sprinkle with the salt and mix well. Set aside for 30 minutes to allow the salt to extract excess liquid.

° After 30 minutes, squeeze out and discard any excess liquid from the ginger, and put the strips into your preserving jar.

° To a saucepan, add a ¼ cup (60ml) of rice vinegar and the water, along with the sugar and beetroot (if using), and warm over a medium heat until the sugar dissolves. Increase the heat to high and allow to boil for 1 minute.

° Pour the vinegar mixture over the ginger strips in the jar and leave to cool.

° Remove the little piece of beetroot and add the remaining ¼ cup (60ml) of vinegar, stir well and seal the jar. Store in the fridge for at least 24 hours, to allow the flavours to develop before eating.

STORE NOTE

The pickled ginger will keep in a sealed jar in fridge for up to 1 month.

Pink-pickled eggs

In my younger days, I ate a whole jar of industrially acid-pickled eggs for a (lucrative) bet; and that still hasn't put me off. But these are in another league altogether. They do rather look like they are a 1960s fabric pattern come to life, but they are as gorgeous to eat as they are pretty to look at. I am not, however, looking to convert those who don't like pickled eggs in the first place.

This method of pickling eggs is not new but a traditional German recipe, lazily but gratifyingly simplified here.

If doing fewer than 18 eggs, I'd still use the same amount of pickling liquid, but a smaller preserving jar; the important thing is that the liquid comes to the top of the jar.

75g raw beetroot, peeled

1 red onion

3 x 15ml tablespoons sea salt flakes

3 x 15ml tablespoons sugar

500ml cold water

500ml red wine vinegar, plus more for topping up later

18 eggs

handful of ice cubes, for cooling the eggs

1 x 1.5 litre preserving jar or any resealable jar with vinegar-proof lid

- Cut the beetroot into dice and drop into a saucepan.

- Halve the unpeeled onion and cut it into slices, and drop these – skin and all – into the pan.

- Add the salt, sugar, water and vinegar and bring to the boil, then let it bubble for 1 minute, before taking off the heat. Leave to steep for 1 day in a cool place.

- Put the eggs into a saucepan, cover with cold water and bring to the boil, and then let it bubble away – not too rambunctiously – for 7 minutes. Take the pan to the sink, drain and run cold water over the eggs until they are cool enough to handle. Transfer them to a large bowl, cover with cold water and, if you can, a handful of ice cubes so that the eggs cool swiftly. If you let hard-boiled eggs cool slowly, they get those grey rings around the yolk.

- After the eggs have had no more than 8 minutes in the iced water, peel them (if they sit for too long, it becomes very difficult to peel the eggs) and put them into your jar. Strain the beetroot and onion liquid into a jug and pour over the eggs in the jar. Now add enough red wine vinegar to come up to the top of the jar (I use about 200ml), then seal the jar with its lid and leave in the fridge for 4 days before eating, turning the jar upside down and then back again at regular intervals.

STORE NOTE

The pickled eggs will keep in a sealed jar in fridge for up to 1 month.

SWEET

SWEET

I love baking. That is no secret. There is something about ushering a cake into being that creates in me a sense of cosiness and serenity, the combination of which is the very essence of this book.

Strangely, I am not much of a cake-eater. Don't be alarmed: not being a slave to a sweet tooth makes me much more demanding of the cakes and cookies I *do* make and eat. It's never sugar-at-any-price: I need to be able to taste and revel in the flavours, and feel lifted out of the ordinary order of things; in short, it must always be a treat. I never make dessert on an everyday basis, but I wouldn't invite friends around my table without offering up something sweet at the end. Mind you, those who don't want to eat sugar are free to abstain. Cooking is about providing sustenance and giving pleasure: no one needs a cake to sustain them, and if there is no pleasure for someone in eating one, then they shouldn't feel any compunction about not doing so.

But part of the balance of life lies in understanding that different days require different ways of eating. A life that banishes sweet things is not a balanced life, but a constrained one and – although this is not the focus of my book – an invitation to obsession that I want to be no party to. I have always noticed that I, who keep a lot of chocolate and ice cream in the house, and bake cakes and cookies, can manage to live very equably with such a sweet stash, whereas friends of mine who make a point of refusing any such devilry, can easily devour every crumb of cake, or tub of ice cream when they visit.

I also want to say that I have no truck here with the "no sugar" bake, simply because anything that tastes sweet is, effectively, made with sugar. A cake that is made with agave syrup, for instance, is not a sugar-free cake, even if this is a fashionably held belief. I'm often – though why, I do not know – asked for diet desserts, and my response is simply "then don't eat dessert". But I am not going to apologize for keeping it sweet: it is a part of life, and, further, a part that is central to the way human society celebrates, and I am more than happy to honour that. Those who disapprove should turn away now.

Many of the cakes below are either gluten-free or dairy-free, or both. Anytime I have friends for supper there are always some in these camps, and since I have invited them because I want them to feel welcome, why would I cook them something they can't eat? I'm not making any health claims here, and am not in a position to – and I'm always mindful of the late Marina Keegan's irritation as a coeliac, at what she felt was the craziness of the Hollywood gluten-free diet – but I can certainly attest to their deliciousness. And if more people can enjoy that, the happier I am.

You will see, though, that I haven't constrained myself in any way with the recipes that follow. The joy I feel in baking translates to the joy to be had in eating. Whatever ingredients I use, the aim is always simple: to give pleasure, both to the cook and the eater, without which, life and the sum of human happiness, in this small but essential way, would be much diminished.

Apricot almond cake with rosewater and cardamom

This is my idea of a perfect cake: simple, beautiful, fragrant and beguiling. I've been making this sort of cake, in one form or another, since my clementine cake in *How To Eat*, and I can't help but feel, with a certain calm excitement, that it has reached its apogee here. This is invitingly easy to make, and while I love the poetry of its ingredients, the cake doesn't overwhelm with its *Thousand-and-One-Nights* scent. Rosewater can be a tricky ingredient: a little, and it's all exotic promise; a fraction too much and we're in bubblebath territory.

One of the things that makes this so easy, is that you can throw all the ingredients into a food processor. But if you don't have one, simply chop the prepared dried apricots and cardamom seeds very finely and then beat together with the remaining cake ingredients.

CUTS INTO 8–10 SLICES

150g "ready-to-eat" dried apricots

250ml cold water

2 cardamom pods, cracked

200g ground almonds

50g fine polenta (not instant)

1 teaspoon baking powder (gluten-free if required)

150g caster sugar

6 large eggs

2 teaspoons lemon juice

1 teaspoon rosewater

non-stick cooking spray or sunflower oil for greasing

TO DECORATE:

2 teaspoons rose petal or apricot jam

1 teaspoon lemon juice

2½ teaspoons very finely chopped pistachios

1 x 20cm round springform cake tin

° Put the dried apricots into a small saucepan, cover them with the cold water, and drop in the cracked cardamom pods with their fragrant seeds. Put on the heat, then bring to the boil and let it bubble for 10 minutes – don't stray too far away from the pan, as by the end of the 10 minutes the pan will be just about out of water and you want to make sure it doesn't actually run dry as the apricots will absorb more water as they cool.

° Take the pan off the heat, place on a cold, heatproof surface and let the apricots cool.

° Preheat the oven to 180°C/gas mark 4. Grease the sides of your springform cake tin and line the bottom with baking parchment.

- Remove 5 of the dried apricots and tear each in half, then set aside for the time being. Discard the cardamom husks, leaving the seeds in the pan.

- Pour and scrape out the sticky contents of the pan into the bowl of a food processor. Add the ground almonds, polenta, baking powder, caster sugar and eggs, and give a good long blitz to combine.

- Open the top of the processor, scrape down the batter, add 2 teaspoons of lemon juice and the rosewater, and blitz again, then scrape into the prepared tin and smooth with a spatula. Arrange the apricot halves around the circumference of the tin.

- Bake for 40 minutes, though if the cake is browning up a lot before it's actually ready, you may want to cover loosely with foil at the 30-minute mark. When it's ready, the cake will be coming away from the edges of the tin, the top will feel firm, and a cake tester will come out with just one or two damp crumbs on it.

- Remove the cake to a wire rack. If you're using apricot jam to decorate, you may want to warm it a little first so that it's easier to spread; rose petal jam is so lusciously soft-set, it shouldn't need any help. Stir a teaspoon of lemon juice into the jam and brush over the top of the cake, then sprinkle with the chopped pistachios and leave the cake to cool in its tin before unspringing and removing to a plate.

STORE NOTE	FREEZE NOTE
Store in an airtight container in a cool place for 5–7 days. In hot weather (or if the central heating's on) keep in fridge.	The cake can be made ahead and frozen for up to 3 months (though the nuts may soften slightly on defrosting). Wrap the fully cooled cake (still on the springform tin base) tightly in a double layer of clingfilm and a layer of foil. To defrost, unwrap and leave it (still on the tin base) on a plate at room temperature for about 4 hours.

Warm raspberry and lemon cake

Although this started off life as more of a trad British bake, rather along the lines of the Marmalade Pudding Cake in *Kitchen*, I prefer it in this incarnation: sweet with almonds and the soft crunch of polenta. This also gives it universal appeal in that it is both dairy- and gluten-free. But if you want a more old-fashioned cake taste, then make it with 200g soft unsalted butter (plus a little more for greasing the tin), which you cream with the sugar and zest, and use 225g plain flour in place of the almonds and polenta. You will also need 4 eggs rather than 3, and – the flour being less sweet than both the almonds and the polenta – I'd advise you warm the lemon juice that goes on top with 2 teaspoons of honey first.

In both cases, this is as good cold as it is warm, though I love the way the scent mingles with the taste when it still has the breath of the oven on it. When cold, however, you can make the cake go further, by slicing it into fingers and eating it daintily with a cup of tea.

I've specified frozen raspberries rather than fresh as they don't go so mushy when baked. However, in either case, the fruit has a tendency to sink a bit, but don't let that bother you.

MAKES 9 SLABS OR 18 FINGERS

150ml light olive oil, plus more for greasing

zest and juice of 1 unwaxed lemon

125g caster sugar

150g ground almonds

75g fine polenta (not instant)

½ teaspoon bicarbonate of soda

1 teaspoon baking powder (gluten-free if required)

3 large eggs

150g frozen raspberries (not thawed)

1 x 20cm square cake tin

○ Preheat the oven to 180°C/gas mark 4, and lightly grease the tin with a dab of olive oil.

○ Beat the oil with the finely grated lemon zest (you'll need the juice later), then add the sugar and mix together. This can be done in a freestanding mixer or by hand with a wooden spoon, or you can blitz all the ingredients, bar the raspberries, in a food processor.

○ In a separate bowl, combine the ground almonds, polenta, bicarb and baking powder and fork together to mix well. Add a spoonful to the oil and sugar mixture, beating all the while, then add 1 egg, followed by about a third of the almond and polenta mixture, and so forth, until all the eggs and the almond and polenta mixture are used up and you have a smooth, sunny, yellow batter.

○ Whether you've mixed the batter with a processor, freestanding mixer, or bowl and wooden spoon, now fold in the frozen raspberries by hand and then spoon and smooth the mixture into the prepared tin. Bake for 40 minutes, by which time the cake will start to come away from the edges of the tin, be brown on top, and a cake tester will come out clean with all but a few golden crumbs (this is meant to be a damp cake).

○ The minute the cake is out of the oven, pour or brush the lemon juice on top and leave until warm (rather than fresh-from-the-oven hot) before eating it.

STORE NOTE	FREEZE NOTE
Store in an airtight container in a cool place for up to 2 days, or in fridge for up to 5 days. In hot weather, keep in fridge.	Leftovers can be frozen, in an airtight container, for up to 3 months. Thaw overnight in fridge, or for 2–3 hours at room temperature.

Liquorice and blackcurrant chocolate cake

Any recipe with liquorice is essentially a divisive one, but I've written of my liquorice-love before, and know there are many more of my persuasion out there. Besides, while my No-Churn Blackcurrant Ice Cream with Liquorice Ripple on **p.336** is definitely a no-go area for any but the true believer, this cake is gentle enough to lure in those who profess initial caution. The chocolate seems to soften the liquorice's dark intensity, and the sharp blackcurrant is a fitting foil and traditional partner; indeed, the inspiration for this cake came from a lifelong love of the blackcurrant and liquorice sweets I ate in my childhood. And it is worth getting the blackcurrants for the top of the cake: they are more than just decorative. I had to pick mine out of a packet of frozen mixed berries, then let them thaw, but it was worth it.

I use Lakrids' Fine Liquorice Powder, but if you're using raw liquorice powder, then reduce the amounts to 3 teaspoons in the cake and ¾ teaspoon in the icing. The point is, the liquorice should not hit you over the head, but become subtly present in the "follow", blooming after the bite. With the quantities below, professed liquorice-haters actually liked the cake; liquorice-lovers, of course, adored it.

By the way, although this cake is dairy-free, by all means substitute semi-skimmed milk if that isn't a consideration. As for the chocolate, if it has a minimum of 70% cocoa solids it should be, in effect, dairy-free but may still contain some traces of milk. So if this is a concern, do check the labelling on the packet to be sure.

CUTS INTO 8–12 SLICES

FOR THE CAKE:

225g plain flour

275g caster sugar

75g cocoa

2 teaspoons baking powder

1 teaspoon bicarbonate of soda

4 teaspoons fine liquorice powder (see Intro)

175ml almond milk

175ml sunflower oil, plus extra for greasing

2 large eggs

250ml hot water, from a recently boiled kettle

200g best-quality blackcurrant jam

FOR THE ICING:

2 x 15ml tablespoons hot water, from a recently boiled kettle

1 teaspoon fine liquorice powder (see Intro)

75g (¼) cup golden syrup; oil the cup before measuring

100g dark chocolate (min. 70% cocoa solids), very finely chopped (see Intro)

TO DECORATE:

100–125g blackcurrants (optional; see Intro)

2 x 20cm sandwich tins (not loose-bottomed)

- Preheat the oven to 180°C/gas mark 4. Prepare your sandwich tins (not ones with loose bottoms as this is a very liquid batter) by greasing with oil and lining with baking parchment.

- Measure the flour, sugar, cocoa, baking powder, bicarb and liquorice powder into a large mixing bowl, and fork to combine, breaking up any lumps.

- Whisk the milk, oil and eggs in a measuring jug. Add these wet ingredients to the dry ones and, still whisking – or move to a wooden spoon if you prefer – beat to mix. Now beat in the boiling water and, when all is combined, pour equally into the 2 tins. It is a tight fit, but don't let that alarm you.

- Carefully put the cakes in the oven and bake for about 25 minutes, by which time they should be coming away from the edges of the tins, feel firm to the touch, and a cake tester should come out clean. A few crumbs may still adhere, as this is a desirably damp cake, but you shouldn't have any actual batter on the cake tester.

- When they're done, stand the cakes in their tins on a wire rack for 10 minutes, then unmould them carefully – they should slip out easily, but they are tender, so be gentle – onto the wire rack, peel away the baking parchment and leave to cool.

- Once the cakes are cool, put 1 cake, flat-side up, on a plate. Spread with the blackcurrant jam and top with the other cake, flat-side down.

- To make the icing, put the hot water and liquorice powder in a small pan and whisk to mix, so that the powder dissolves, then add the golden syrup and bring to a boil. The second it starts bubbling, turn off the heat (but leave the pan on the hob) and add the finely chopped chocolate. Swirl the pan, making sure the chocolate is covered and is starting to melt, and leave for a scant minute, then whisk until you have a glossy icing. Pour this onto the centre of the top of the cake and, using a small spatula, ease it to the edges, letting some bits drip a little down the sides. If you want, top with blackcurrants, making sure that – if they're frozen – they are completely thawed and drained. And if you do want to add the blackcurrants or any other sort of decoration, move fast as the icing sets quickly!

STORE NOTE	FREEZE NOTE
Store in an airtight container (or under a cake dome) at cool room temperature for up to 5 days.	The cake can be made ahead and frozen, without icing. When cool, very carefully wrap cake layers in a double layer of clingfilm and a layer of foil. Freeze for up to 3 months. To defrost, unwrap and place on a wire rack for 2–3 hours.

Dark and sumptuous chocolate cake

This cake. It confounds me. It delights me. I almost want to leave it there.

But I should explain: I never ever thought I would be in raptures about the joyfulness of a – yes – vegan chocolate cake. This isn't the voice of prejudice but was – "was" being the operative word – the conclusion of experience.

It's true that I first made a version of it – the recipe kindly given to me by Caroline Stearns, my technical guru in the kitchen – when I was giving a supper for a vegan friend, but I now make this as my chocolate cake of choice for people where dietary restrictions are *not* an issue, and I don't even need to explain it's vegan. No need to offer explanations: you just need to offer the cake. On top of everything else, it's incredibly simple to make.

My version has coconut oil in the cake, and coconut butter in the icing, but of course you can use vegetable oil in the cake, and vegan margarine for the icing if you prefer. The combination stipulated in the ingredients list, however, creates a cake and icing of such depth and fudginess that I never veer from it, even though I know the shopping list is a tiny bit demanding. But once you've tasted it, you too must surely concur that a cake as good as this can be as demanding as it likes. Besides, it asks nothing of you in the kitchen beyond some simple stirring. You are not required to get a mixer out, or do any heavy lifting at all: this is a simple bowl-and-wooden-spoon number. Both the coconut oil and coconut butter need to stand out of the fridge for a good couple of hours before using. I often take them out the night before, as then they are easier to measure out.

Please check the labelling on the chocolate you buy. It needs, whatever your concerns, to be dark (minimum 70% cocoa solids for my taste), but if you need this to be absolutely dairy-free or vegan, make sure it says so on the packet.

I hate the worthy association that comes with vegan cakes, and celebrate this one by scattering rose petals and chopped pistachios over it.

FOR THE ICING:

60ml cold water

75g coconut butter (this is not the same as oil)

50g soft dark sugar

1½ teaspoons instant espresso

1½ x 15ml tablespoons cocoa

150g dark chocolate (min. 70% cocoa solids, see Intro), finely chopped

FOR THE CAKE:

225g plain flour

1½ teaspoons bicarbonate of soda

½ teaspoon fine sea salt

1½ teaspoons instant espresso powder

75g cocoa

300g soft dark brown sugar

375ml hot water, from a recently boiled kettle

90ml (75g if weighed when solid) coconut oil

1½ teaspoons cider vinegar or white wine vinegar

1 x 15ml tablespoon edible rose petals

1 x 15ml tablespoon chopped pistachios

1 x 20cm round springform cake tin

- Start with the icing, though first preheat the oven to 180°C/gas mark 4 and pop in a baking sheet at the same time. Put all of the icing ingredients except the chopped chocolate into a heavy-based saucepan and bring to the boil, making sure everything's dissolved. Then turn off the heat – but leave the pan on the hob – then quickly add the finely chopped chocolate and swirl the pan so that it is all underwater, so to speak. Leave for a scant minute, then whisk until you have a darkly glossy icing, and leave to cool. I find this takes exactly the amount of time the cake takes to make, cook and cool. But do give the icing a stir with a spatula every now and again.

- Line the bottom of your springform cake tin (you will need a good, leakproof one as this is a very wet batter) with baking parchment.

- Put the flour, bicarb, salt and instant espresso and cocoa in a bowl and fork to mix.

- Mix together the sugar, water, coconut oil and vinegar until the coconut oil has melted, and stir into the dry ingredients, then pour into the prepared tin and bake for 35 minutes. Though do check at the 30-minute mark to see if it is already done. When it's ready, the cake will be coming away from the edges of the tin and a cake tester will come out clean, apart from a few crumbs. This is a fudgy cake and you don't want to overdo it.

- Once the cake is cooked, transfer the tin to a wire rack and let the cake cool in its tin.

- Turn to your icing, and give it a good stir with a spatula to check it is at the right consistency. It needs to be runny enough to cover the cake, but thick enough to stay (mostly) on the top. So pour over the unmoulded cake, and use a spatula to ease the icing to the edges, if needed. If you wish to decorate, now is the time to do it. In which case, sprinkle joyously with rose petals and chopped pistachios or anything else that your heart desires; otherwise, leave it gleaming darkly and, indeed, sumptuously. Leave to stand for 30 minutes for the icing to set before slicing into the cake.

STORE NOTE	FREEZE NOTE
Store in an airtight container (or under a cake dome) at room temperature for up to 5 days.	The cake can be made ahead and frozen, without icing. When cool, carefully wrap cake in a double layer of clingfilm and a layer of foil. Freeze for up to 3 months. To defrost, unwrap and place on a serving plate at room temperature for 3–4 hours.

Thyme and lemon bundt cake

I love thyme and sprinkle it wantonly in my cooking, but I wanted a cake that relied on it as a leading ingredient, not merely as a decorative flourish. Besides, with a rosemary loaf cake under my belt (in *Feast*), I had no doubt that it would work. And it does. Don't be alarmed at the amount of thyme in the cake batter, as it doesn't overwhelm. It charms.

I've specified buttermilk in the ingredients list, but you can use runny plain yogurt in its stead. Or, easier still, make your own buttermilk – my fallback position – by adding 1 tablespoon of lemon juice (since you will have lemons to hand for this recipe; otherwise you can use white wine vinegar or cider vinegar instead) to 250ml semi-skimmed milk and letting it stand for 20 minutes before you need it, stirring before use.

Now, a cautionary word: even when the cake looks bronzed and ready, you need to make sure that it's cooked through around the funnel. Otherwise, not only will it be the devil to unmould, but you will also find the cake disappointingly undercooked (however brown it looks on the surface) once you slice into it.

If you don't have a bundt tin, then you can make this in a 20cm square cake tin (approx. 5.5cm deep). It makes quite a high cake, almost the full height of the tin, and takes between 1 hour to 1 hour 20 minutes at the oven temperature below (and check that it is cooked all the way through to the centre before removing it from the oven).

CUTS INTO 10–14 SLICES

450g plain flour	3 large eggs
¾ teaspoon baking powder	250ml buttermilk (see Intro)
¾ teaspoon bicarbonate of soda	120g icing sugar
200g soft unsalted butter	non-stick cooking spray (or sunflower oil and plain flour) for greasing
2 unwaxed lemons	
small bunch fresh thyme	1 x 10-cup (2.5 litre capacity) bundt tin or 20cm square cake tin approx. 5.5cm deep
250g caster sugar	

° Preheat the oven to 170°C/gas mark 3, slipping in a baking sheet at the same time. Spray the inside of your bundt tin with non-stick cooking spray, or brush on a paste made of 2 teaspoons of plain flour mixed with 2 teaspoons of oil, making sure you get into all the crevices of the tin. Leave the bundt tin upside down over a

piece of newspaper or baking parchment while you get on with making the cake batter. (And keep this piece of paper once you've put the batter in the tin, as it'll come in handy for the icing part.)

- Combine the flour, baking powder and bicarb in a bowl, and fork to mix.

- Put the butter in the bowl of a freestanding mixer or a regular mixing bowl, grate in the zest of both lemons and beat until creamy.

- Strip 4 tablespoons of thyme leaves from the sprigs, and add along with the caster sugar, and beat again until you have a light fluffy mixture.

- Now, one by one, beat in the eggs and, after the last one, slow down your mixing and add a third of the flour mixture, followed by a third of the buttermilk, and so on until both the flour mixture and buttermilk are used up.

- Finally, beat in the juice of 1 of the lemons and transfer this mixture to the prepared bundt tin. Place on the baking sheet in the oven and bake for 1¼ hours, though start checking after 1 hour. Don't be alarmed if it looks like there's too much batter for the bundt tin: all shall be well, and all manner of things shall be well. In other words, the cake will rise but then sink back down comfortably.

- When a cake tester comes out clean, remove the cake to a wire rack and leave in its tin for 15 minutes before carefully unmoulding. This is always a tense moment, but if the tin's been sprayed or greased adequately, and the cake is fully baked, you should have no problem. Besides, it's that moment of breathless tension which makes the dramatic unmoulding and unveiling all the more gratifying.

- When the cake is cool, slip the piece of newspaper or baking parchment under the wire rack, then sieve the icing sugar into a bowl and beat in the juice of the remaining lemon until you have a glaze that is thin enough to run down the cake – I reckon on 2½–3 tablespoons – but thick enough to act as a tangy glue for the thyme leaves you are about to sprinkle on top. Or you can pour this directly over the cake on its serving plate. Duly pour the sherbetty glaze over the cake, and immediately scatter with thyme leaves and the odd sprig or two. How many you add is entirely up to you, but I tend to strew with abandon.

STORE NOTE	FREEZE NOTE
Store in an airtight container in a cool place for up to 5 days.	This cake can be frozen, without icing, for up to 3 months. Wrap cake in a double layer of clingfilm and a layer of foil. To defrost, unwrap and place on a wire rack at room temperature for about 5 hours.

Pumpkin bundt cake

I love the harvest-festival feel of a pumpkin cake, even if the pumpkin does come out of a can. The first time I made this, I didn't ice it, just dusted the cake with icing sugar and served it alongside a bag of frozen mixed berries that I'd thawed, stirring a little finely grated orange zest into the fruits as I tipped them, still frozen, into their bowl. Then, I felt I really had to do something with the half can of pumpkin I had left over, and so came up with the No-Churn Brandied Pumpkin Ice Cream (**p.334**), which goes especially well here should you choose to serve the bundt while it still has a little residual warmth about it. But don't feel bad if you want to eat this as a coffee-or-tea-accompanying cake; in which case, ice it as below.

Yes, this is the second of three bundt cakes for your delectation, but it seems to me that if you own such a tin (and I am in possession of one that creates a cake that looks like a cross between an old-fashioned mother-of-the-bride hat and a Catherine wheel) you will want to get as much use out of it as possible.

However, if you don't have a bundt tin, use a 20cm square cake tin (approx. 5.5cm deep) instead. This makes quite a high cake, almost the full height of the tin, and will need 45–55 minutes' baking time at the oven temperature below (and check it is cooked all the way through to the centre before removing it from the oven).

CUTS INTO 10–14 SLICES

300g soft light brown sugar

250ml sunflower oil

zest and juice of 1 orange, preferably unwaxed

3 large eggs

400g plain flour

2 teaspoons bicarbonate of soda

2 teaspoons ground cinnamon

½ teaspoon ground allspice

300g pumpkin purée (from a 425g can – save the rest for the No-Churn Brandied Pumpkin Ice Cream on p.334)

non-stick cooking spray (or sunflower oil and plain flour) for greasing

FOR THE ICING:

200g icing sugar

2½–3 x 15ml tablespoons orange juice (using orange from above)

small square dark chocolate for grating

1 x 10-cup bundt tin (2.5 litre capacity) or 1 x 20cm square cake tin approx. 5.5cm deep (see Intro)

° Preheat the oven to 180°C/gas mark 4. Spray your bundt tin with non-stick cooking spray, or make a paste by mixing 2 teaspoons of oil and 2 teaspoons of flour and brush it all over the insides of the tin, making sure you get into all of the crevices. Leave upside down on a piece of newspaper or baking parchment to drain off any excess oil while you prepare the cake.

- In the bowl of a freestanding mixer (although you could do this by hand), beat together the sugar, oil, the finely grated zest of half the orange and 2 tablespoons of its juice until smoothly combined. You'll need to stop and scrape down the bowl once or twice.

- Add the eggs, beating again.

- Measure the flour, bicarbonate of soda and spices into another bowl, forking everything together lightly so that it's all mixed well.

- Then beat the pumpkin purée into the cake mixture, before finally adding the flour and spices and folding to combine. Once you have a smooth cake batter, carefully fill your oiled bundt tin with this mixture.

- Bake for 45–55 minutes, though I always start checking at 40. The cake should be coming away from the edges of the tin and a cake tester will come out clean. Remove to a wire rack, leaving the cake to cool in its tin for 15 minutes.

- Gently prise the cake away from the tin with your fingers, paying particular attention to the part around the funnel, then turn out the cake onto the wire rack and leave to cool completely.

- To ice the bundt, stand it on the plate of your choice, then sieve the icing sugar into a bowl and gradually whisk in the orange juice, beginning to slow down after the second tablespoon, just to make sure you get the consistency you want. Once you have a smooth icing that's thick enough to stick to the cake, but with just enough runniness to drip down the sides a little, start spooning it over the top of the cake, letting it move naturally on its own: it will run down the architectural grooves of the cake, rather beautifully of its own accord; don't worry if it drips a little onto the plate as – for me, anyway – this adds to its charm. Sometimes, if I have a little icing left over, I can't stop myself doing a bit of a frenzied Jackson Pollock (as you can see from the photo).

- Grate the chocolate on top, to finish: even a small square gives you too much, but it's no great sacrifice to eat what you don't use.

STORE NOTE	FREEZE NOTE
Store in an airtight container in a cool place for up to 1 week.	Freeze, without icing, for up to 3 months. Wrap the cake in a double layer of clingfilm and a layer of foil. To defrost, unwrap and place on a wire rack at room temperature for about 5 hours.

Cider and 5-spice bundt cake

Most of the time I refer to this as my Cider and 5-Spice Gingerbread, but I changed the name out of concern for those who expect a little more gingeriness from their gingerbead (although anyone is free to boost the amount of ginger at will). But, actually, the tender crumb has the lightness of a cake rather than the damp heaviness (gorgeous though that is) of a gingerbread. Besides, I felt it only proper to accord the magnificently aromatic 5-spice seasoning its star role. I have since found that there are many variants of 5-spice powder out there. While generally I presume on a mixture of star anise, cloves, cinnamon, Sichuan pepper and fennel seeds, I also love the versions that have liquorice and dried mandarin peel. But what I've found is that all types work, even the one or two brands that erroneously add garlic: a couple of people (one here, and one in the States) have made it with this version, and both vouch that the garlic is not detectable. Still, when you're shopping, it's best to check the ingredients label and go for one without garlic if you can.

If you want to intensify the ginger element, without doing a lot more peeling and grating (or don't want to use alcohol), then use 250ml ginger beer in place of the cider.

Either way, this is wonderful enough plain as it is, though I have something of a *faiblesse* for the gleaming accompaniment of the Smoky Salted Caramel Sauce on **p.342**, as you can see from the picture.

One last note: if you don't have a bundt tin, you can make this in a 20cm square cake tin (approx. 5.5cm deep), in which case it will need 50–55 minutes' baking, or until a cake tester comes out clean and the cake is firm to the touch. Let the cake cool in the tin, before unmoulding and wrapping (see overleaf).

CUTS INTO 10–14 SLICES

250ml cider, preferably dry or at least not sweet

175ml sunflower oil

100g soft dark brown sugar

300g (250ml) black treacle (use an oiled 1-cup measure for ease)

3 large eggs

3cm piece (15g) fresh ginger, peeled and finely grated

300g plain flour

2 teaspoons baking powder

¼ teaspoon bicarbonate of soda

½ teaspoon freshly grated nutmeg

2½ teaspoons Chinese 5-spice powder

1½ teaspoons ground cinnamon

non-stick cooking spray or sunflower oil for greasing

1 x 10-cup (2.5 litre capacity) bundt tin or 1 x 20cm square cake tin approx. 5.5cm deep (see Intro)

- Open the cider so that it loses its fizz. Preheat the oven to 170°C/gas mark 3, and grease your bundt tin with non-stick cooking spray, or simply oil it, and leave the tin upside down on a piece of newspaper or baking parchment while you get on with the batter.

- Measure the oil, brown sugar and (whether you're weighing it or going for volume and using a cup measure, always lightly oil the receptacle for the treacle first and it will slide out easily) black treacle into a bowl.

- Pour in the cider and crack in the eggs, add the ginger and beat till smooth. While I use a freestanding mixer to make this cake, it's simple enough by hand: in which case, beat the eggs together first before adding to the other ingredients.

- In another bowl measure out the flour, baking powder, bicarb, nutmeg, 5-spice and cinnamon, and fork through to combine.

- Gently tip the dry ingredients into the wet treacly mixture, beating as you go to make a smooth batter. Scrape the sides and the bottom of the bowl well to make sure there aren't any pockets of flour.

- Pour the dark and aromatic batter into the prepared tin: it will be very runny, but don't be alarmed. Place in the oven to bake for 45–50 minutes, but start checking after 40. When the cake's ready, it will start to come away from the sides of the tin and a cake tester should come out clean; that's to say, not wet, but with some crumbs adhering to it. Transfer the bundt to a wire rack for about 30 minutes, then use your fingers to help prise the cake away from the edges of the tin, most particularly around the funnel, and turn out. Leave to cool completely before wrapping, first in parchment and then foil, as it tastes best if eaten the next day. I don't always manage this.

STORE NOTE	FREEZE NOTE
The cake can be kept loosely wrapped in its parchment and foil, in an airtight container at cool room temperature for up to 1 week.	The fully cooled cake can be tightly wrapped in a double layer of clingfilm and a layer of foil and then frozen for up to 3 months. To defrost, unwrap and place on a wire rack and leave at room temperature for about 5 hours.

Matcha cake with cherry juice icing

I've had an *idée fixe* in my head for some time now about the making of a matcha cake. And ever since I saw a picture of a recipe for doughnuts with cherry juice icing, I knew the latter had to play some part in my culinary life. You will have noticed that I have (subtly, I hope) a bit of a green-and-pink theme dancing through the book, so I suppose it was inevitable that these two – the matcha cake and the cherry juice icing – would need to be realized together. I love the evocation of Japanese cherry blossom alongside the equally Japanese matcha – and I am childishly delighted that a cake so beautifully vibrant, so magically tinted, can be achieved without food colouring. Please don't think for one moment that this is the product of the Concept Kitchen. It tastes as exquisite as I'd dreamt it could, or it wouldn't have found its way to these pages.

Good-quality matcha, that greenest of green tea powders, is expensive, but I've found other uses for it so, once bought, it does have more play in your kitchen (see **pp.338** and **348**). Think of it as a culinary investment. My favourite matcha for this is organic Izu Matcha by Tealyra (I am happy enough with the Aiya Beginner's Matcha for the latte on **p.348**, but find it too mild here), which is not cheap but by no means among the most costly. I don't recommend buying a lesser variety, for the simple reason that it will still be expensive, and will neither taste as good nor be as green as the real thing. There's no point doing all this and ending up with something dusty and khaki. Yes, this is a luxury cake, and must be savoured as such.

I find that making a chiffon-style cake – in which the eggs are separated and the whipped whites folded into the batter – makes for a softer texture, which is much needed here, as the matcha powder would dry out a regular sponge. However, you can be left with a slight indentation at the top of the cake, as it rises more on cooking, inevitably to fall. If the indentation is minimal, you can reduce the icing to 200g icing sugar mixed with 3 tablespoons of cherry juice (bought in a bottle, not arduously squeezed by hand, I should add), but otherwise proceed as below. Should cherry juice (not acerola, which is yellow) elude you, try pomegranate juice. And if that fad hasn't hit where you are, then push a few raspberries through a sieve and mix the red juice with a little water.

One final note. Strictly speaking, chiffon cakes should not be made in non-stick and ungreased tins (which impede their rise), but I have only non-stick cake tins, and all the times I've made this, I have had no trouble.

CUTS INTO 12–14 DELICATE SLICES

1 x 15ml (7g) tablespoon Izu Matcha (see Intro)

80ml hot water, from a recently boiled kettle

3 large eggs, separated

120g caster sugar

60ml sunflower oil

110g plain flour

1 teaspoon baking powder

250g icing sugar

4 tablespoons pure organic cherry juice (not acerola)

1 x 20cm springform cake tin (preferably not non-stick)

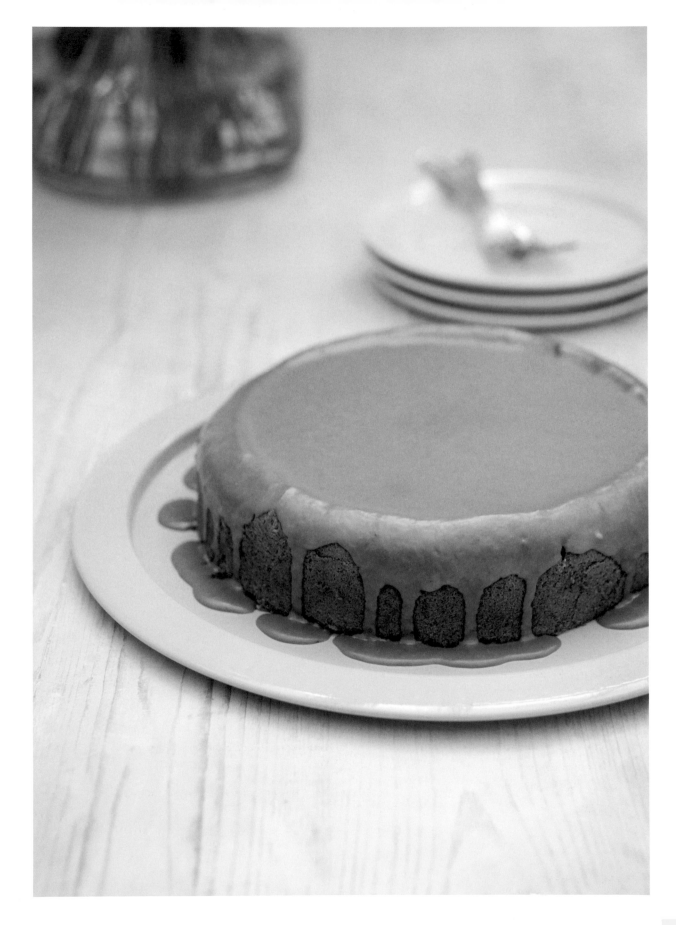

- Preheat the oven to 180°C/gas mark 4. Line the base of your springform tin with baking parchment, but don't grease the tin.

- Put the matcha powder in a small bowl and whisk in the hot water until smooth. Leave to cool slightly.

- Put the egg whites in a separate bowl and whisk to floppy peaks. Still whisking, add 3 tablespoons of the caster sugar and combine, then set aside for a moment.

- Put the egg yolks and remaining caster sugar in another bowl and whisk until pale. Whisk in the matcha liquid followed by the oil. Sieve over and fold in the flour and baking powder.

- Add a dollop of the egg white mixture and fold in, then follow up with the remainder. Gently pour the mixture into the springform cake tin and bake for 25–30 minutes, until a cake tester comes out clean. Do not even think of opening the oven door before 20 minutes to check, as it could make the cake deflate.

- Let the cake cool completely in its tin, sitting on a wire rack. The cake will shrink back slightly as it cools. Run a spatula around the edge of the cake and unspring from the tin. Put a plate on the top of the cake, flip it over, then remove the base of the tin, peel away the baking parchment and carefully sit the cake, bottom-side down, on a plate or cake stand.

- Once the cake is ready to ice, sieve the icing sugar into a bowl and whisk in the cherry juice a little at a time to make an opaque but still runny glacé icing. The cake may have a slight dip on top and this amount of icing allows for this, though it does mean it will pool out pinkly as you cut the cake (I find this rather pretty). Ice the top of the cake and let the icing run down the sides a little. Leave for up to 1 hour to set: it will still be a little runny, but any longer and it starts to lose its gleam.

STORE NOTE	FREEZE NOTE
Store in an airtight container in a cool place for 2–3 days.	The fully cooled, un-iced cake can be frozen, tightly wrapped in a double layer of clingfilm and a layer of foil, for up to 1 month. You may find it easier to leave the cake on the springform tin base when freezing. To defrost, unwrap (carefully remove cake from the tin base if left on) and place on a wire rack at room temperature for about 3 hours.

Date and marmalade Christmas cake

This cake tastes like Christmas pudding – a very, very good Christmas pudding – the sort the Quakers (as I'm fond of quoting) once magnificently condemned as "the invention of the scarlet whore of Babylon". It's rich, damp, treacly and so heady, it doesn't even need the traditional alcohol in it. It also happens to be gluten- and dairy-free, and is a last-minute cake, so very useful if you haven't got round to making that family recipe that needs to be baked ahead and fed with brandy for 6 months.

I like to use a wonderful home-made marmalade (thanks to Helio Fenerich, who also supplied me with the Italian Veal Shank Stew on **p.185**), which is good and bitter and rather soft set, and it's a miracle I can keep it long enough to use in this cake. But there are many good marmalades out there in the shops. Just bear in mind that the dates have their own rich and fudgy sweetness (on top of all the other dried fruit) so don't go for anything too jammy: Frank Cooper's Original Oxford Marmalade or Wilkin & Sons "Tawny" Orange would be my choice; in other words, go for a marmalade with treacly depth, and one that provides that *frisson* of bitterness.

And while I adore the deep caramelly taste of medjool dates (the fruit of the biblical kings), you can use dried dates – the sort styled "ready to eat" – in their stead.

One final thing: the finely chopped almonds came, as did the ground almonds, from a packet – any chopped nuts would do, but that nubbly texture, among all the plump-soaked fruit, is most desirable.

CUTS INTO APPROX. 14 SLICES

250ml strong black tea	2 teaspoons ground ginger
500g medjool dates	½ teaspoon ground cloves
150g natural colour glacé cherries	200g good-quality marmalade (see Intro), plus more to brush on the cake
150g dried cranberries	
150g sultanas	200g ground almonds
175g dark muscovado sugar	100g chopped almonds
175g coconut oil	3 large eggs, beaten
2 teaspoons ground cinnamon	
	1 x 20cm springform cake tin

- Preheat the oven to 150°C/gas mark 2. Using your springform cake tin as a template, cut out a baking parchment circle for the bottom, and then make a lining for the sides of the tin that is about 6cm higher than the height of the tin itself. Do this by making a very long rectangular strip of baking parchment, then fold the long bottom edge in by about 2cm, as if turning up a hem, then take a pair of scissors and snip into this hem at intervals as if to make a rough frill. Curl this around the inside of the tin, with the frilly edge flat on the bottom, and then sit your parchment circle on top of the frilled bit to hold it in place.

- Make your tea: I just pour 250ml boiling water over a teabag, let it steep, and make sure I take out the bag before adding the tea to the pan. Remove the stones from the dates, and snip each date into 4 pieces, using scissors. Halve the glacé cherries, also using scissors. Of course, you can use a knife if you prefer.

- Get out a saucepan that will take all the ingredients, including the tea, and put everything in it except for the almonds and eggs. Place on the heat, stirring to mix, and stir every now and again until it comes to a bubble. Then turn down the heat and let it simmer for 10 minutes, stirring frequently. The stirring not only helps the dates break up and "dissolve", but it also keeps the heat even and stops the mixture catching on the bottom of the pan. After 10 minutes, take the pan off the heat and let the batter stand for 30 minutes; an hour wouldn't matter.

- Stir in the ground and chopped almonds, followed by the beaten eggs, and when it's all combined — though frankly I could eat the batter just like this — pour it into the prepared tin and even out the top with a spatula, then bake for 1½–1¾ hours. The sides will be coming away from the tin, and the cake, while squidgy, should leave only a slight stickiness (rather than any actual batter) on a cake tester.

- Remove to a wire rack, brush with about 3 tablespoons of marmalade and let the cake cool in its tin (if your marmalade is firm, you may need to warm it a bit first to make it brushable — 20–30 seconds in the microwave, or warmed through in a small saucepan should do). Leave for a day before eating. I like to brush a little more bitter marmalade on top again, before slicing and serving. Obviously, you must feel free to decorate further and more seasonally if you wish.

MAKE AHEAD NOTE	STORE NOTE
The cake can be made 1 week ahead. Wrap the cooled cake in a double layer of baking parchment or greaseproof paper and a layer of foil. Store in an airtight container in a cool place.	Once cut, store the cake – still wrapped in baking parchment and foil – in an airtight container for up to 1 month.

Gluten-free apple and blackberry pie

Generally, my way of tackling gluten-free baking is simply to exclude flour altogether – as various recipes both here and on my website testify – because, unless you are a coeliac or are cooking for a coeliac, I don't really see the point of trying to come up with substitutes, which all too often are lesser choices rather than equal alternatives. However, I was cooking for a late-diagnosed coeliac, and one who felt sorely deprived of pie, and clearly this was a sad state of affairs that I couldn't let stand. After an amount of research, I found my pie pastry in *The How Can It Be Gluten Free Cookbook*, published by the estimable America's Test Kitchen. I did have to quash my qualms about xanthan gum (which, despite its name, is a powder) and I'm glad I did: this pastry is indeed no lesser choice – you'd have to tell people it was gluten-free in order for them to realize – and is a public service on behalf of pie-deprived coeliacs everywhere.

I love the look of a pie baked in one of those old-fashioned looking cast-iron skillets – and I wouldn't want to cook without them generally – but you can just as easily use a pie dish, though go for a metal rather than ceramic one. Although this recipe makes enough dough to line and cover a 22cm pan or dish, I am faced with the choice, in my kitchen, between a 20cm or 25cm diameter pan, so I use the former.

Should you want to make this dairy-free, then use the same weight of coconut oil (when solid) as butter, replace the sour cream with soy or coconut yogurt, and put the pan or dish, once lined with pastry dough, in the fridge for 5 minutes before adding the fruit.

FOR THE FRUIT FILLING:

1 x 15ml tablespoon (15g) unsalted butter

2 medium Bramley apples (approx. 500g), peeled, cored and sliced or chopped

2 x 15ml tablespoons (30g) white granulated sugar

½ teaspoon ground cinnamon

250g blackberries

⅛ teaspoon xanthan gum

FOR THE PASTRY:

200g cold unsalted butter

80ml ice-cold water

3 x 15ml tablespoons (45ml) sour cream

1 x 15ml tablespoon rice vinegar

365g gluten-free plain flour

1 x 15ml tablespoon (15g) white sugar

1 teaspoon salt

½ teaspoon xanthan gum

TO BAKE:

1 egg white, lightly whisked (till just frothy)

½ teaspoon white granulated sugar

1 x 20 or 22cm pie dish or cast-iron frying pan

○ Start with the filling. Melt the butter in a wide, heavy-based pan, then add the sliced or chopped apples, sugar and cinnamon, turning everything about in the pan, and cooking for about 3 minutes or until the apples soften and make a caramelly liquid in the bottom of the pan. Add the blackberries, stir gently, then take off the heat, mix in the xanthan gum and leave to cool.

○ Now for the pastry. Cut the cold butter into 5mm cubes and place on a plate in the freezer for 15 minutes while you get on with the rest of the ingredients.

○ Mix the water, sour cream and rice vinegar together in a jug or bowl.

○ Tip the gluten-free flour, sugar, salt and xanthan gum into a food processor and blitz quickly to combine.

○ When the butter's had its 15 minutes of fame in the freezer, add it to the flour mixture in the processor and give about 10 pulses, until the butter is the size of large peas.

○ Pour in half the sour cream mixture and pulse till incorporated. About 3–5 pulses should do it: the mixture will be crumbly and quite fine.

○ Pour in the remaining sour cream mixture and process until the dough just begins to come together, clumping around the blades.

○ Tip out the pastry and form into 2 equal-sized balls, then flatten each into discs, wrap in clingfilm and put in the fridge for 40 minutes to rest. Preheat the oven to 200°C/gas mark 6, and slip in a baking sheet to heat up at the same time.

- When the discs of pastry have had their time to rest in the fridge, take 1 of the discs and roll out between 2 pieces of greaseproof or parchment paper. It is important not to add any flour to the pastry during the rolling process.

- Roll out the pastry so that it is big enough to line the bottom and sides of your dish or pan, with about 4cm of overhang. Take off the top layer of greaseproof or parchment, then turn the pastry upside down over your dish and carefully peel off the remaining paper.

- Ease the pastry into your dish, pressing it into the sides. Take out the remaining disc of pastry and roll out in the same way. Then tip the apple and blackberry mixture into the pie case and dampen the lip of the pastry with a little of the frothy egg white. Peel away the top layer of paper off the pastry lid and flip it over the top of the filled pie, discarding the last remaining layer of paper.

- Cut around the overhang of pastry with a knife and then seal the edge by either crimping or pressing it down with the prongs of a fork. Cut a few slits in the centre of the pie for steam to escape, then paint the top with the egg white and sprinkle with the sugar.

- Bake for 30–40 minutes, or until the pastry is cooked and golden. Remove from the oven and let the pie sit for 15–30 minutes before slicing.

MAKE AHEAD NOTE	STORE NOTE	FREEZE NOTE
Pastry dough can be made 2 days ahead. Wrap in clingfilm and store in fridge, and let it stand at room temperature for 20–30 minutes before rolling. Very chilled dough may need to stand for 30 minutes at room temperature before rolling. Filling can be made 1 day ahead. Once cool, transfer to an airtight container or covered bowl and store in fridge until needed. Pie can be assembled 3–4 hours ahead of baking, but glaze just before baking. The pie will keep warm for up to 1 hour after baking if left in a warm place.	Store in fridge in an airtight container or loosely covered with clingfilm or foil for up to 5 days. Best reheated before serving. Reheat portions in an oven preheated to 150°C/gas mark 2 for 20–30 minutes.	Pastry dough can be frozen: wrap discs of dough tightly in clingfilm and put in a resealable bag or wrap in foil. Freeze for up to 3 months and defrost overnight in fridge. Freeze leftover portions in airtight containers. Defrost overnight in fridge and reheat as Store Note.

Bitter orange tart

Since my Seville Orange Tart in *How To Eat*, I've never stopped feeling the urgent need to use Seville oranges for their short season between December and February (as you will see elsewhere in this book), but that bitter orange taste is too good to forsake during the long months that Seville oranges are not about. Then I simply try to recreate their floral sharpness by using regular orange and lime juices in something approximating a 2:1 ratio. And although I am not someone who uses the deep freeze as one great, efficiently stacked culinary filing cabinet, I do try and make little packages of the zest and juice of 4 Seville oranges just for this; then when I run out, I use the eating orange and lime combo.

This is more than a simplified revision of the *How To Eat* recipe: it uses a crushed gingernut-and-butter base in place of home-made pastry, and is even more acerbically – and excitingly – sharp than its predecessor. I love its cheek-squeaky, sherbetty bitterness, but I serve a small pot of good honey alongside, and urge everyone (to the point of irritation) to drizzle some over as they eat.

I have to say, that when Seville oranges *are* in season, this tart looks like a disc of winter sunshine on the plate – and tastes like it, too. I love it particularly after the Asian-Flavoured Short Ribs or Italian Veal Shank Stew (**pp.179** and **185**), but don't want to restrict its application in any way. I must also add that the curd is just as fabulous spread over toasted crumpets or proper white bread.

FOR THE BASE:

250g gingernuts or plain ginger biscuits

75g soft unsalted butter

FOR THE CURD FILLING:

3 large eggs

2 egg yolks

100g caster sugar

zest and juice of 4 Seville oranges (about 200ml juice) or use 60ml lime juice (from 2–3 limes) and 140ml orange juice (from 1 large or 2 medium oranges)

150g soft unsalted butter, cut into 1cm cubes

TO SERVE:

good runny honey

1 x 24cm loose-bottomed, shallow flan tin (approx. 5cm deep)

° Process the ginger biscuits until crumbled and no longer whole, then add the butter and process again, patiently waiting until it begins to clump and look like damp, dark sand. If you don't have a processor, put the ginger biscuits in a freezer bag or resealable plastic bag, and bash with a rolling pin or similar heavy implement, even if it has to be one with less comedy value. Melt the butter, and transfer the crumbs to a bowl. Mix in the melted butter until the crumbs are evenly coated.

° Tip into your flan tin, and carefully spread the biscuit base all around the tin and up the sides; you can do this with your hands or the back of a spoon.

° Put the tin in the fridge, to allow the biscuit base to harden, for at least 1 hour – although it may take up to 2 hours if your fridge is stacked. I often find it easier to get the base done in advance, so it's coolly ready and waiting, in which case, I do it up to 2 days ahead.

° Once your base is set firm you can get on with your curd filling. In a heavy-based saucepan – off the heat – whisk together the eggs (both the whole eggs and the yolks) and sugar, making sure you incorporate them well.

° Add the zest (grate gently so you don't get the pith, too) and juice from the oranges along with the cubes of butter, then put the pan over a medium heat and cook, stirring constantly; I use a small flat whisk for this.

° This thickening process will take about 5–7 minutes, but do take it off the heat regularly during this time, while you carry on whisking, to prevent it from getting too hot. Once the curd has thickened, take it off the heat, keep whisking for about 30 seconds, and carry on doing so as you pour it straight into a jug (it makes about 550ml). Then place a piece of dampened baking parchment or greaseproof paper on top of the filling (this will stop it forming a skin), and let it cool in the fridge for about 30 minutes.

○ Once the filling has cooled, but not set solid, pour and scrape it into your biscuit-lined tin and spread it out evenly.

○ Let the tart set further in the fridge for at least 4 hours (or overnight), and up to 2 days, before unmoulding. This is best done while it is still cold – so don't take it out of the fridge for more than 5–10 minutes before you want to cut it. Then serve in slices, with a little pot of honey for people to drizzle over as they wish.

MAKE AHEAD NOTE	STORE NOTE
Base can be made 2–3 days in advance and stored in fridge until needed, covered loosely with clingfilm. Once firm, the base (in its tin) can also be wrapped tightly in a double layer of clingfilm and a layer of foil and frozen for up to 1 month. Defrost in fridge for 2–3 hours before filling. Curd can be made 2 days ahead. Fill the tart and refrigerate for about 4 hours, until the curd has become firmer, then tent loosely with foil, trying not to touch the surface of the tart.	Leftovers can be stored in fridge for 2 days. The tart base will soften gradually as the tart stands.

Salted chocolate tart

I have always avoided making chocolate tarts, not out of laziness (I love a bit of pastry-making, in the right mood), but because I have never really felt that the pastry served the chocolate, or was worth the effort here. This is my simple solution: make a base out of chocolate biscuits. And the filling is just as easy to make, too. Not that you'd know from the taste. I never lie about how effortless something is to make, but no one will believe me on this one. I think the hit of salt is crucial: it subtly counters the richness of all the chocolate, so even if you don't normally go in for the sweet-salt combo, don't be tempted to leave it out. Halve the amount of salt, if you must. I am having a bit of a smoked salt moment (see the Smoky Salted Caramel Sauce on **p.342**) and urge you to try the flakes in general and, in particular, here.

If you want to, of course, you can use Bourbon biscuits for the base: Oreos give that dramatic espresso-blackness, but the more Aztec-earth brown of the Bourbon base will highlight the darkness of the filling.

CUTS INTO 14 SLICES

FOR THE BASE:

2 x 154g packets Oreos (28 biscuits in all)

50g dark chocolate (min. 70% cocoa solids)

50g soft unsalted butter

½ teaspoon smoked sea salt flakes (see Intro)

1 x 23cm deep-sided (approx. 5cm deep), loose-bottomed flan tin

○ Snap the biscuits into pieces and drop them into the bowl of a food processor. Do likewise with the chocolate, then blitz them together until you have crumbs. Add the butter and salt, and blitz again until the mixture starts to clump together. If you're doing this by hand, bash the biscuits in a freezer bag until they form crumbs, finely chop the chocolate and melt the butter, then mix everything, along with the salt, in a large bowl with a wooden spoon or your hands encased in disposable vinyl gloves.

○ Press into your tart tin and pat down on the bottom and up the sides of the tin with your hands or the back of a spoon, so that the base and sides are evenly lined and smooth. Put into the fridge to chill and harden for at least 1 hour, or 2 hours if your fridge is stacked. I wouldn't keep it for longer than a day like this as the Oreo crust tends to get too crumbly.

FOR THE FILLING:

100g dark chocolate (min. 70% cocoa solids)

25g cornflour

60ml full-fat milk

500ml double cream

50g cocoa, sieved

2 teaspoons instant espresso powder or strong instant coffee powder

75g caster sugar

1 teaspoon vanilla paste or extract

2 teaspoons extra-virgin olive oil

¾ teaspoon smoked sea salt flakes

° Finely chop the chocolate. Put the cornflour into a cup and whisk in the milk until smooth. (I find it easier to use cups for the liquids – in which case the milk measure is equivalent to an American quarter cup, and you'll need 2 cups of cream.)

° Pour the cream into a heavy-based saucepan into which all the ingredients can fit and be stirred without splashing out of the pan, then add the finely chopped rubble of chocolate, the sieved cocoa (or just sieve it straight in), espresso or instant coffee powder, sugar, vanilla paste or extract, olive oil and smoked salt. Place over a medium to low heat and whisk gently – I use a very small whisk for this, as I'm not aiming to get air in the mixture, I'm just trying to banish any lumpiness – as the cream heats and the chocolate starts melting.

○ Off the heat, whisk in the cornflour and milk mixture until it, too, is smoothly incorporated, and put the pan back on a low heat. With a wooden spoon, keep stirring until the mixture thickens, which it will do around the 10-minute mark, but be prepared for it to take a few minutes more or less. Take the pan off the heat every so often, still stirring, so that everything melds together, without the cream coming to a boil. When ready, it should be thick enough to coat the back of a wooden spoon, and if you run your finger through it (across the back of the spoon) the line should stay.

○ Pour into a wide measuring jug or batter jug (it should come to about the 600ml mark). Now run a piece of baking parchment or greaseproof paper under the cold tap, wring it out and place the damp, crumpled piece right on top of the chocolate mixture, then put the jug into the fridge for 15 minutes. The mixture will still be warm, but will be the right temperature to ooze into the base without melting it.

○ Pour and scrape the mixture into the biscuit-lined flan tin and put back in the fridge overnight. Don't leave it longer than 24 hours, as the base will start to soften.

○ Take out of the fridge for 10 minutes before serving, but unmould straight away. Sit the flan tin on top of a large tin or jar and let the ring part fall away, then transfer the dramatically revealed tart to a plate or board. Leave the tin base on.

○ Slice modestly – this is rich and sweet, and people can always come back for more – and serve with crème fraîche; the sharpness is just right here. Leftovers will keep in the fridge for 4–5 days, but the base will soften and the sides crumble a bit. That will not detract from your eating pleasure too much, but I still like to give it its first outing at optimal stage!

MAKE AHEAD NOTE	STORE NOTE
Base can be made 1 day ahead. When firm, cover and keep refrigerated until needed.	Store the tart in fridge until needed. Leftovers will keep in fridge for 4–5 days. The base will soften gradually as the tart stands.
Tart/filling can be made 1 day ahead. Fill tart and refrigerate overnight, until set. Tent with foil, trying not to touch the surface of the tart.	

Honey pie

As anyone who follows me on Instagram (I'm @nigellalawson for anyone asking) knows, I have something of an obsession with The Four & Twenty Blackbirds Pie Shop in Brooklyn and nothing but gratitude for their mission to share the pie-love. It all started with their Salty Honey Pie, and this is my version of it. Nothing much is different – why mess with perfection? – but mine does have an easier-to-make pie crust, a pastry for those with (apologies to Mel Brooks) Pie Anxiety. I've fiddled with the balance of ingredients in the filling – this latter point is hardly worth mentioning, but I feel any deviation from a recipe should be openly made. And, by the way, you shouldn't have to limit yourself to just one of their pies: luckily, *The Four & Twenty Blackbirds Pie Book* exists to put that right. I find the saltiness here tempers the rich, honeyed sweetness, but if you prefer to embrace its intensity head on, reduce the salt in the filling to 1 teaspoon. But in either case, it's essential you use sea salt flakes, not pouring salt.

Pie-pedants will insist it is, in fact, a tart, since it doesn't have a pastry lid, but this is an American recipe, and if pastry is involved in America, it's a pie. OK? Anyway, why would you not want to glory in the chance to make something called Honey Pie?

Now, you know that I am not one for mean portions. So believe me when I say you must cut this into modest slices. Partly because it is very intense, and partly because it is just too annoying if people don't finish, and you could have had some slices left for when they've gone.

CUTS INTO 14 SLICES

FOR THE PASTRY:

225g plain flour

½ teaspoon fine sea salt

125ml light and mild olive oil

60ml full-fat milk

FOR THE PIE FILLING:

100g soft unsalted butter

150g caster sugar

1 x 15ml tablespoon fine polenta (not instant) or cornmeal

2 teaspoons sea salt flakes

1 teaspoon vanilla paste or extract

175ml (250g) good runny honey

3 large eggs

150ml double cream

2 teaspoons cider vinegar

TO SPRINKLE ON TOP:

¼ teaspoon sea salt flakes

1 x 23cm deep-sided (approx. 5cm deep), loose-bottomed flan tin

- First, mix the flour, salt, oil and milk to form a rough, slightly damp, dough. You can do this by hand or at low speed in a freestanding mixer.

- Tip out into your flan tin, and press patiently over the base and a little up the sides of the tin. I find a mixture of fingers, knuckles and the back of a spoon the easiest way to go. Put into the freezer for at least 1 hour. I tend to do this the day before, but in any event, you bake from frozen.

- Preheat the oven to 180°C/gas mark 4 and pop in a baking sheet at the same time.

- Melt the butter in a medium saucepan. Take it off the heat and leave to stand for 5 minutes, then beat in the sugar, polenta or cornmeal, 2 teaspoons of sea salt flakes and the vanilla paste or extract.

- When all the above ingredients are incorporated, stir in the honey – oiling the bowl or jug you're measuring it in first – and beat in the eggs, followed by the cream and vinegar.

- Take the pastry-lined flan tin out of the freezer and pour the honey mixture into the case, then place on the baking sheet in the oven to bake for 45–50 minutes, turning it around after 30, at which time it will still seem very uncooked. When it's ready, it will be a burnished bronze on top, puffy at the edges and set in a soft jellied way in the middle (and it carries on setting as it cools).

- Remove to a wire rack, sprinkle with the ¼ teaspoonful of sea salt flakes, and leave to cool – this will take about 2 hours. I like this best when properly cold.

- To unmould easily, sit the flan tin on top of a large jar or tin and let the ring part fall away, then transfer the liberated pie to a plate or board. I manage to get the pie off the flan base easily, but if you feel safer leaving the metal base on, then do. Slice modestly – this is rich and sweet, and you will want leftovers for yourself – and serve with clotted cream or crème fraîche.

MAKE AHEAD NOTE	STORE NOTE
The crust can be made up to 1 month ahead. Once frozen, wrap the crust (in its tin) in a double layer of clingfilm and a layer of foil. Bake directly from frozen.	Leftovers should be refrigerated as quickly as possible. Store in fridge, loosely covered with clingfilm, for up to 3 days.

Lemon pavlova

Ever since my first pav in *How To Eat*, I have been something of a pavaholic. For me, acidity is key. I never understood why anyone would pile sweet fruit on top of something that is essentially – and dreamily – a cross between a marshmallow and a meringue. So naturally, a lemon pavlova made perfect sense. I had the idea – yes, really – from the actor Michael Sheen. This didn't come in the form of a personal tip, I should admit. I saw him create a great pile of lemony pavs on BBC Two's *The Great Comic Relief Bake Off*, and it inspired me. *Diolch* Michael (if I may).

You will note there are a lot of flaked almonds required: that is because they are the topping of the pav and not mere decoration; the crunch they offer is essential.

I make this with a jar of shop-bought lemon curd, but obviously I wouldn't stop you from making your own. Should you want, proceed as follows: whisk together 2 large eggs, the yolks from 2 further large eggs and 150g caster sugar in a heavy-based saucepan (off the heat). Add the finely grated zest and juice of 2 unwaxed lemons and 100g soft unsalted butter, cut into 1cm cubes or teaspooned out into similar-sized blobs, and put the pan over a medium heat, stirring constantly with a little flat whisk, until thickened. This will take around 5–7 minutes, but keep taking it off the heat – stirring or whisking all the while – at regular intervals during this time. When thickened, pour and scrape into a cold bowl and let it cool, stirring occasionally.

I am childishly excited about this pavlova: a reminder that good ideas come unbidden, much as happiness does.

SERVES 8–12

6 egg whites (feel free to use egg whites from a carton, such as Two Chicks, if wished)	50g flaked almonds
375g caster sugar	300ml double cream
2½ teaspoons cornflour	1 x 325g jar lemon curd (see Intro)
2 unwaxed lemons	

- Preheat the oven to 180°C/gas mark 4 and line a baking tray with baking parchment.

- Beat the egg whites until satiny peaks form, then beat in the sugar a spoonful at a time until the meringue is stiff and shiny.

- Sprinkle the cornflour over the meringue, then grate in the zest – a fine microplane is best for this – of 1 lemon and add 2 teaspoons of lemon juice.

- Gently fold until everything is thoroughly mixed in. Mound onto the lined baking tray in a fat circle approximately 23cm in diameter, smoothing the sides and the top with a knife or spatula.

- Place in the oven, then immediately turn the temperature down to 150°C/gas mark 2, and cook for 1 hour.

- Remove from the oven and leave to cool, but don't leave it anywhere cold as this will make it crack too quickly. If you think your kitchen is too cool, then leave the pavlova inside the oven with the door completely open. When you're ready to eat, turn the pavlova onto a large flat plate or board with the underside uppermost – I do this before I sit down to the meal in question and let it stand till pudding time. This is so the tender marshmallow belly of the pav melds with the soft topping.

- Toast the flaked almonds, by frying them in a dry pan over a medium to high heat until they have started to colour. Shake the pan at regular intervals and don't let them burn. This doesn't take more than a minute or so. When they're done, remove to a cold plate so that they don't carry on cooking.

- Whip the cream until thick and airy but still with a soft voluptuousness about it, and set it aside for a mo.

- Put the lemon curd into a bowl and beat it with a wooden spoon or spatula to loosen it a little. Taste the lemon curd (if it's shop-bought) and add some lemon zest and a spritz of juice if it's too sweet.

- With a light hand, a glad heart and a spatula, spread the lemon curd on top of the meringue base. Now top with the whipped cream, peaking it rather as if it were a meringue topping. Sprinkle with the zest of the remaining lemon – you can grate this finely or coarsely as you wish – followed by the flaked almonds, and serve triumphantly.

MAKE AHEAD NOTE	STORE NOTE
Meringue base can be made 1 day ahead. Store in an airtight container until needed.	Leftovers can be stored in fridge, loosely covered with clingfilm, for up to 1 day.
Curd can be made up to 3 days ahead. Cover and store in fridge until needed. Stir before using.	
Almonds can be toasted a week ahead. When cold, store in an airtight container at room temperature until needed.	
Assemble the pavlova about 1 hour ahead of serving.	

Old Rag Pie

Old Rag Pie is not the most glamorous name for something which, while being incredibly simple to make, will have you, and anyone who eats it, in raptures. The name is the English translation for the Greek *Patsavouropita*, created by bakeries as a way of using up old scraps of filo pastry: the "old rags" indicated by the title. They'd just go along their counters, collect up all the bits and turn them into this pie. For this reason, you don't need to worry about keeping your filo covered as you go, as is normally advised. It doesn't matter if it dries out a little as you make it, indeed this can even be desirable.

In Greece, there are two variants, one sweet, one savoury, but this version is the brainchild of my friend Alex Andreou (a bona fide – if it's not too rude to go into Latin here – Greek from Mykonos, and the source of other recipes here, too) which merges the two, adding honey to salty feta, to create what I can best describe (in taste terms) as a Greek cheesecake.

I have made this with a variety of filo pastries, and I have found that the more widely available brands are too damp and too heavily sprinkled with flour to do the job well. Luckily, those brands make a frozen filo, which doesn't seem to suffer from the same problems, which is why I stipulate this, below. (The other benefit of using frozen filo is that – given that feta has such a long shelf life – you can keep all the ingredients to make this in your freezer, fridge and storecupboard without an extra visit to the shops.) However, should you be lucky enough to have access to good-quality, authentic filo, then please use fresh. And if you plan to freeze the pie before baking it, then you will definitely have to start with fresh, not frozen filo for sure. Since the packets of frozen filo come in 270g weights, that is what I have used, but another 75–100g or so wouldn't go amiss. So, if you can buy this in bigger packets, or are buying fresh by weight, go ahead, but don't break open a second packet for it.

I'm afraid this Patsavouropita does make for an annoyingly difficult tin-washing-up later, but when you eat this, you'll know it's worth it. Tip: use bio washing powder for clothes, or a dishwasher powder, rather than washing-up liquid when you soak.

100g soft unsalted butter	2 large eggs
1 x 270g packet frozen filo pastry, thawed	150ml full-fat milk
250g feta cheese	1 x 15ml tablespoon sesame seeds
2 teaspoons grated Parmesan	1 jar good runny honey (such as Greek thyme honey or orange blossom honey)
2 teaspoons fresh thyme leaves or 1 teaspoon dried	
	1 x 20cm square cake tin

- Melt the butter in a small saucepan, then take it off the heat.

- Line your cake tin with a layer of filo, making sure it comes up the sides; you will need to use more than one sheet. Then pour 1 tablespoon of melted butter over the pastry.

- Using one third of the remaining filo sheets, tear and scrunch the sheets up and drop them loosely in the tin. Then crumble in half the feta, sprinkle with 1 teaspoon of Parmesan and just under ½ teaspoon of thyme leaves (or ¼ teaspoon of dried thyme) and pour a third of the remaining melted butter over the top.

- Repeat, so that you use up all but a little of the butter and a small amount of thyme. For the last layer, you can use larger pieces of filo "rags" (as it's the lid), filling the tin a little more tightly, but still scrunching them.

- Fold the edges of overhanging filo over themselves, and pour the remaining butter on top. Using the sharp point of a knife, make 2 cuts down and 2 cuts across into the filo-packed tin, from edge to edge to create 9 sections. It's important that you don't use a blunt knife, as you don't want to drag the filo or press down on it.

- Beat the eggs with the milk, then pour over the contents of the tin. Sprinkle the last bit of thyme along with the sesame seeds on top. Let it stand for at least 30 minutes in a cool place before baking. If 2 hours is easier for your timetable, then put it in the fridge. And you can do this in advance (see Note, right).

- Heat the oven to 200°C/gas mark 6, and bake the pie for 30 minutes. When it's ready, the pastry will be golden and puffed up, and the inside set.

- Let it stand for 10 minutes, then spoon 1 tablespoon of the honey over the top.

- Cut into slices or slabs – using a serrated bread knife and sawing action to prevent squishing the filo on top too much, then pushing the knife down to cut through. Serve the pie directly from the tin and put the jar of honey, with a spoon in it (or you can pour it into a jug) on the table for people to add extra as they eat.

MAKE AHEAD NOTE	STORE NOTE	FREEZE NOTE
The pie can be made 1 day in advance and kept in fridge. Pie can also be frozen at this stage, in which case cook from frozen, as Freeze Note.	The pie is best on the day it is made, but leftovers can be stored in fridge, on a plate covered with clingfilm or in an airtight container, for up to 2 days. Slices can be reheated in an oven preheated to 150°C/gas mark 2 for 15–30 minutes, until piping hot. Cool for 5 minutes before serving (this will crisp up the filo again).	Wrap tin tightly in a double layer of clingfilm and a layer of foil. Freeze for up to 1 month. To cook from frozen, unwrap the tin and put into a cold oven, then turn the oven on to 200°C/gas mark 6 and bake for 45–55 minutes. If the top browns too much (check at about 40 minutes), cover with foil. Make sure the pie is piping hot in the centre before removing from oven. Leftovers can also be frozen, tightly wrapped in a double layer of clingfilm and then put into a resealable bag or wrapped in foil, for up to 1 month. Thaw overnight in fridge and reheat as Store Note.

Chocolate chip cookie dough pots

My children love a chocolate chip cookie so gooey on the inside that I can't really make the outside firm enough to let the cookies keep integrity of form. This, then, is the solution: a cookie dough you bake in a little dish, and then eat with a spoon, dolloped with ice cream or crème fraîche as desired. The recipe itself I've adapted from one I found on a favourite website, thekitchn.com, and very grateful I am, too.

If you don't own any ramekins, or similar, know that you could just use a pie dish; I used one that measures 20cm diameter at the base and 24cm diameter at the lip, and it needed 5 minutes' longer cooking time. But the ramekins give you a better goo-to-crust ratio, and that's what these are all about.

I know I blamed my children for them (what else are children for?), but don't think of these just as junior fare: any time you're having friends over for supper and don't know what to make for pudding, this is the answer.

SERVES 6

150g plain flour

½ teaspoon fine sea salt

½ teaspoon bicarbonate of soda

110g soft unsalted butter

85g soft light brown sugar

1 teaspoon vanilla paste or extract

1 large egg

170g dark chocolate chips

6 x ramekins approx. 8cm diameter x 4.5cm deep (approx. 200ml capacity)

○ Preheat the oven to 180°C/gas mark 4, and measure the flour, salt and bicarb into a bowl, forking together to mix.

○ With an electric mixer, or by hand, beat the butter and sugar until you have a light and creamy mixture, then add the vanilla paste or extract and the egg, beating again to incorporate.

○ Gently fold in the flour mixture, then, once it's all mixed in, fold in the chocolate chips.

○ Divide the dough between 6 ramekins (you will need about 4½ tablespoons of batter for each one). Using a small offset spatula (for ease) or the back of a teaspoon, spread the mixture to cover the bottom of the ramekins, and smooth the tops.

○ Place the ramekins on a baking sheet and bake in the oven for 13–15 minutes. They will still be quite gooey inside, but the top will be set, and they should be golden brown at the edges and just beginning to come away from the sides of the ramekins.

○ Leave to cool for 5–10 minutes before serving. You can spoon a scoop of ice cream on top of each one or serve with cream or crème fraîche on the side. They will set as they cool down, so don't dally now.

MAKE AHEAD NOTE	FREEZE NOTE
These can be made up to 6 hours ahead, then covered with clingfilm and stored in fridge. Allow to come up to room temperature before baking.	Wrap each ramekin tightly in a double layer of clingfilm and put in resealable bags or wrap each in a layer of foil. Freeze for up to 3 months. Bake directly from frozen, adding an extra 2 minutes to the baking time.

Nutella brownies

When I made these the first time, I put them on the table after supper and I have never seen a plateful of anything go down so fast. Naturally, I have been making them a lot ever since. As the ingredients – yes, all of them – are among my kitchen basics, I know I always have the wherewithal to make these, unplanned. Having said that, this is one of those recipes which is actually better the following day, not that it's likely you'll get a chance to find out.

MAKES 16 SQUARES

4 large eggs

pinch fine sea salt

250ml (270g) Nutella

½ teaspoon icing sugar

1 x 20cm square cake tin

○ Preheat your oven to 180°C/gas mark 4. Line the base and sides of your cake tin with baking parchment.

○ Break the eggs into a mixing bowl, then add the salt and beat, using a freestanding mixer with the whisk attachment or electric handheld whisk, until they have more than doubled in size and are pale, aerated and mousselike; this will take about 5 minutes.

○ Measure the Nutella into a microwave-safe jug, filling it up to the 250ml mark, and microwave for 1 minute at 750 watt. Or you can soften it in a heatproof bowl over (but not in) a saucepan of simmering water for 3–4 minutes, stirring occasionally, until warm and slightly runny.

○ Stir the heated Nutella, then pour it in a continuous thin stream onto the eggs, whisking as you go, until all the Nutella is combined. This will knock the volume out of the eggs quite a bit, but don't worry about it.

○ Pour this mixture into your prepared cake tin and bake for 17–20 minutes, by which time the top will be dry, and the middle tender but set in a slightly jellied fashion.

○ Leave to cool completely in the tin; the mixture will shrink away from the sides a little as it does. Once cool, cut it into 16 squares, arrange them on a plate and dust with a little icing sugar pressed through a fine tea strainer or sieve.

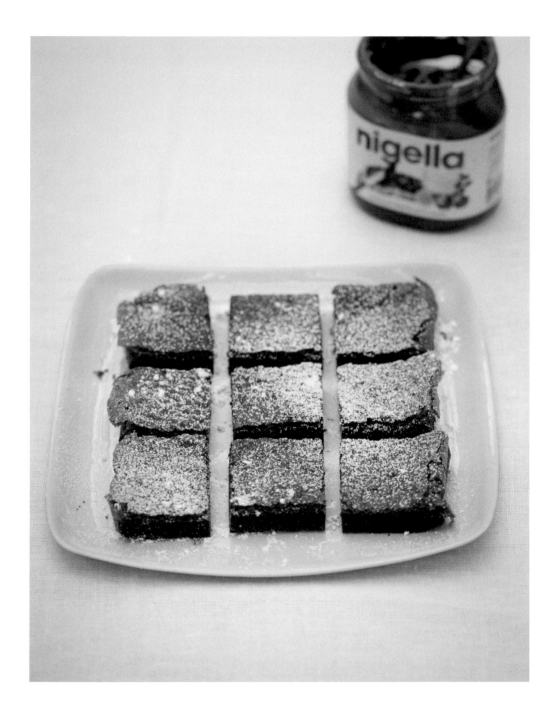

STORE NOTE	FREEZE NOTE
Store in an airtight container in a cool place for up to 5 days or in fridge for up to 1 week. In hot weather, store in fridge.	Stack the squares in an airtight container with baking parchment in between the layers. Freeze for up to 3 months. To defrost, put squares on a wire rack and leave at room temperature for about 1 hour, or defrost overnight in fridge.

Flourless peanut butter chocolate chip cookies

I can't seem to stop making these, and as I make them, so they get eaten. Luckily, they are extraordinarily easy to throw together. And, incidentally, they are gluten- and dairy-free. Do check the ingredients list on the peanut butter if you do absolutely need this to be gluten-free (were you to be baking them for a coeliac, for example) as brands vary. I'm afraid health-food-shop-type peanut butter (the sort I like on my toast) doesn't work here.

These do soften if left overnight – though there are those who actively prefer them this way – and are crisper when freshly cooked, though they will be fine from any other point of view in an airtight container for up to a week. Good luck with that.

MAKES 16 COOKIES

225g smooth peanut butter, such as Skippy

100g soft light brown sugar

½ teaspoon bicarbonate of soda

pinch fine sea salt

1 large egg

1 teaspoon vanilla paste or extract

50g dark chocolate chips (I use Dove's Farm here, which are good and small, and are also free from gluten, milk and soya)

○ Preheat the oven to 180°C/gas mark 4.

○ In a bowl, beat together the peanut butter, brown sugar, bicarb and salt.

○ Beat in the egg and vanilla extract, but not too vigorously: just to mix them; gently does it.

○ Stir or fold in the chocolate chips, then line 1 or 2 baking sheets with baking parchment.

○ Scoop out heaped tablespoonfuls of the cookie dough onto the lined sheets, placing them about 5 or 6cm apart, then bake for 10 minutes, until they're slightly darker around the edges. They will look undercooked but will be the perfect texture once cooled (if you can wait that long).

○ At any rate, leave them on the baking sheets for 10 minutes, as they will be very fragile. Then transfer gently to a wire rack to cool. This takes another 10 minutes; I tend to cave in after 5.

MAKE AHEAD NOTE	STORE NOTE	FREEZE NOTE
Form the dough into mounds and freeze on a baking sheet lined with baking parchment. Once solid, transfer to a resealable bag and freeze for up to 3 months. Bake directly from frozen, adding 1 minute to the baking time.	Store in an airtight container at cool room temperature for up to 1 week.	Put baked cookies in a resealable bag, or stack in an airtight container with baking parchment between the layers. Freeze for up to 3 months. Defrost on a wire rack for about 1 hour.

Buckwheat triple chocolate cookies

For those of you not yet familiar with the term procrastibaking, this is a prime example of the genre, and while I have certainly pioneered the practice, the brilliant coinage is one Aya Reina's – I feel it deserves wider circulation, and many congratulations. I was in the middle of the photo shoot for this book when I first made these – I was putting off typing up some recipe changes (admin holds not the greatest lure for me) – and was suddenly gripped by an urgent need to make these cookies. (There's not a book of mine when I haven't gone off-piste from my shoot list to go rogue and introduce a hitherto unplanned recipe.) The recipe itself is adapted from londonbakes.com, which in turn is an adaptation from the book *Chocolate Magic* by Kate Shirazi: this is the story of cooking.

I've fiddled with amounts a bit, only because I wanted a little less sugar and a lot more chocolate, but the star here is the buckwheat, not only because it makes these cookies gluten-free, but mainly because I feel it brings its own nutty flavour and unique texture, creating a cookie that has softness and a shortbready bite, as well as a subtle smokiness. Those who like a truly chewy cookie might find these a little cakey, but I like chewiness in a cookie and yet find constant excuses to make these. They are meltingly good, and entirely sui generis.

Buckwheat flour – rather more exotically *farine de sarrasin* in French, and it's the French flour I habitually use – is in itself always gluten-free, but (as with oats) it is often contaminated by the presence of gluten, depending on the factories in which it is produced. So if you are making these because you need them to be gluten-free, rather than just going for the flavour of the flour, make sure the packet is labelled as such before you start.

MAKES APPROX. 25 COOKIES

150g dark chocolate chips	½ teaspoon fine sea salt
125g dark chocolate (min. 70% cocoa solids)	60g soft unsalted butter
125g buckwheat flour	125g soft dark brown sugar
25g cocoa, sieved	1 teaspoon vanilla paste or extract
½ teaspoon bicarbonate of soda	2 large eggs, fridge-cold

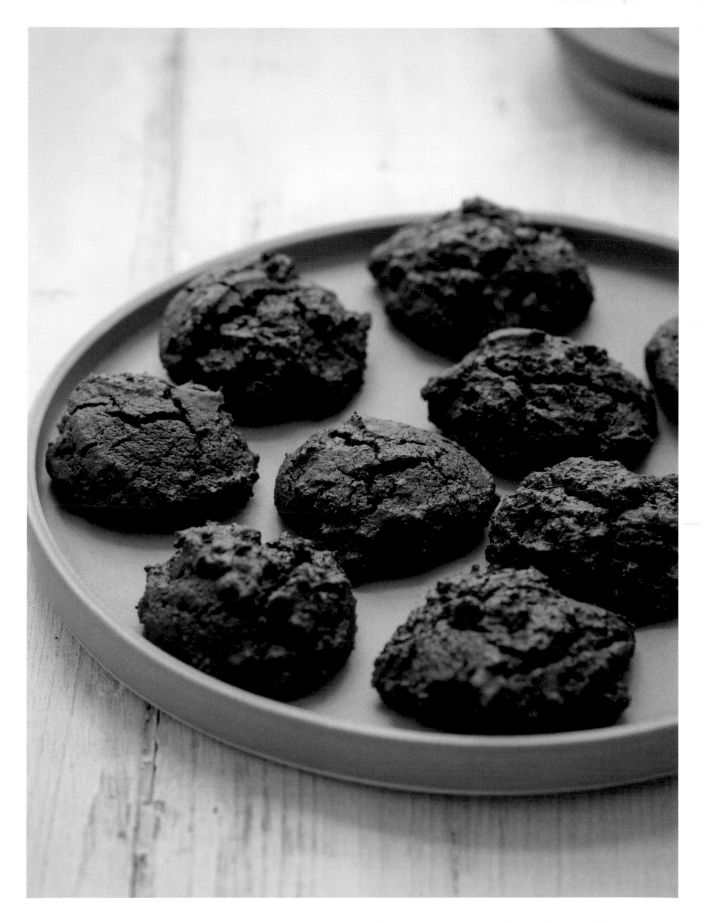

- Clatter the chocolate chips out into a flattish dish and put this in the fridge while you get on with making the batter. It wouldn't hurt to sit them in the freezer, either. I do this so that the chips don't melt too much while baking, leaving you with nuggets of intense chocolatiness.

- Preheat the oven to 180°C/gas mark 4 and line a couple of baking sheets (or 1 if baking in 2 batches) with baking parchment.

- Roughly chop the dark chocolate, and melt it either in a suitable bowl in the microwave or over a pan of simmering water. Set aside to cool a little.

- In another bowl, mix together the buckwheat flour, cocoa, bicarb and salt, and fork to make sure everything's well combined.

- In yet another bowl (I use my freestanding mixer here, but a bowl and a hand-held whisk or, indeed, wooden spoon and elbow grease would work, too), cream together the butter and sugar with the vanilla extract until a dark caramel colour and fluffy, using a spatula to scrape down the sides of the bowl if necessary. Beat in the cooled, melted chocolate then the fridge-cold eggs (I find this means one doesn't then have to refrigerate the dough before baking) one by one, and when both are absorbed into the butter and sugar mixture, scrape down the sides of the bowl again, turn the speed down and carefully beat in the dry ingredients.

- Using a wooden spoon or a spatula, fold in the cold chocolate chips, then dollop rounded tablespoonsful of the dough onto a lined baking sheet, leaving about 6cm between each one. Put the bowl with the remaining cookie dough in the fridge while the first batch is underway.

- Bake for 9–10 minutes, by which time the cookies will be just set at the edges, but otherwise seem undercooked, then remove the sheet from the oven and let the cookies sit on the warm tray for another 10 minutes before transferring them to a wire rack to cool.

- When the tray is cool, or you have another one lined and ready to go, take the bowl of dough out of the fridge and proceed as before.

MAKE AHEAD NOTE	STORE NOTE	FREEZE NOTE
The cookie dough can be made ahead, then covered and stored in fridge for up to 3 days. If the dough is too firm to scoop into tablespoons, let it stand at room temperature for 20 minutes.	Store in an airtight container in a cool place for up to 5 days.	Form the dough into mounds and freeze on a baking sheet lined with baking parchment. Once solid, transfer to a resealable bag and freeze for up to 3 months. Bake directly from frozen, adding 1 minute to the baking time. Baked cookies can also be frozen in resealable plastic bags for up to 3 months. Defrost on a wire rack at room temperature for about 1 hour.

Seed-studded Anzac biscuits

Anzac biscuits, purportedly sent to those serving in the Australian and New Zealand Army Corps during the First World War, significantly contained no ingredients that could spoil on the long voyage. Although I think it is important to remember Anzac Day in the proper fashion each 25 April (this was the date of the first Anzac landing at Gallipoli in 1915), I don't feel it is necessary to make the biscuits as hard, dry and durable as they needed to be then. So, I have taken liberties and added pumpkin seeds, sunflower seeds and sesame seeds, which might not last a long-distance journey without refrigeration, but make for a much more beguilingly textured biscuit. They are like less stodgy flapjacks in biscuit form.

Now, there are those who like their Anzac biscuits crisp, and those – like me – who like them on the chewier side (I also like mine made with sprouted oats). To accommodate both tastes, I have cooked those you see in the picture overleaf in 3 different ways. On the left, the crispest biscuit, cooked with regular oats, for 12 minutes; in the middle, biscuits made with sprouted oats and cooked for 12 minutes; and on the right, my biscuits of choice, using sprouted oats and cooked for 10 minutes. However, don't get hung up on the sprouted oat issue. A far more decisive factor is the cooking time. Those with hotter ovens than me may find the range closer to 8–10 minutes than 10–12.

100g soft unsalted butter	125g plain flour
100g soft light brown sugar	50g unsweetened desiccated coconut
2 x 15ml tablespoons golden syrup	100g sprouted or porridge oats (not instant)
½ teaspoon bicarbonate of soda	25g pumpkin seeds
2 x 15ml tablespoons hot water, from a recently boiled kettle	25g sunflower seeds
	25g sesame seeds

- Preheat the oven to 180°C/gas mark 4 and line 2 large baking sheets with baking parchment (or use 1 if baking in batches).

- In a decent-sized saucepan, big enough to hold all of the ingredients, melt the butter, sugar and golden syrup together, then take off the heat.

- In a bowl, dissolve the bicarbonate of soda in the hot water, then add to the butter mixture in the saucepan.

- Now add the remaining ingredients to the saucepan and combine well.

- Scoop rounded tablespoons of the mixture onto the lined baking sheets, leaving about 2–3cm between these dollops to allow room for the biscuits to spread as they bake, then slightly flatten them with a spatula or the back of a spoon.

- Bake for 8–10 minutes (or a little longer if you want them wholly crisp) until golden brown, swapping the baking sheets over and rotating them halfway through cooking. When cooked, the biscuits will still feel slightly soft, but will harden to a desirable chewiness once cooled.

- Remove from the oven and let the biscuits stand on their sheets for 5 minutes, before using a wide cranked spatula to transfer them to a wire rack to cool.

STORE NOTE	FREEZE NOTE
Store in an airtight container at cool room temperature for up to 1 week. The crisper version of the biscuits will soften slightly over time.	Put cooked biscuits into a resealable bag, or stack in an airtight container with baking parchment between the layers, and freeze for up to 3 months. Defrost individual biscuits on a wire rack for about 1 hour before eating.

No-churn brandied pumpkin ice cream

I have made no-churn ice creams ever since *How To Eat*, but it's fair to say that the One-Step No-Churn Coffee Ice Cream in *Nigellissima* marked the beginning of my flirtation with condensed milk as a simplifying ingredient in lazy ice-cream making. There are people too pure for this kind of dalliance but, while I respect them, I am not among them.

The genesis of this particular recipe is the Pumpkin Bundt Cake on **p.289** or, rather, the fact that having made it, I had a small amount of pumpkin purée left over. I paired it with half a tin of condensed milk, added cream, fresh nutmeg and a splosh or two of brandy and, *eccoci*, a gorgeously spiced and – strange though it sounds – warm-flavoured ice cream. Eat it with its mothercake or the Cider and 5-Spice Bundt Cake on **p.293** or, be radical, and cast it in the role of brandy butter alongside your pudding this Christmas. Those who celebrate Thanksgiving should need little encouragement to bring it out alongside a warm apple or, obviously, pumpkin pie, and it is a damn fine accompaniment to pecan pie, too.

MAKES APPROX. 1 LITRE

125g pumpkin purée (from a can – use the leftover purée from the Pumpkin Bundt Cake on p.289)

½ x 397g tin (150ml) condensed milk

300ml double cream

1 teaspoon freshly grated nutmeg

3 x 15ml tablespoons brandy

2 x 500ml empty ice-cream tubs or airtight containers (or 1 x 1 litre tub or airtight container)

° Combine the pumpkin purée and condensed milk in a bowl, and stir to mix.

° Add the cream and whisk until it begins to thicken.

° Grate the nutmeg over the ice cream and whisk in the brandy as you pour it in a slow trickle.

° Decant into your airtight container or containers and freeze overnight. Take it out of the freezer for 10 minutes to soften before serving.

MAKE AHEAD NOTE	STORE NOTE
The ice cream can be made and frozen up to 1 week ahead.	Leftover ice cream should be returned to freezer as quickly as possible, and is best eaten within 1 month.

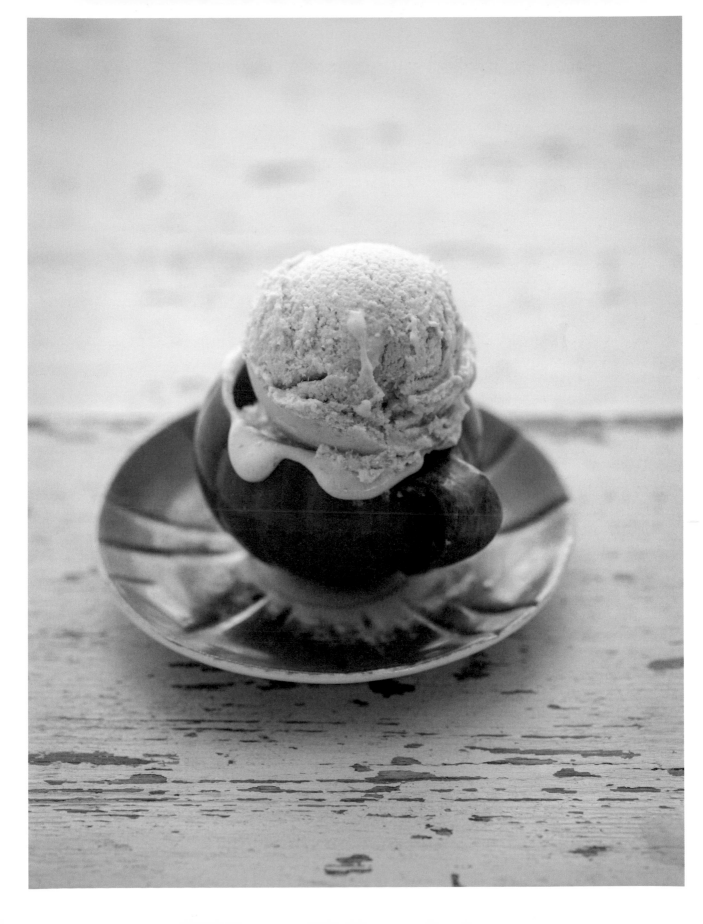

No-churn blackcurrant ice cream
with liquorice ripple

As with the Liquorice and Blackcurrant Chocolate Cake on **p.280**, this ice cream is inspired by my favourite boiled sweet. And in ice cream form, these flavours – the fresh sharpness of the currants gorgeously countered by the almost dizzyingly pungent hit of the liquorice – are particularly compelling, as both are conveyed through the smooth, soothing, melting medium. This is not one for liquorice-loathers, however. Especially given that I go for the uncompromising rasp of salty liquorice syrup here and, indeed, anywhere I can find an excuse for it.

I keep an old 1 litre ice-cream tub (it measures 18 x 12 x 7cm) for this, as you need a surface area not provided by the 500ml cylindrical ice-cream tubs I normally prefer. Obviously, any similarly dimensioned airtight container would do.

Blackcurrants are often fiendishly hard to come by, but you might be able to find them frozen. Usually I am reduced to picking them out of a packet of frozen mixed berries by hand. If you can't get up to 150g, use 100g blackcurrants and increase the lemon juice to 3 tablespoons.

150g frozen or fresh blackcurrants	3 teaspoons salty liquorice syrup
2 tablespoons lemon juice	
½ x 397g can (150ml) condensed milk	1 x 1 litre empty ice-cream tub (approx. 18 x 12 x 7cm) or similar-sized airtight container
300ml double cream	

○ Put the blackcurrants into a small saucepan (do not thaw them, if using frozen) with the lemon juice, put on a lid and cook over a medium heat for 5 minutes, by which time you should have a runny, deep-tinted liquid bobbled with berries. Pour into the bowl you're going to mix the ice cream in and use a fork to mash to a textured purée; it's good to have bits of sharp berries in the smooth ice cream later. Leave to cool.

○ Stir the condensed milk into the cold currant purée and, when combined, pour in the double cream and whisk until thickened. Pour half of this mixture into your container. Now dip a pointy teaspoon into the liquorice syrup and drizzle it over the ice-cream mix, either zigzagging or just in stripes across, refuelling when your teaspoon's empty with a further ½ teaspoonful.

○ Top with the remaining half of the ice-cream mix, and do the same again with the liquorice syrup. Now, get a skewer and squiggle through – making the sort of shapes in the ice cream you might make in the air were you holding a sparkler – so that the glossy liquorice ripples through the pink cream and you end up with an edible example of Florentine marbling.

○ Put on the lid and freeze overnight, until set. Take it out of the deep freeze 10–15 minutes before serving, to allow it to soften. And do I have to tell you to bring the jar of liquorice syrup to the table to pour more over as you eat?

MAKE AHEAD NOTE	STORE NOTE
The ice cream can be made and frozen up to 1 week ahead.	Leftover ice cream should be returned to freezer as quickly as possible, and is best eaten within 1 month.

No-churn matcha ice cream

I love matcha ice cream, and this version gives me particular pleasure. Yes, it's ridiculously easy to make, which is gratifying, but more glorious – and important – is the perfect balance between the sophisticated bitterness of the matcha powder and the uncompromisingly childish sweetness of the condensed milk. You would never imagine such an uncouth ingredient could be a factor in the exquisite outcome here.

I first made this during the photo shoot for this book, as a spontaneous off-piste recipe, simply because I had the matcha still out on the counter from the making of the Matcha Cake (**p.295**) and I have to say it has emerged as one of my absolute favourite recipes.

Should you ever be making the Molten Chocolate Babycakes from *How To Be A Domestic Goddess*, I urge you to serve this alongside.

MAKES APPROX. 1 LITRE

½ x 397g tin (150ml) condensed milk

300ml double cream

2 x 15ml tablespoons Izu Matcha green tea powder (see Intro to Matcha Cake on p.295)

2 x 500ml empty ice-cream tubs or airtight containers (or 1 x 1 litre tub or airtight container)

- Put the condensed milk in a bowl, and stir to loosen. Add the cream and whisk until it begins to thicken.

- Then whisk in the green tea powder until you have a whipped green cream.

- Decant into your airtight container or containers and freeze overnight.

- Take the ice cream out of the freezer to soften for 10 minutes before serving.

MAKE AHEAD NOTE	STORE NOTE
The ice cream can be made and frozen up to 1 week ahead.	Leftover ice cream should be returned to freezer as quickly as possible, and is best eaten within 1 month.

No-churn white miso ice cream

This is a domino-effect leftover story. I had some pumpkin purée left from the bundt cake on **p.289**, so I made the Brandied Pumpkin Ice Cream (**p.334**). That left me with half a tin of condensed milk open, so I made this. I am afraid this is how I operate. Still, I should also say, in my defence, I have always wanted to make a simple, no-churn version of a white miso ice cream, along these lines, ever since having the real thing at The Shiori, a tiny Kaiseki restaurant in London that I would much prefer to keep my secret, but won't.

The idea of a miso ice cream may sound strange, but think of salted caramel, only subtler and deeper at the same time. (And if it's actual salted caramel ice cream you want, see nigella.com for my No-Churn Salted Caramel Bourbon Ice Cream). I like it with a skinny drizzle of salty liquorice syrup over it, but perhaps a softer introduction would be to try it with a thick drip of golden syrup. But it's wonderful plain, with a wafer or in a cornet, or dolloped alongside the Cider and 5-Spice Bundt Cake (**p.293**) while it's still warm, or the Gluten-Free Apple and Blackberry Pie on **p.302**.

MAKES APPROX. 1 LITRE

100g sweet white miso

½ x 397g tin (150ml) condensed milk

300ml double cream

2 x 500ml empty ice-cream tubs or airtight containers (or 1 x 1 litre tub or airtight container)

- Combine the miso paste and condensed milk in a bowl, and stir to mix and loosen. Then add the cream and whisk until it begins to thicken.

- Decant into your airtight container or containers and freeze overnight.

- Take the ice cream out of the freezer to soften for 10 minutes before serving.

MAKE AHEAD NOTE	STORE NOTE
The ice cream can be made and frozen up to 1 week ahead.	Leftover ice cream should be returned to freezer as quickly as possible, and is best eaten within 1 month.

Smoky salted caramel sauce

I first made this sauce for *Stylist* magazine, as part of what became almost an entire issue (I was guest editor) given over to the allure of salted caramel. I have never stopped making it. I don't care if the hipster crowd feel that salted caramel is no longer cool and new. Food is either good or it isn't, and while fashion relies on quick-change, taste – if it is authentic, rather than faddish – endures.

I have made a small adjustment to my original recipe. I have since come across Maldon smoked sea salt flakes, and they take this to another level of delectability. But any good soft flaked sea salt will do. It is all about that unholy trinity of fat, sugar, salt. Look, I'm not asking you to live off it!

Tip: one Christmas, I turned this into a Salted Caramel Brandy Butter, by beating 2 tablespoons of this sauce (when cold) along with 2 tablespoons of brandy into 150g soft, unsalted butter. It was a very good Christmas.

SERVES 6, AS A SAUCE FOR CAKE OR ICE CREAM

75g unsalted butter	50g golden syrup
50g soft light brown sugar	125ml double cream
50g caster sugar	2 teaspoons smoked sea salt flakes, or to taste

° Melt the butter, sugars and syrup in a small, heavy-based pan and let it simmer for 3 minutes, swirling the pan every now and then.

° Add the cream and the smoked salt and swirl again, then give it a stir with a wooden spoon, and taste. Go cautiously so that you don't burn your tongue, and see if you want to add more salt, before letting it cook for another minute, then pour into a jug to serve.

MAKE AHEAD NOTE	STORE NOTE	FREEZE NOTE
The sauce can be made ahead and stored in an airtight container in fridge for 1 week. Remove the sauce from fridge about 1 hour before serving, until it has come up to room temperature, or warm it very gently in a saucepan.	Leftover sauce should be refrigerated as quickly as possible and stored in an airtight container in fridge, where it will keep for up to 1 week from the day of making. Do not reheat the sauce more than once.	The sauce can also be frozen for up to 3 months. Defrost the sauce overnight in fridge before serving. Defrosted sauce should be used within 1 week.

BEGINNINGS

BEGINNINGS

I am not going to keep you long: no one wants to be engaged in vigorous conversation first thing in the morning. But this chapter has been a delight for me and has changed the way I think about my breakfast: I now look forward to it. We all know that breakfast is supposed to be the most important meal of the day, but it has always been the one time I actually have to force myself to eat. Because of this, I have generally had one breakfast – egg on toast – which I repeated, automaton-like, just because I knew I had to eat something, and didn't want to think about it. In other words, for a brief hour in the morning, I turned into one of those alien people who aren't thinking about food all the time. Luckily, these recipes have saved me. True, I still often decide the night before (much like, when I worked in an office, I took out the clothes for the next day when I went to bed) to remove the burden of decision-making on the morning itself. But what I am left with is the joy of anticipation, the pleasure of eating, and the feeling that the new day is to be celebrated.

I have chosen to finish the book with this appropriately named chapter, rather than start with it, because I feel that out of endings come new beginnings, and the recipes that follow are my kitchen *carpe diem*.

Matcha latte

When I first read about these, I confess I thought them a ridiculous fad. Now, I am a total convert. Yes matcha is expensive, but making these at home is nothing compared to what you'd pay at a coffee shop. And there is a reason the beautiful green matcha powder costs a lot: the tea is tended carefully, grown under cover (to boost its green colour, and keep it tender) and harvested by hand, for a start. There are too many unproven health claims made in its name, though it is certainly rich in antioxidants and high in L-Theanine levels, and L-Theanine – a water-soluble amino acid which has been found to help with anxiety and promote "relaxed alertness" – works in conjunction with the tea's caffeine content to improve cognition. So, all in all, a good start to the day, I'd say.

Being a builder's-tea-drinker on the whole, I find this is the perfect tea for a non-coffee-drinker who wants something with froth and get-up-and-go. And the amount of milk certainly keeps one full (I think of it as a meal of a drink). I like mine made with oat milk (and I buy one especially made for baristas, as it froths fantastically) but otherwise do use almond milk (and, if you're a sugar-taker, which I'm not, sweetened almond milk) or other milk of your choice.

Matcha powder varies tremendously in taste and price: my favourites are the Izu Matcha by Tealyra and Aiya Beginner's Matcha Izumi, in that order.

SERVES 1

1½ teaspoons matcha powder, plus more if you're making a pattern on top

2 x 15ml tablespoons hot water, from a recently boiled kettle

¾ cup (175ml) milk of your choice

° Spoon the matcha powder into a mug, add the hot water and combine using a frothing mixer, such as an Aerolatte.

° Warm the milk in the microwave for 1½ minutes, or in a saucepan on the hob, till steaming hot, then remove and froth until it has almost doubled in volume.

° Pour half the milk into the matcha paste and combine, using the frother, then top with the rest of the milk. If you want to feel like a barista in your own home, buy a pack of stencils made just for this purpose (they saw me coming) and place the one of your choice on top of the mug as you dust the cut-out parts with matcha powder.

Rhubarb and ginger compote

I haven't written a book yet without a recipe for rhubarb ("like a sharp-tongued best friend, who makes everything more interesting" in the words of the *Los Angeles Times* food writer, Russ Parsons) and I am not about to start now.

Here, the rhubarb's sharpness is given extra pep by copious amounts of ginger and, dolloped on to yogurt in the morning with a sprinkling of chopped pistachios, is a beautiful, uplifting and invigorating start to the day. I exult in the glorious pinkness of forced rhubarb from the famous Yorkshire Triangle, when it's in season.

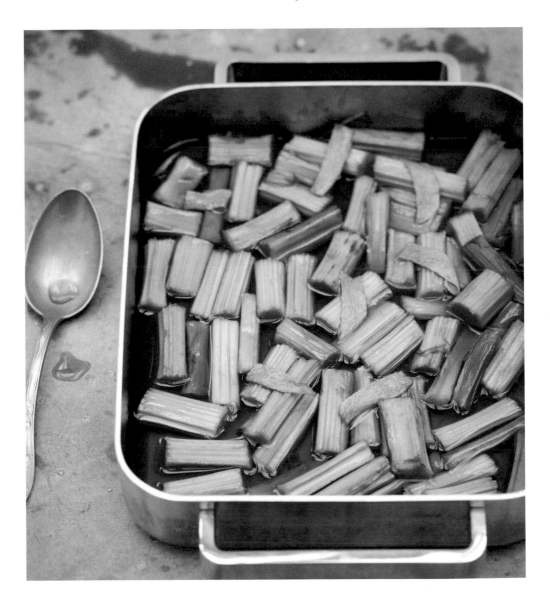

MAKES APPROX. 600ML, ENOUGH FOR 6–10 PORTIONS, DEPENDING ON WHAT IT'S SERVED WITH

800g rhubarb (trimmed weight)	200g caster sugar
10cm piece (50g) fresh ginger, peeled	

- Preheat the oven to 190°C/gas mark 5. Chop up the rhubarb: thin sticks should be cut into 5–6cm batons; fat stems should be cut into 3cm chunks. The point here is just to make sure that all the rhubarb cooks evenly. Put into an ovenproof dish or roasting tin in which the rhubarb can sit in one layer; I use one measuring approx. 29 x 25 x 5cm.

- Cut the peeled ginger into thin-ish slices lengthways, then cut these slices in half across. Add to the rhubarb and, using your hands, toss to mix. Now add the caster sugar and gently mix in: you may prefer to use spatulas for this, but I don't mind getting my hands sticky. With clean hands, cover with a sheet of foil, making sure the edges are sealed tightly, and put in the oven for 45 minutes. It may be wise to check at 30 minutes and turn the mixture gently to help all the sugar dissolve, and I mean gently: you don't want to break up the rhubarb and risk turning it into mush. Certainly, I like the rhubarb pieces to be discrete entities.

- After 45 minutes, or when the rhubarb is tender, but still holding its shape, and the sugar has turned to a pink syrup with the rhubarb's juices, take out of the oven, remove the foil lid and let it stand for 5–10 minutes to cool a little, and then strain gently into a large sieve suspended over a bowl or a wide-necked jug. Pour the pink liquid into a saucepan and put on the hob over a high heat to reduce. You could always do this using the tin you've just cooked the rhubarb in, if it can go onto direct heat. Let it bubble away until reduced by half. If you're doing this in a saucepan, this will take about 5–7 minutes, and it'll be a lot quicker in an oven tin. You can go in and check for taste and viscosity.

- When the puce syrup's reduced, pour it into a jug or bowl to cool a little – if you want warmth rather than heat from the ginger, pick out the strips of ginger from the rhubarb at this point – and then pour over the rhubarb. Leave the dish of rhubarb to cool completely for about 2 hours, before covering and putting in the fridge until the morning, or for up to 5 days, or portion up for the freezer for further future breakfasts.

STORE NOTE	FREEZE NOTE
Cooled compote will keep, covered, in fridge for up to 5 days.	Can be frozen for up to 3 months. Defrost overnight in fridge.

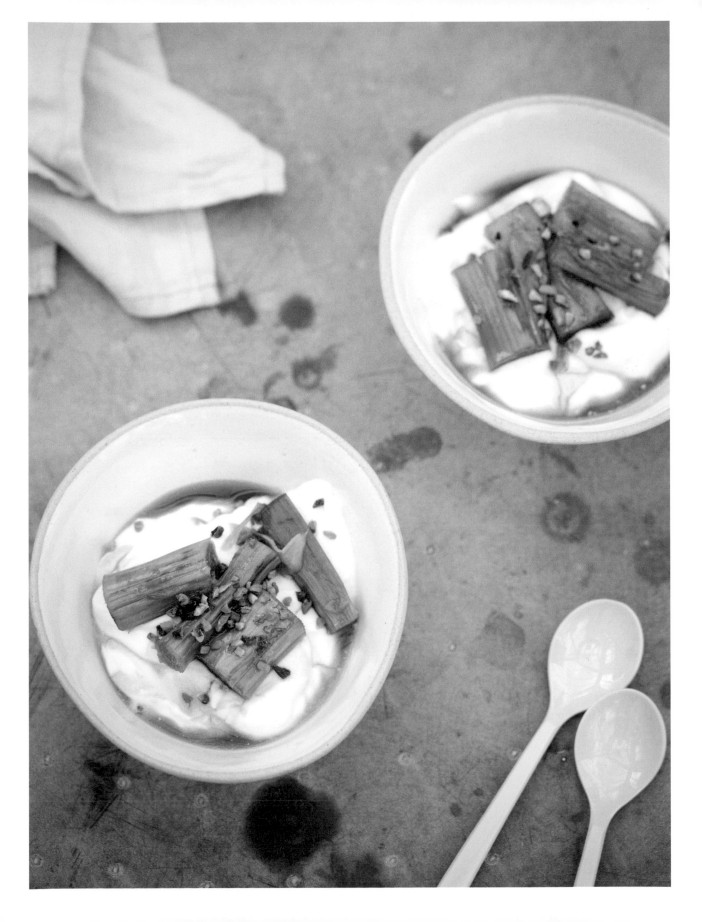

Spiced apple and blueberry compote

I love an old-fashioned dish of stewed Bramley apples: they strike that all-important balance between soothing and astringent, which makes them the perfect, edible wake-up call.

This fantastically-hued blueberried version, with its warm spices, loses none of that desirable sharpness, but do add more maple syrup if you want a sweeter compote, and anyway, the sweetness of blueberries varies enormously. Should you want to eat this dolloped onto a bowl of tangy yogurt, you may want to drizzle a little extra maple syrup over, too.

MAKES APPROX. 500ML, ENOUGH FOR 4–6 PORTIONS, DEPENDING ON WHAT IT'S SERVED WITH

3 Bramley apples (approx. 750g total), peeled and quartered

100g blueberries

1 stick cinnamon

1 whole clove

¼ cup (60ml) water

2 x 15ml tablespoons maple syrup, or more to taste

- Chop the apple quarters into fairly small pieces and drop these into a heavy-based saucepan that comes with a tight-fitting lid.

- Add the blueberries, cinnamon stick, clove and water, put the lid on and place over a medium to low heat. In about 2–3 minutes, you can lift the lid up to check that the scant amount of water is bubbling. Replace the lid, and let it cook for about 10–15 minutes, giving a vigorous stir every 3 minutes or so with a wooden spoon. This is just to make sure that nothing sticks to the bottom of the pan, and so that you can aid the delicious disintegration of the fruit.

- When everything is cooked and stirred to a purée (bar the odd speck) take the pan off the heat, add 2 tablespoons of maple syrup and beat exuberantly with your wooden spoon, but don't break up the cinnamon stick. You should have a ridiculously magenta, spiced and sharp compote in front of you. Taste to see if you want any more maple syrup, and add accordingly, then leave to cool.

STORE NOTE	FREEZE NOTE
Cooled compote will keep, covered, in fridge for up to 5 days.	Can be frozen for up to 3 months. Defrost overnight in fridge.

Avocado toast with quick-pickled breakfast radishes

Avocado toast is my favourite breakfast, lunch, tea, supper, and I know I am not alone in this. Crowned with some, appropriately named, breakfast radishes, it makes a breakfast that will see you through for hours on those days when you're frightened that lunch may be late. Breakfast, or French, radishes, are long in shape, with their red fading to white at one end; these are much easier to cut into juliennes for pickling. But if an evening's quick pickling isn't for you, then just cut a radish or two in the morning and scatter the peppery crimson strips over your greenly luscious avocado.

SERVES 1–2

FOR THE PICKLED RADISHES:

175g breakfast radishes

125ml rice vinegar

125ml cold water

2 x 15ml tablespoons sugar

2 teaspoons sea salt flakes

2½ teaspoons whole pink peppercorns

FOR THE AVOCADO TOAST:

½ teaspoon sea salt flakes, or to taste

2 teaspoons lime juice

1–2 slices bread of your choice

1 ripe avocado

¼ teaspoon dried chilli flakes

1–2 x 15ml tablespoons chopped fresh dill

1cm (5g) fresh ginger, peeled and grated

○ Cut off the beards and the stems of the radishes, and then slice into eighths lengthways (if they are very skinny, then quarters will do). Put into a small bowl.

○ Put the rice vinegar, water, sugar, salt and peppercorns into a small saucepan and bring to the boil. Turn off the heat, and stir to make sure the sugar and salt are dissolved, then pour over the prepared radishes, patting them down with the back of a spoon for a minute or two until they are all submerged. Leave to cool, then put some in the fridge overnight for tomorrow's breakfast, before transferring the remainder to an airtight jar with a vinegar-proof lid and keeping for up to 1 month, and many future breakfasts.

○ Add the salt to the lime juice, and toast your bread. While it's cooling a little, fork the flesh of the avocado to a rough mash in a bowl with the ¼ teaspoon of chilli flakes, 1 tablespoonful of chopped dill and the freshly grated ginger, for extra pep. Now add the salt and lime juice, stirring it first, and fork to combine. Taste for seasoning. Spread the toast with the zingy avocado, top with radishes, pickled or otherwise, and sprinkle with some more chilli flakes and dill to taste.

Breakfast banana bread with cardamom and cocoa nibs

I positively will everyone in the house not to eat the bananas so that they overripen and I have an excuse to make this. I love all the variants of banana bread I have ever made – much more than I do bananas – but this one is on another level. The smoky bitterness that emanates from both the cardamom and cocoa nibs offers a subtle foil to the natural and rich sweetness of the bananas. As this is for breakfast, it isn't terribly sweet, so feel free to up the sugar to 250g if you have a sweet tooth and want to indulge it. It is also excellent (and tastes sweeter) when toasted and spread with unsalted butter.

2 very ripe or overripe bananas (250–275g total in their skins)	1 ¼ teaspoons baking powder
2 large eggs	1 teaspoon bicarbonate of soda
200ml plain (runny) yogurt or buttermilk	2 teaspoons ground cardamom, or seeds from 1 x 15ml tablespoon cardamom pods, ground
125ml light and mild olive oil	50g cocoa nibs
325g plain flour	
200g soft light brown sugar	1 x 2lb/900g loaf tin approx. 23 x 13 x 7cm

○ Preheat the oven to 170°C/gas mark 3, and pop a paper liner into your loaf tin (or line the bottom with baking parchment and grease the sides with a little sunflower oil).

○ I do the whole thing using a freestanding mixer, but a bowl and an electric whisk, or a wooden spoon and plenty of elbow grease would be fine. Mash the bananas (and if you're not using a freestanding mixer, use a fork and a smallish bowl first, otherwise the flat paddle of a freestanding mixer will do) and beat in 1 egg at a time, followed by the yogurt or buttermilk, then the oil, and beat it all together. I measure the flour, sugar, baking powder, bicarb and cardamom into a bowl, and whisk together, while this is going on.

○ Slow the speed down while you add the dry ingredients, gradually, beating all the while, and then turn the speed slightly higher again, and beat for 1 minute until all the dry ingredients are incorporated. You may have to scrape the bowl down and give a short final beat if you notice any flour sticking to the edges of the bowl. Then, using a rubber spatula or wooden spoon, fold in the cocoa nibs by hand and transfer the mixture to your prepared tin and thence to the oven for 1 hour (it is wise to start checking at 45 minutes) or until a cake tester comes out clean.

○ Sit the loaf tin on a wire rack and leave the banana bread in the tin until cold. Slip it out, in its paper liner (or baking parchment), and wrap with more parchment and then kitchen foil and keep for a day – if you can – before eating.

STORE NOTE	FREEZE NOTE
Store in an airtight container in a cool place for up to 1 week.	Can be frozen for up to 3 months. Wrap cake in a double layer of clingfilm and a layer of foil. To defrost, unwrap and put on a wire rack at room temperature for about 5 hours. Or wrap individual slices in clingfilm and put into a resealable bag, and defrost by toasting on a low heat.

Breakfast bars 2.0

I have a breakfast bar recipe in an earlier book, but this is the new, improved version: gluten-free, dairy-free and enough seeds to make you start sprouting. I've used no sugar, but before you start thinking this is virtuously sugar-free (which I could claim it to be), remember that the sweetness that comes from the dates is, in essence, sugar, though certainly it's unprocessed and full of fibre at the same time. There are a lot of ingredients, but you need a good mixture to give crunch and chew – and all manner of smugness-inducing nutrients – though you can fiddle about with them. You can, for example, use sunflower seeds in place of flaxseeds, or half and half rather than all flaxseeds, as below, and you can also use puffed rice (gluten-free if needed) or buckwheat flakes in place of cornflakes. In theory, cornflakes (and oats) should be gluten-free, but if crucial, make sure it's stipulated on the packet.

If you can't get hold of medjool dates, then use 350g pitted dried dates and up the water to 400ml. And they'll take about 10, rather than 5, minutes to cook until they're soft enough to mash to a purée.

Make these bars at the weekend, and you'll be set up for the week if you're someone who needs to grab-and-go in the morning. They come in pretty handy for that 4pm slump, too.

MAKES 16 BARS

250g medjool dates	50g cocoa nibs
2 teaspoons ground cinnamon	25g chia seeds
325ml cold water	25g cornflakes (gluten-free if required)
75g goji berries	100g organic porridge oats (not instant)
75g pumpkin seeds	
150g brown flaxseeds	1 x 20cm square baking tin

° Preheat the oven to 180°C/gas mark 4, and line the bottom and sides of your tin with baking parchment. Pit the dates and tear them with your fingers into a small saucepan, add the cinnamon, cover with the water, bring to the boil and let bubble for 5 minutes. Turn off the heat, and beat with a fork until you have a rough purée.

° Put all the remaining ingredients into a large bowl, add the date mixture and mix until everything is combined. I wear a pair of disposable vinyl gloves for this.

° Squodge into your prepared tin and bake in the oven for 30 minutes, until firm and set, and golden on top and darker around the edges. Leave to cool in the tin before cutting into pieces.

STORE NOTE	FREEZE NOTE
Store in an airtight container in a cool place or in fridge for up to 1 week.	Wrap bars individually in clingfilm or foil and put in a resealable bag, or stack bars in an airtight container with baking parchment in between the layers. Freeze for up to 2 months. To defrost, put bars on a wire rack and leave at room temperature for about 2 hours.

Chai muffins

Taking tea in muffin form seems ideal for breakfast, and the warm spices of chai bring scented richness without heft. I've made these dairy-free, but if you want to, you can easily use semi-skimmed milk in place of the almond milk, below. And if you can't get the white spelt flour, which is magnificent in muffins, use 300g plain flour and 100g plain wholemeal (not bread) flour instead. I want to make it as easy as possible for you to make these, as this is a particularly splendid specimen of muffin.

Talking of which, it makes sense to steep the milk, leave it to cool, and measure out all the ingredients, putting the eggs by the side, the night before, so that you can shimmy into the kitchen in the morning and bake up a batch without adding a furrow to your brow.

225ml unsweetened almond milk

2 Chai teabags

1 teaspoon ground cinnamon

400g white spelt flour

2½ teaspoons baking powder

150g soft light brown sugar

75g natural skin-on almonds, roughly chopped

2 large eggs

150ml sunflower oil

1 x 12-bun muffin tin

○ Warm the almond milk with the contents of the 2 teabags (I just rip them open over the pan) and cinnamon – stirring to mix – and leave to cool.

○ While the milk's cooling, preheat the oven to 200°C/gas mark 6 and line your muffin tin with paper cases.

○ In a large bowl, measure out the flour, baking powder, sugar and all but 2 tablespoons of the chopped almonds, and combine well.

○ When the milk has cooled, add the eggs and oil, then whisk well.

○ Add the liquid ingredients to the dry ingredients, using a wooden spoon. Don't be too efficient about this: a slightly lumpy batter makes for lighter muffins.

○ Divide the mixture between the muffin cases (it will fill them well), then sprinkle equally with the remaining almonds and bake in the oven for 20–25 minutes, or until a cake tester comes out clean and the muffins are slightly risen and pleasingly golden on top.

○ Remove to a wire rack to cool for about 10 minutes before devouring.

STORE NOTE	FREEZE NOTE
Best eaten on day they are made, otherwise store in an airtight container for 1–2 days. Reheat in an oven preheated to 150°C/gas mark 2 for about 8 minutes. Best served warm.	Stack fully cooled muffins in an airtight container with baking parchment between the layers, or wrap individually in clingfilm then put in a resealable bag. Freeze for up to 3 months. Defrost on a wire rack for about 1 hour. Reheat as Store Note.

Buckwheat, banana and carrot muffins

These may not be the most splendid muffins you have ever cast your eye on, but they will be some of the most delectable you ever bite into. The reason they keep their magnificence hidden is that buckwheat flour is gluten-free, and so the muffins do not rise much as they cook. But the important thing – and this is not always the case with gluten-free baking – is that they are lush and light. The banana, carrots and ground almonds keep the muffins wonderfully succulent, but it is the toasty nuttiness of the buckwheat that is the stand-out star here. On the subject of which, while buckwheat itself has no gluten, some flour manufacturers do warn of cross-contamination from other flours milled on site, so if it is a matter of urgency, do check that it says gluten-free on the packet.

MAKES 12

1 ripe banana

zest and juice of 1 unwaxed lemon

75g soft light brown sugar

2 large eggs

150ml light and mild olive oil

150g buckwheat flour

50g ground almonds

½ teaspoon bicarbonate of soda

2 teaspoons gluten-free baking powder

250g carrots, peeled and grated

1½ teaspoons sesame seeds

1 x 12-bun muffin tin

○ Preheat the oven to 200°C/gas mark 6 and line your muffin tin with paper cases.

○ Mash the banana in a large bowl with the finely grated zest and juice of the lemon, and then whisk in the sugar, eggs and oil until smooth.

○ In another bowl, large enough to take all the ingredients later, combine the buckwheat flour, ground almonds, bicarb and baking powder, and mix thoroughly with a fork.

○ Now, pour the bowl of wet ingredients into the bowl of dry ingredients, add the grated carrots, and stir with a wooden spoon till everything's just combined.

○ Using an ice-cream scoop, or however you find this easiest, fill each muffin case. This mixture will give you enough to fill each almost right to the top. Sprinkle with the sesame seeds and bake in the oven for 15–20 minutes.

○ When the muffins are ready, a cake tester should come out clean. Remove the tin from the oven to a wire rack. I like to take the muffins out of the tin straightaway and sit them directly on the rack, but then 1) I've got asbestos hands and 2) I'm very impatient. I'll leave it to you to take them out when you feel comfortable handling them. I love these best warm, but the juiciness provided by the carrots and banana means they are also good cold.

STORE NOTE	FREEZE NOTE
Best eaten on day they are made, otherwise store in an airtight container in a cool place for up to 5 days. Reheat in an oven preheated to 150°C/gas mark 2 for 5–7 minutes.	Stack fully cooled muffins in an airtight container with baking parchment between the layers, or wrap individually in clingfilm then put in a resealable bag. Freeze for up to 3 months. Defrost on a wire rack for about 1 hour. Reheat as Store Note.

Pomegranate muesli

My maternal grandmother used to mix up her Bircher muesli every night so it would be ready for her breakfast tray in the morning. I loved watching her quiet absorption and practised deftness as she went about this evening ritual, even if it did let me know it was bedtime. But I just couldn't get on with her muesli, and still can't: I cannot abide the shredded apple in the milk that traditionalists insist upon. I fear this is an extravagant muesli my grandmother would not approve of; she'd look particularly askance at the fact that I buy my pomegranate seeds in tubs. But it makes me happy – and she'd want that.

I find oat milk optimal here, but feel free to use the milk of your choice, of course. And in theory, oats should be gluten-free, but if this is crucial, do check the packaging to be sure.

SERVES 1

¼ cup (25g) jumbo or sprouted oats (not instant)

²/₃ cup (150ml) milk of your choice, plus more as needed

2–3 soft dried apricots

1–2 x 15ml tablespoons chopped natural skin-on almonds or flaked almonds

2 x 15ml tablespoons pomegranate seeds

runny honey, to dribble over on serving (optional)

○ Measure the oats into a bowl and pour the milk over. Snip in the dried apricots: I find it easiest to use scissors and let the pieces drop into the bowl. Give it a good stir, then cover with clingfilm and leave overnight in the fridge or in a cool place.

○ The next morning, stir it again – you shouldn't need to add any more milk, as I make this quite runny to start off with – just to combine the swollen oats and fruit with the milk still left at the top, then stir in half the chopped almonds and pomegranate seeds, and sprinkle more of both on top, to taste. Those with a sweet tooth might want to drizzle some honey over.

Toasty olive oil granola

This is a pared-down — though most definitely luxurious — granola, in the sense that it has no dried fruit in it. Nor does it clump together, as it is markedly less sweet than standard versions. In other words, what it's not is the sort of granola that's like confectionery through the back door, and I very much prefer it.

I like this with almond milk and sometimes toss in a few fresh berries too — blackberries being my favourite here — though it is also good eaten with yogurt and blueberries. And I have been known to eat it by grabbed handfuls straight from the jar.

MAKES ENOUGH TO FILL 1 X 1.5 LITRE JAR

300g rolled oats (not instant), preferably organic

2 teaspoons ground ginger

2 teaspoons ground cinnamon

1 teaspoon sea salt flakes

100g natural skin-on almonds

75g sunflower seeds

75g pumpkin seeds

50g brown flaxseeds

50g flaked almonds

25g sesame seeds

125ml extra-virgin olive oil

125ml maple syrup

1 x large baking sheet approx. 46 x 34 x 1.5cm

° Preheat the oven to 150°C/gas mark 2 and line your baking sheet with baking parchment.

° Tip the oats into a large bowl, add the spices and salt and mix well (I use my hands for this).

° Now add all the nuts and seeds, and mix well again.

° In a measuring jug, combine the oil and maple syrup, then pour the mixture into the oats, nuts and seeds and, with either a fork, or hands encased in disposable vinyl gloves, mix to combine. Tip onto the prepared baking sheet, and move it around so that it covers the tray evenly.

° Put in the oven to toast gently for 30 minutes and then, with spoons or spatulas, turn it to help toast the underside as well. Put back in the oven for another 30 minutes, and then sit the tray on a wire rack until the granola's cold.

STORE NOTE
Store in a sealed jar or an airtight container for up to 1 month.

Maple pecan no-wait, no-cook oats

This features prominently in my notional breakfast schedule because it is pretty well instant and needs absolutely no forethought. It is, if not a life-saver, then certainly a good-mood-preserver, and much called upon when I have to bolt out of the door and need something I can make last minute. But it also gets creamier as it stands, so by all means, mix it up before you go to bed, if you want.

SERVES 1

²/₃ cup (150ml) plain yogurt

½ teaspoon ground cinnamon

4 teaspoons maple syrup

4 teaspoons fine oat bran

4 teaspoons crumbled pecans

° Tip the yogurt into a bowl and stir in the cinnamon, followed by 2 teaspoons of the maple syrup and then the 4 teaspoons of oat bran.

° In a little cup, mix the crumbled pecans with the 2 remaining teaspoons of maple syrup and spoon over the oat-bowl. That's all, folks.

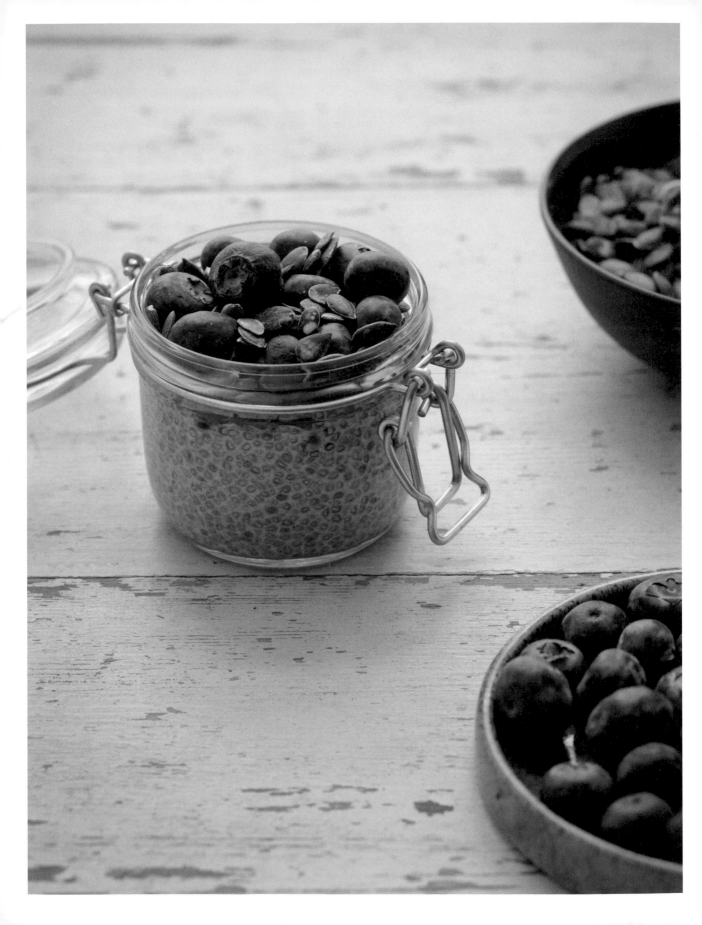

Chia seed pudding with blueberries and pumpkin seeds

Well, blow me down if I don't love chia seed pudding. It certainly took me by surprise, anyway. Chia seeds don't have any taste in themselves, which is why I scent the milk they're soaked in with cinnamon, rosewater and orange flower water, thereby giving myself a taste of exotica at breakfast. The deal about chia seeds (apart from the fact that they are meant to be a Force for Good in the world, nutritionally speaking, about which I have no view) is the texture, and this is not for everyone. The pudding that emerges, once the seeds have swollen in the milk, is tapioca-like, for sure, but then, I liked frogspawn at school, too. Those who are hesitant about trying it, should be reassured by the fact that its glorious (to me) glutinousness is tempered by the crunch of pumpkin seeds and the juicy brightness of berries.

SERVES 1

¾ cup (175ml) almond milk

½ teaspoon ground cinnamon

½ teaspoon rosewater

½ teaspoon orange flower water

1½ teaspoons black or white chia seeds

⅓ cup (approx. 50g) blueberries

2 x 15ml tablespoons pumpkin seeds

1 x 250ml preserving jar or other resealable jar

- Since the chia seeds need to be stirred frequently once they've gone into the milk, I find it best to make these in small preserving jars, so that I can shake 'em up easily, rather than uncovering clingfilm, stirring, re-clinging and repeating this dull procedure regularly. So: fill your jar with milk, stir in the ground cinnamon (which will not be absorbed, but still float about the surface at this stage), then add the rosewater, orange flower water and chia seeds, seal with the lid and shake. And then shake 3 or 4 times over about 15 minutes or so before putting in the fridge to soak overnight.

- Open the lid, and give the now-glutinous pudding a stir, then top with blueberries and pumpkin seeds before eating. (This has the virtue of turning your breakfast into a portable feast.) Or decant the pudding into a bowl, and mix the seeds and berries more thoroughly.

Fried egg and kimchi taco

This is definitely *the* breakfast for the morning after the night before. I don't leave it for those obviously infrequent occasions, however. If I can find an excuse for getting *kimchi* – a Korean pickle that has fire and tang – into something, I will, and at 11am on a Saturday morning when I am happily (and with a clear head) mooching about the house in need of something that serves both as a late breakfast and an early lunch, I can often be found wolfing this down.

SERVES 1

1 soft corn tortilla	1 large egg
2 x 15ml tablespoons sunflower oil	pinch sea salt flakes
½ fresh red chilli, de-seeded (or not, as desired) and finely chopped	¼ cup (4 x 15ml tablespoons) kimchi

° Put a cast-iron or heavy-based frying pan of about 20cm diameter on the heat, and when hot, warm the tortilla in it: give it a minute on one side, then turn over and give it 30 seconds on the other, then remove to a waiting plate.

° Add the oil and half of your chopped chilli, then once the chilli has paled a little in the hot oil, crack in the egg, sprinkle the yolk with a pinch of sea salt flakes, and spoon the chilli-flecked oil over until the white is set. Transfer to the middle of the waiting tortilla.

° Add the kimchi around the egg, and sprinkle both egg and kimchi with the remaining chilli. I then like to pierce the yolk, smear it over the kimchi and tortilla, halve it to form a half-mooned sandwich – and apply to face.

Sweet potato, black bean and avocado burrito

Since I am in the habit of having ready-baked sweet potatoes around the house, I never need to cook them especially to make this, but if you need to start from scratch, and want to make just enough for this, know that the ½ cup of sweet potato, below, is the mashed interior of a 170g sweet potato baked for 1 hour in a 220°C/gas mark 7 oven, then left to cool. And while I've used canned beans here, were you to have any leftover Cuban Black Beans (see **p.214**), then obviously use those.

I've used cup measures here, as not only is it much easier at breakfast time, even at a weekend, but also the perfect burrito is really more about the ratio of ingredients rather than their exact measurements.

2 x 25cm burrito wraps

½ cup (approx. 125g) cold mashed sweet potato

2 x 15ml tablespoons plain yogurt

1 teaspoon pimentón picante or paprika

1 teaspoon ground cumin

2 fat pinches sea salt flakes

1 cup (about ¾ x 400g can/170g) black beans, drained

2 small ripe tomatoes, roughly chopped

¼ cup (4 x 15ml tablespoons) chopped fresh coriander, plus more for sprinkling

1 ripe avocado, halved, stoned and sliced

⅓ cup (about 30g) grated Cheddar or other cheese of your choice

° Preheat the oven to 200°C/gas mark 6.

° Place the 2 wraps in front of you. Mix – a fork is all you need for this – the mashed sweet potato with the yogurt, pimentón or paprika, cumin and a good pinch of salt and spread this over the 2 wraps.

° In a bowl, mash the black beans slightly with the back of a fork, then add the chopped tomatoes, another pinch of salt and the chopped coriander and stir to mix. Divide this between the 2 sweet-potato-sticky wraps, then do the same with the sliced avocado, and top, equally, with the grated cheese. Transfer to a baking sheet and cook for 5 minutes. If the wraps won't fit together on the same sheet, either use two sheets, or cook one burrito at a time, sharing each one – eaten unrolled – in succession.

° Either eat rolled up as is proper with a burrito, or – and this makes them go further – cut into quarters and then eat as you might a pizza, curling the softer pointy end of the triangle over the crunchier flat end, for the perfect breakfast – indeed, anytime – sandwich.

Oat pancakes with raspberries and honey

If you promise pancakes to an 8-year-old, these are decidedly not the pancakes they will have in mind, though this doesn't mean they aren't for the rest of us. Think of them rather like the oatcakes you might have with cheese, only in pancake form; as with regular fluffy pancakes, however, it is what you eat with them that creates the magic. Here, I've made a honey and raspberry syrup, and the mixture of the soft, oaty cakes, the honey and the raspberries has a decidedly Scottish flavour. This leads me to think this could be good with a wee nip of whisky somewhere in the mix and, in deference to the great Hibernian dessert, Cranachan, a dollop of whipped cream.

The lack of flour means that they are gluten-free (though because of cross-contamination where they are made, you should look for porridge oats that say as much on the packet, if this is crucial). And while you can use regular full-fat milk, I much prefer oat milk, which richly enhances their flavour, as well as making them dairy-free for those for whom that is a concern. Though in which case, banish all thought of the whipped cream now.

150g runny honey

150g frozen (or fresh) raspberries

100g porridge oats (not instant), preferably organic

¼ teaspoon sea salt flakes

1 teaspoon baking powder

1½ teaspoons ground cinnamon

100ml oat milk or any other sort you wish

1 egg

1 teaspoon vanilla paste or extract

1 teaspoon sunflower oil

- ○ Warm the honey and raspberries in a small saucepan over a medium heat, stirring frequently, until the raspberries have thawed. This shouldn't take more than 3 minutes or so. Take the pan off the heat.

- ○ Put the oats and salt in a blender or a food processor with the small bowl fitted, and process until you get the consistency of flour, a mealy flour to be sure, but it should still be fine-ground.

- ○ Tip into a bowl and stir in the baking powder and cinnamon.

- ○ In a measuring jug, whisk together the milk, egg and vanilla, and then stir the wet mixture into the dry, until thoroughly combined. If the batter thickens too much, add more milk. And do not let this batter rest, as otherwise it will thicken too much.

- ○ Pour ½ a teaspoon of oil onto a smooth, non-stick griddle (or large cast-iron or heavy-based frying pan) and, with a piece of kitchen roll, smear it over the whole surface. Put the griddle on a medium heat and, when hot, add the batter, using a quarter-cup measure but only filling it two-thirds full. You should get 4 pancakes at a time, and they will need around 2 minutes a side. Generally, when cooking pancakes, you turn them over when you see bubbles coming to the uppermost side, and while that still holds true, the bubbles are rather understated here. So slip a spatula underneath a pancake after 2 minutes to see if the underside looks cooked, and then when it is, flip it, and the rest of the pancakes, over and cook for another 2 minutes. As always, do not press down on the pancakes as they cook, and do not flip them more than once. When you've cooked the first 4, pile them on a plate, and cover with a clean tea towel, then oil the pan again and proceed as before.

- ○ Serve immediately – the oats carry on drinking up liquid, and the pancakes will dry on standing – with the warm raspberry honey poured on top.

Dutch baby

I've only ever eaten Dutch babies in the States, where they are brought out to you at the table with great pomp: great pancakes puffed up and golden, still in the cast-iron skillets they were cooked in. Obviously, I had to make my own at home. Not being a restaurant, I don't want to be juggling with heavy pans, giving each person their own, so I've made mine a giant one for sharing; this ain't no baby, that's for sure. It's a wonderful thing to whip up when you have people for breakfast at the weekend: firstly, because it looks so magnificent, and secondly, because you don't have to stand at the stove like a short-order cook.

The "Dutch" of the title doesn't in fact refer to Holland, or anything to do with that country, but rather owes its name to the fact that this particular pancake comes from the German-American community known as the Pennsylvania Dutch and would originally have been served with melted butter, sugar and lemon, and indeed they often still are.

This kind of baked pancake is really a feature of much Northern European cooking: the Swedes have their *ugnspannkaka* just as we have our Yorkshire Pudding. It takes an American, however, to decide to start making them for breakfast.

While you can, of course, serve this mega-pancake just sprinkled with granulated sugar and lemon juice or, for a more diner taste, with a side order of bacon and maple syrup, I like it tumbled with berries and dusted with icing sugar with a bowl of crème fraîche within arm's reach. I confess, I also add an ooze of maple syrup as I eat.

SERVES 4–6

3 large eggs

1 x 15ml tablespoon caster sugar

150ml full-fat milk

100g plain flour

1½ teaspoons vanilla paste or extract

pinch salt

freshly grated nutmeg

25g unsalted butter

TO SERVE:

icing sugar

berries

crème fraîche

maple syrup

1 x 25cm cast-iron frying pan, or 1 x small roasting tin approx. 28 x 21 x 4.5 cm

° Preheat the oven to 220°C/gas mark 7, and straightaway put your pan into the oven to heat up while you prepare the batter.

° Beat the eggs with the caster sugar in an electric mixer until light and frothy. Whisk in the milk, flour, vanilla, salt and grated nutmeg, and beat until you have a smooth but thin batter.

° Wearing a thick oven mitt, remove the pan from the oven and put the butter carefully into the hot pan or tin and swirl it to melt, then quickly pour in the batter and return it to the oven.

° Bake until puffed and golden brown, about 18–20 minutes.

° Serve dusted with icing sugar, and a tumble of berries, if the idea appeals; otherwise, see Intro.

MAKE AHEAD NOTE

The batter can be made the night before. Cover and refrigerate until needed. Whisk briefly before using.

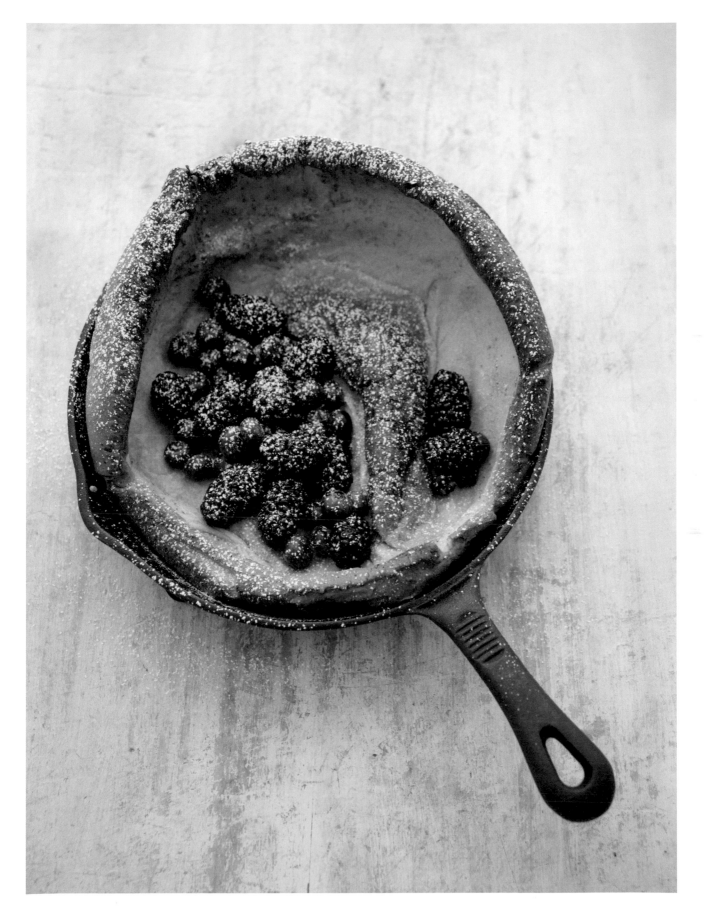

French toast soldiers with maple syrup

I am not normally in favour of cutesiness, but something came over me at the photographic shoot for this book – perhaps more hysteria than whimsy – and I felt compelled to wash out the egg I'd cracked for the French toast, before painstakingly removing every bit of membrane and then filling the shell with maple syrup. In my everyday life, I simply pour the maple syrup into a pair of egg cups, then dunk in my French toast soldiers. But certainly, the tableau I have created here better conveys the pun.

I like to use a thin slice of sour and dense pain Poilâne (it really is *French* French toast), but any good solid sourdough (or other) would do. I would advise against using plastic sliced bread, or anything aerated.

And I should add, this makes as good a midnight feast as it does a breakfast.

2 slices sourdough bread, crusts removed	1 teaspoon (5g) butter
1 egg, carefully broken to reserve the egg shell	¼ teaspoon sunflower oil
2 x 15ml tablespoons full-fat milk	maple syrup, to serve
1 teaspoon vanilla extract or paste	

○ Cut each slice of sourdough bread into 2 fingers or soldiers. This should give 4 fingers that can just about fit into your egg shell (or, more easily, into cups) filled with maple syrup.

○ Whisk the egg, milk and vanilla extract or paste in a shallow dish that the soldiers will fit in. Soak the soldiers in this for 2 minutes a side, by which time they should be quite sodden but not falling to pieces, and there will be a little egg mixture left in the bottom of the dish.

○ Heat the butter and oil in a cast-iron frying pan or a heavy-based, non-stick frying pan, and, once the butter has melted, cook the soldiers for 2 minutes a side over a medium heat. You want the eggy bread to colour gently and become golden on either side, but not scorch too much.

○ Once the soldiers have had their time, take them out of the pan and arrange them on a plate, with an egg cup ready.

○ Rinse the egg shell before popping it in the egg cup and filling with maple syrup or, more sensibly, fill a couple of egg cups (or a little bowl) with maple syrup, as much or as little as you like. However you have served the maple syrup, dip the French toast fingers into it, and eat in solitary splendour, savouring the moment.

Baked French toast with plums and pecans

This is the French toast recipe you need if cooking for a crowd. I find it particularly easy, since you can prepare it all the night before, which seems a good move should you be having people for brunch or – more pertinent still – have them staying overnight and need to provide breakfast.

Actually, you *need* really to get started a whole day ahead, so that the bread has time to stale (though you can do this more quickly in a low oven). Yes, obviously it would make more sense to do this with stale brioche, but you are unlikely to have 500g stale brioche, surely. I, being lazy, buy ready-sliced brioche for this, though do use proper brioche (or, indeed, challah), and cut it into thin-ish slices, no more than 1.5cm thick.

CUTS INTO 12 SLABS

1 sliced brioche loaf (approx. 500g)

butter for greasing

2 x 570g cans red plums in light syrup

6 large eggs

50g caster sugar

500ml double cream

500ml full-fat milk

½ teaspoon ground nutmeg

FOR THE STREUSEL TOPPING:

50g chopped pecans

2 teaspoons ground cinnamon

2 teaspoons (10g) soft unsalted butter

125ml maple syrup

1 x ovenproof dish approx. 30 x 20 x 5cm, or
1 x oval ovenproof dish approx. 33 x 23cm

- Cut each slice of brioche in half, so that you have triangles, and place these on wire racks to dry out: this could take about 6 hours, or up to a day, depending on the weather; or put them on a wire rack or directly on the oven shelf in an oven preheated to 100°C/gas mark ¼ for 15–20 minutes (turning halfway).

- When the bread's stale, lightly grease your ovenproof dish with butter, and drain the cans of plums in a sieve over a batter jug or bowl. Remove any stones from the plums, and reserve the syrup. Tip the drained, pitted plums into the bottom of the dish. Arrange the staled brioche slices, overlapping, on top of the plums, and get on with the custard.

- Whisk together the eggs, sugar, cream, milk and nutmeg and pour over the brioche slices, pressing the bread to help it soak up its rich drink. Cover with clingfilm and leave in a cool place for up to 2 hours or in the fridge overnight. If you have time, let it come to room temperature before putting it in the oven.

- Preheat the oven to 180°C/gas mark 4. Make the streusel topping by mixing the chopped pecans, cinnamon and butter together in a bowl until you have a dark clumpy mess, and then dot this on top of the custard-soaked brioche slices. Bake in the oven for 45–50 minutes, by which time the top will be risen and bronze, and the custard set. If baking from fridge-cold, add an extra 10–15 minutes to the cooking time. When it's ready, remove from the oven and let it stand for 10–20 minutes before serving.

- Pour the light plum syrup you've saved from the cans into a saucepan and boil until reduced to 250ml (this should take about 6–7 minutes). You might have to check a couple of times while it's bubbling away, so keep a heatproof measuring jug handy. When you've got your 250ml, or thereabouts, add the maple syrup and warm through, then pour into the jug or a couple of warmed smaller jugs for serving.

MAKE AHEAD NOTE	STORE NOTE
Pudding can be assembled up to 1 day ahead. Cover and store in fridge (remove from fridge 1 hour before baking). Topping can be made 1 day ahead. Cover and store at cool room temperature. Syrup can be made 1 day ahead. Store in an airtight container or sealed jar in fridge. Can be warmed gently in a saucepan on a low heat before serving.	Cool leftovers, then cover and refrigerate within 2 hours of making. Will keep in fridge for up to 2 days. Eat cold, or reheat individual portions in the microwave in short bursts, following manufacturer's instructions.

Soda bread buns with fennel seeds and cranberries

I recommend eating one of these for breakfast with lots of unsalted butter, which gives all the sweetness I need, but if you want a sweeter bun, add 50ml runny honey along with the yogurt and egg. Like any soda bread, these buns are as good eaten with a slice of cheese, as they are with butter and jam, and the slightly more exotic scent of the fennel seeds and the bursts of tart flavour from the cranberries, don't stop these from having the cosiness of a – perhaps fictional – Irish parlour. And while they are not something I would knock up for an everyday breakfast, when I've got time on my hands I love to get said hands working a dough to conjure up a batch of these. A cursory glance at the recipe will show you how gratifyingly easy they are to make.

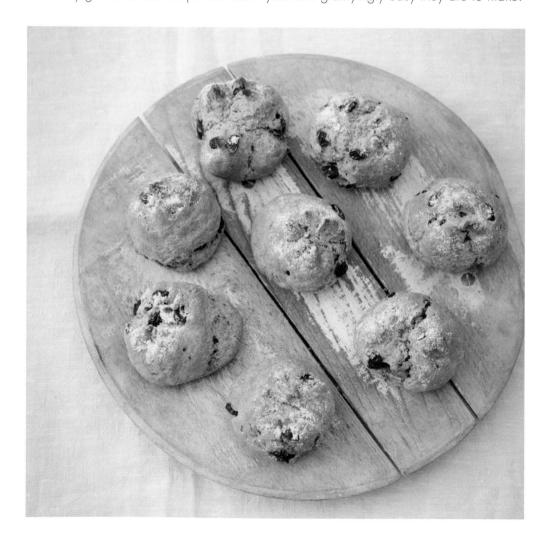

50g unsalted butter	¾ teaspoon bicarbonate of soda
150g plain flour	¾ teaspoon ground allspice
100g plain wholemeal (not bread) flour, plus more for cutting and sprinkling	150ml runny plain yogurt or buttermilk
1 teaspoon fine sea salt	1 large egg
1½ teaspoons baking powder	75g dried cranberries
	2 teaspoons fennel seeds

- Melt the butter and then leave it to cool a little. Preheat the oven to 220°C/gas mark 7, and line a baking sheet with baking parchment.

- In a large bowl, combine both flours, the salt, baking powder, bicarb and ground allspice, and use a fork to mix well.

- In a measuring jug, or similar, whisk the yogurt or buttermilk together with the egg, and then whisk in the cooled, melted butter.

- Pour the jugful of wet ingredients over the bowl of dry ingredients, then add the dried cranberries and fennel seeds, and stir to mix with a wooden spoon. I then do the final bit of mixing with my hands once the dough seems to be coming together.

- Turn the damp or sticky dough out onto a floury surface, and then cut the ball of dough in half, and then each half into 4 pieces, so that you have 8 bits in total. Shape each piece of dough into a rough ball and place on your lined baking sheet with some space between them.

- Take a pair of scissors and snip a small "X" shape into the top of each one, then – using your fingers – sprinkle a little wholemeal flour over each bun.

- Bake in the oven for 15 minutes, or until the buns are brown and sound hollow when tapped underneath. Let them cool for about 10 minutes before you eat them.

MAKE AHEAD NOTE	STORE NOTE	FREEZE NOTE
Dough can be prepared up to 3 months ahead and frozen. Shape dough into buns, put on lined baking sheet and, once solid, transfer to resealable plastic bag and into freezer. Bake from frozen, sprinkling with a little wholemeal flour, and add 2 minutes to baking time.	Buns are best eaten on day they are made. Store leftovers in an airtight container for 1–2 days. Reheat in oven preheated to 150°C/gas mark 2 for 8–10 minutes, or split buns in half and toast under preheated grill.	Baked buns can be frozen in resealable bags for up to 3 months. Thaw on wire rack for about 2 hours and reheat as Store Note.

Oven-baked egg hash

I include this here, as nothing says "weekend breakfast" better than an egg hash,
but you will no doubt find yourself rustling it up for suppers just as gladly. Yes, there
is a bit of chopping involved, but since you don't have to peel the potatoes, this
doesn't take too much time or effort. In fact, the whole brunch dish is wonderfully
undemanding, though I'm glad to say, also irrefutably rewarding.

SERVES 6

3 x 15ml tablespoons olive oil

750g waxy potatoes

1 red onion, peeled and roughly chopped

2 teaspoons cumin seeds

2 teaspoons black mustard seeds

2 red peppers, de-seeded and cut into roughly
3–4cm squares

1 teaspoon sea salt flakes

6 eggs

TO SERVE:

Simple Salsa on p.120 or bottled hot sauce

chopped fresh red chillies

- Preheat the oven to 220°C/gas mark 7. Pour the oil into a large bowl. Cut each potato into 1cm slices, then quarter each slice, and drop these slices, as you go, into the bowl.

- Add the chopped onion, along with the cumin seeds, mustard seeds, chopped peppers and salt, and toss everything together patiently until evenly coated in oily seeds, then tip out onto a large baking tin (I use one approx. 40 x 30cm) in a single layer.

- Bake for 35–40 minutes, or until everything is cooked through and the potatoes are beginning to crisp.

- Take the tray out of the oven and crack one of the eggs into a cup or small bowl, then push the potatoes aside to make a little gap and slip the egg straight into it. Proceed likewise with the remaining eggs, making sure they're evenly spaced on the tray.

- Whack it back into the oven for 5 minutes, until the whites of the eggs are set and the yolks still slightly runny. Then eat immediately, serving a small dish of chopped red chillies and either a bottle of hot sauce or – for preference – the salsa on **p.120** alongside.

MAKE AHEAD NOTE

The potatoes can be cut 1 day ahead. Submerge in a bowl of cold water, cover and refrigerate. Drain and thoroughly pat dry before using.

INDEX

- Dairy-free recipes
- Gluten-free recipes

Refers to baking and sweet recipes only.

ACKNOWLEDGEMENTS

In order to keep this page from sounding like the breathy gush of an Oscar acceptance speech, I will keep my thanks brief, and hope that any terseness is not construed as lack of gratitude on my part. Indeed, I am profoundly grateful and in ways that could not adequately be expressed here, first and foremost to Gail Rebuck, who inspired me to write this, and buoyed me up while I was doing so. The same thanks must likewise be conveyed to Mark Hutchinson and Ed Victor, and also to Caz Hildebrand and Keiko Oikawa whose art direction and photography, respectively, brought the book you hold in your hands to life. Nor could it have come into being without the ministrations of Clara Farmer, Parisa Ebrahimi, Hettie Potter, Yasmin Othman, Caroline Stearns, Camille Blais, Linda Berlin, Violette Kirton, Megan Hummerstone, Zuzana Kratka and Zoe Wales.

I am also grateful for the good will and generosity of Mud Australia (and in particular, the London outpost), Le Creuset, Netherton Foundry, Grain & Knot, David Mellor, Mason Cash, Fermob, Workshop Living, La Fromagerie, and more particularly my fishmonger, Rex Goldsmith, of The Chelsea Fishmonger, Adam and Daniel of HG Walter, my butchers, and my greengrocer, Andreas, of Andreas Veg.

Finally, I thank my family, my friends, my readers: your support, encouragement and enthusiasm along the way was what turned this project into a book.